Be About Beauty

University of New Orleans Press
Manufactured in the United States of America
All rights reserved
ISBN: 9781608011667

Cover Artwork: Adriene Cruz
Cover Photo: Art Alexander
Back Cover Photo: Alex Lear
Interior Design: Ann Hackett

UNIVERSITY OF NEW ORLEANS PRESS
unopress.org

Be About Beauty

KALAMU YA SALAAM

This collection is dedicated to: our organization AHIDIANA (1973 – 1985) & all the comrades and supporters who worked and struggled in concert with me all along the way.

CONTENTS

BE ABOUT BEAUTY

one

I hit earth between the end of World War 2 and the beginning of what was called the Korean Conflict: March 24, 1947. Born Vallery Ferdinand III, my son jokes that if I hadn't changed my name, he could have been Vallery Ferdinand IV. People who know me as an adult and who knew my father when he was a middle-aged man say I look like him. I never talked with my father about the wars in which he served. I had no interest. I was young. Black in White America. Eventually a devotee of jazz.

There was only one record I remember Big Val listening to. For most of the fifties and early sixties, we alternated celebrating Mardi Gras at the Ferdinands or at the Robinsons. Frank Robinson was my daddy's best friend—from what I understand, their deep friendship was a long story that included Daddy asking Mr. Robinson to look out for our mother while Daddy was in the army. Anyway, if it was our turn, Big Val would invariably cook one of his specialties (indeed, other than red beans and rice, it was his only specialty that I remember): oysters encircled by bacon slices, pierced with a toothpick, and deep fried in Crisco shortening. And, regardless of whatever else music we played on Carnival Day, you had to hear, usually two or three times, both sides of Duke Ellington's *A Drum Is A Woman*. In Duke's words, the recording was about Madam Zajj, a real swinging chick—"was, is and always will be a real swinging chick."

Inola Copelin Ferdinand, my mother, was an elementary school teacher and the eldest daughter of Noah Copelin, a Baptist minister who was known in some circles by his pre-religious nickname, Dude Copelin, rather than the honorific Reverend Copelin that denoted his better-known calling. Inola was a petite woman, under five feet tall, married to a big man, by whom she birthed and with whom she parented three strapping sons—what a family we were, except we were ordinary-looking in our part of the world.

We lived in an area that was called Lower Nine, below the Industrial Canal in a semi-rural and overwhelmingly Black part of New Orleans. Two blocks from our house and across the levee were the swamps where we used to play; one block in the other direction was a farm: cows, horses, pigs, chickens. We picked blackberries from the empty lots surrounding our house and caught crawfish in a small canal one block up toward the city. In fact we were surrounded by water: twenty blocks from the Mississippi River, the whole neighborhood was ribboned with canals, most of which are now subterranean; they were open when I was growing up in that place that shaped us, whose many distinctive physical features are now long gone.

We walked Civil Rights picket lines after high school and spent most weekends canvassing door-to-door for voter registration in various neighborhoods citywide. That's how I learned to talk with people; to be comfortable with ordinary, working class Black folk whom I didn't know personally; to help people cross the hurdles the state of Louisiana erected to keep us from gaining our rights. I and both my siblings were brought up in the movement. Whether it was picking up something from the corner store or giving people rides in the evening, it was unthinkable not to help, not to take the time to clean up trash on both sides of the street from corner to corner or help seniors tote whatever they were carrying on the long walk from the bus stop. Later it was no trouble to take bicycle rides to the drugstore, ten blocks there and back, to pick up a prescription for the elderly couple in the next block. We cut a lot of grass in empty lots and even chopped down more than a few trees. Even when we were too young to be full-fledged carpenters, my brothers and I would carry lumber and, with two hands, drag pails of nails or ten gallon buckets of paint; as adolescents we would expertly wield a hammer, a hatchet, and tirelessly work a cross-cut hand saw. We literally helped neighbors build their homes.

As children we were expected to labor, to be cheerful helping hands, not withstanding the fact that before we finished high school we had achieved more formal education than any number of the parents of our childhood playmates. Knowing who we were, people expected Mrs. Ferdinand's boys to help them decipher the mumbo jumbo of government letters and summonses. In many ways, we were brought up as working members of a hard-working community.

On the other hand, White people were another country. When James Baldwin published his 1962 novel of the same title (*Another Country*), his book was officially banned in New Orleans, a censoring that we, of course, ignored. I remember a young sister reading Baldwin's subversive novel while riding on the Galvez bus, which ran the five or so miles downtown from Canal Street. It would take forty-five minutes to an hour to get home if the bridge wasn't up, which it usually was, so the journey generally took far more than an hour.

By the sixties there were three bridges across the Industrial Canal that lead into the Lower Ninth Ward, but when I was coming up there were only two: the main bridge on

St. Claude Avenue and the back way, a small bridge at what we called Florida Walk that had one lane for cars (you had to take turns in either direction) plus a set of railroad tracks. The thing about the back way was that it had the Florida Housing Project, which was all White, on one side, and then a canal plus a set of tracks before the all Black Desire Housing Project: that's right, both railroad tracks and a canal separated Blacks from Whites. The ironic thing is that these neighborhoods, composed of federally funded housing units located in different parts of New Orleans, were the only legally mandated, racially segregated residential areas. Every place else in New Orleans you could find Blacks and Whites living next to, around the corner from, or a couple of blocks over from each other. Since those early days of my youth, while the city's landscape has changed drastically, we are effectively more residentially segregated by both race and class today than we ever were pre-Civil Rights.

Indeed one of my indelible childhood memories is living with my mother's parents while my daddy was away at war. The Copelins had a telephone (Franklin-8103) and the White people who lived in the house across the yard at the corner didn't, so they sometimes came over to use ours. Meanwhile, across Lizardi Street there was an empty lot where we played ball but also half a block away, next to the empty lot, was a public park with a baseball diamond and a swimming pool, surrounded by a chain link fence. A segregated park. We Blacks couldn't play ball there but our White neighbors could use our phone. That's just the way life was in the fifties in Lower Nine.

The third bridge, the Judge William Seeber Bridge, which we all simply called the Claiborne Bridge, and which was a four lane structure that ran across the Industrial Canal, quickly became a major link on the lower end of the main and only roadway that crossed the breadth of New Orleans. The Claiborne Bridge was inaugurated in 1957. It was a point of family pride that the day it opened we were among the first cars to cross the bridge. Once the bridge opened, the Galvez (to Delery) bus ran all the way into Lower Nine and had only one stop after St. Maurice (which was the street we lived on). My mother's older brother, Uncle Sherman, resided on that last street, Delery, where the Galvez bus would turn around to crawl back to Canal Street—in the fifties probably three-quarters of the bus lines ended and/or started at Canal Street. Indeed, down where we lived, you had to turn around if you wanted to stay in New Orleans: the Mississippi River was on one side, the swamps on the other, and just an empty field, a wooded area, and Jackson military barracks separated us from a completely different jurisdiction, St. Bernard Parish, the redoubt of arch segregationist Leander Perez.

I graduated St. Augustine High School in 1964, dropped out of college within a year and joined the army after enduring some duress from my mother. I had not registered for the draft, but Vietnam was raging and she was sure they were coming to get me. I should say she was "afraid" they were coming to get me. There was no need to say who "they" were. Like mosquito-filled nights, we saw the government, the police, the sheriff or whatever other manifestations of civil authority as constant environmental blights. One way or another, I would spend most of my adult life, as Jimmy Baldwin was wont to say, going to meet the man.

I wanted to be a writer. Before she died, Narvalee, my mother's youngest sister, affectionately told me I always had my head stuck up in some book. Looking back it's easy to see that in addition to my personal literary desires I was reared to be an activist. We Ferdinand boys all were NAACP field workers, distributing meeting flyers, pushing petitions, and circulating the details about the latest legal stipulations endlessly afflicting our people. I, being the oldest, was blessed to come in on the tail end of the sit-in movement. When

I first got arrested, which is how movement people measured time, I was over a year away from finishing high school. Every night I had a lot to think about as I fell asleep going over the day's activities.

Given that this was New Orleans, rhythm & blues, jazz, and gospel were much more common than literature. Otis Reddings' bama-ma-lam-ma shouting and hometown hero Ernie K-Doe's rhythmic exhortations filled my ears and heart; to this day those songs remain touchstones in my psyche. My mother did play piano for the Sunday school sessions before "big" church, but there was no piano at home, and I don't remember any other music-making going on. Yet somehow, my brothers and I all grew up loving music.

While I was in the army, I took up the drums and became pretty good at it. Kenneth, the brother just under me, was then and remains now a hell of a trumpet player; regardless of whatever else in life he's gone on to do professionally, he remains a serious musician, keeps his black-and-white band hat and shining, golden horn ever ready either in his bedroom or near his front door. Keith, my younger brother, played clarinet and eventually became a cardiologist but, in keeping with his future profession, seemed to enjoy the physical exertion of dancing much more than sitting down and blowing on a reed instrument.

For me the die was cast when I was young. Another aunt, Neomi, had a small library; seemed like I devoured ten or twelve Frank Yerby novels when I hiked over to her Lower Nine house to babysit my younger cousins. Even years later, well after all my family older than me are long gone, I have not deviated from my upbringing, have held fast to my crescent city dreams. Hurricanes and floods notwithstanding, I've never stopped calling New Orleans home, never stopped digging Black music, never stopped reading literature, especially Black literature. And, of course, have never stopped writing.

This then is a collection of writings from a Lower Ninth Ward Black boy. Although I have literally been around the world and even though I now live in Algiers, on New Orleans' west bank side of the Mississippi River, I am still very much a product of an isolated slice of black New Orleans known in the sixties and the seventies as the Mighty Nine.

two

I credit Mrs. O. E. Nelson, my eighth grade English teacher, with turning me on to Langston Hughes, who immediately became my patron saint. I never went to school in Lower Nine. Early on there were no schools for me to go to below the canal. Besides, up until seventh grade, we went to school wherever my mother taught third grade. My first public school was at Fisk, way uptown off Tulane Avenue near Jefferson Davis Parkway. Mrs. Paige was my kindergarten teacher; her daughter Maneza was in the same grade as me. Maneza eventually would work for Delta Airlines, and many, many years later I ran into her one time at New Orleans' Louis Armstrong Airport. (I recognized her from her name tag.) For fifth and sixth grade, it was Phillis Wheatley Elementary School, around the corner from the famed Dooky Chase's Restaurant. My mother's friend Mrs. Wilson was my sixth grade teacher who shocked us one afternoon by writing "pussy" on the blackboard and challenging us, virtually daring us, to tell her what the word meant. After that I was a big boy and was sent on my own to Rivers Frederick Junior High School in the Seventh Ward, which marked the beginning of my exploring the city alone, unsupervised, and way beyond ordinary walking distance from the two-bedroom brick home my father had purchased utilizing a VA loan. In fact, he actually bought the plot of land, and we would drive the fifteen or so blocks from my grandparent's house as our new home was under construction.

I fondly remember his pride when he showed us where our new home would be. When we moved in there, it was almost like living in the country. There were only two other families living on the block: the Masons at the corner and the Townsends across the street. We drove out to St. Bernard Parish and hiked up the river levee to literally dig up boxes of St. Augustine grass that we loaded in the trunk and ferried home to be re-planted in our front and back yards. My mother wanted a flower garden like the beautiful roses that lined the long driveway that stretched from the front sideway to the back of the Copelin home. My daddy, being the country man he was, agreed to a flower bed across the front of our house, but along the walkway, from the sidewalk to the front door, he planted strawberries; they had pretty white blossoms, and you could eat them. Of course we had a small garden in the backyard behind the garage, plus he planted a pecan tree, which as young boys my brothers and I would take running starts and leap over, though it quickly grew too tall for any of that.

Seventh, eighth, and ninth grades were the best years of all my formal schooling in terms of both book learning and social education. Actually the Civil Rights Movement was more influential than school. Although I spent most of my daylight hours in the classroom, unusual for New Orleans, I never attended class in the neighborhood in which I lived, hence I didn't have childhood friends with whom I both grew up and matriculated with. I spent a lot of time by myself, looking out the windows of city busses, criss-crossing the urbanscape. I can remember riding home after school when I had gone to meet my father at the Veterans Hospital where he worked as an army-trained laboratory technician. The VA was only a few blocks from the main library. So, I would hang out at the library until it was time to meet my father at the end of his work day, and then we would catch the bus home together. My daddy always carried a copy of

Reader's Digest, and from him I learned that travel time was reading time. In later years I came to realize that although he didn't have a college education, he was constantly trying to improve himself. Modeled on my father, as an autodidact I didn't waste a long commute daydreaming or dozing off. Instead I would break out my unfailing companion: a newspaper, a magazine, or, more likely, a thick book.

Mr. Conrad, my seventh grade industrial arts teacher, also taught photography after school. From saving grass-cutting money to buy a Yashica twin lens reflex camera to the bunch of instruments I've acquired in a lifetime of taking photographs, myopic Kalamu has always been looking at the world with a lens that would enable "the picture man" to write with light.

Seventh grade at Rivers Frederick was the first time I attended school without my mother. I loved it. Looking back I'm certain that some of those teachers were members or sympathizers with Marcus Garvey's UNIA, which had a very strong chapter in New Orleans. On November 18, 1927, it was reported that 500 Negroes stood on the New Orleans docks in the rain to bid farewell when Mr. Garvey was deported aboard the S.S. Saramacca. My elderly history teacher, Ms. Green, had probably been there. The version and vision of history she taught us was heroic. For the Easter break, while everybody else in the school system was listening to the lambs, this lady had us literally doing revolutionary plays. I played Crispus Attucks: "a desperate Black man who is ready to fight and die for my freedom."

How could I not love it? Nevertheless, it was only many years later that I realized that it was really the teachers and not just the lessons that deeply moved me. Many of those Black teachers—Mrs. Nelson, Mr. Conrad, Ms. Green, and a number of others such as Mr. Blanchard, who encouraged my budding affinity for mathematics—indeed, for most of them, teaching us was more than a job: our instruction was a social commitment. I took the love and excellence of their teaching for granted. They supplemented the meager state resources with their own pocket money to purchase books, equipment, and other pedagogical materials that the state of Louisiana refused to pay for, but which our teachers deemed essential to our development. Our teachers loved us. Each of us, all of us, were their children, and they were loving and responsible parents.

I was also informally mentored by young men in the neighborhood, especially one of the Bethune brothers who taught me chess. One day I walked down to his house in the next block and knocked on the side of his house, which was a way to make sure people heard you if they were in their backyard or something. I don't believe I ever knew his phone number or if he even had a phone. He was bare-chested when he opened the door and ushered me in. As I stepped into the dining area, a young woman was retreating to a side room. I saw her slipping a dress over her head and with her hands smoothing it down her hips. My man—I believe his name was Ronald; all the Bethune brothers had names that started with "r"—saw me see the unnamed woman. He matter-of-factly told me that since he had been in the army he had to have a woman around. I understood the words but didn't fully appreciate the feeling until a handful of years later, when I was in the army.

Charlie Bickham, who was an officer in the NAACP Youth Council and who had an amazing gift of gab, got drafted. The following year he was on leave over the Christmas holidays, and I saw him rambling down the Black entertainment district of Claiborne Avenue, the only street that ran the full length of New Orleans from St. Bernard Parish where we lived, all the way across town to Jefferson Parish to the west of the city. Over fifty-some years hence, I still run into Raphael Cassimere, who led the Youth Council. He's married to the vivacious Inez, who lived on Gordon,

I believe that was the street, or maybe one or two blocks over from Gordon, perhaps Roffinac, but I believe it was Gordon. In any case her residence was a little less than a mile from our house, and I, or my brother and I, would walk her safely home after Youth Council meetings. Back then Inez was the Youth Council secretary. At the time, all of the people I hung with were in college or had been in the army, and I watched them closely, learning how to conduct myself as a young man.

Those were my formative years. Like most teenaged males, I went through the big three: Puberty. Girls. Hours alone. But what I really enjoyed was reading, especially a trio of personal avatars. After Langston Hughes, who was and for me always will be number one, it was James Baldwin, and then LeRoi Jones. There were others, such as Carl Sandburg, whose collected poems I read in high school, or John Steinbeck, whose novel *East Of Eden* was a marvel to me. Additionally there were all those writers Hughes introduced to me in his autobiographies, especially all the African writers—for example Peter Abrahams' *A Wreath For Udomo* was an important novel in the development of my personal pan-African consciousness; however, none of the other writers were as influential as was my literary trinity. I never met Langston Hughes, but I did get to know James Baldwin (even walked with him through Armstrong Park as a film crew shot us ambling about, although none of the footage was eventually used). LeRoi Jones changed his name to Amiri Baraka, and he and I worked together for years in various political and cultural formations.

For me, both my physical and intellectual development happened concurrently. By 1964, when I graduated from the Catholic high school that I hated but which my parents sent me to because academically it was the best schooling available to young Black men at that time, I was disinclined to become a successful member of the Black petite bourgeoisie. Afterwards, as a young adult, off and on, I was employed as part of the managerial class in different positions. I had the training and the smarts to chase and even pluck a tail feather from the ever-fleeting bird of the American dream, but I had no real interest in pursuing that particular branch of social ornithology. My heart was always in activism and the arts. Throughout my life, I would walk away from more than a few good paying jobs because I didn't want to make a career out of being a professional factotum for a system I despised.

three

You have to go down the road a bit before you can recognize the patterns that you essentially repeat in your intimate relationships and in your life choices, regardless of the religious or ideological positions you believe you are consciously selecting. Some of the most difficult aspects of negotiating life are the broken promises and betrayals by people close to you, those contradicting and conflicting experiences that are hard to understand and/or withstand. Not only do they blindside you, but the ruptures, the disappointments, the emotional traumas are always deeply painful: the person you thought you loved who turned out to love you and someone else as well, maybe even loved the rival slightly more than you; the organizational position you steadfastly held only to find out a couple of top officials had gotten rich off a compromise; the knee bent to political and religious figures who were in fact false gods whose promises were not only hollow but ultimately both unfulfilling and dishonest. But hey, those experiences are the taste tests that teach you how to distinguish between sugar and salt (or in some cases, sugar and shit), a difference that you initially couldn't tell just by looking. Indeed, haven't we all, innocent true believers as only youths can be, been caught seeking a taste of honey only to end up with a rancid bite of bitterness?

But the worse part of growing up is the realization that sometimes it really wasn't them, or her, or him, or it; sometimes, it actually was you. Or, as the old song says: nobody's fault but mine. We all, or at least most of us, have sweet memories, and we all also have self-inflicted wounds. When you first engage diverse, new experiences, you can't tell in advance what they'll be like. Nor can you forecast what you'll be like when you come out on the other side of growing up. But after you've learned your life lessons, if you survive, if you are smart enough to be self-reflective, and if you successfully engage the tough, tough task of trying to figure out the meanings of your experiences, afterwards, "Maybe next time" is all you can say—the best any of us can say—as we push forward trying, sometimes in vain, not to make the same mistake twice, and certainly not thrice.

My three years in junior high school, seventh through ninth grade at Frederick, developed my dual life-long loves: photography and writing. Then three years in high school at St. Augustine, literally a Black Baptist young man plopped into a light-skinned Catholic Creole society; a lost year dropping out of college—imagine me from New Orleans, freezing cold, confused and confounded by a winter at Carleton College in Northfield, Minnesota; three years in the army, two years at Fort Bliss in El Paso, Texas, bracketing a year in the mountains of South Korea, which was an even colder clime than Minnesota. That was the itinerary of my journey from adolescence to adulthood.

That year following my discharge from the army was the major line of demarcation. I was never the same afterwards. For example, that's when I permanently gave up drinking—Jack Black (Jack Daniels, black label) with water back, was my drink of choice. Chilled Taylor's Cream Sherry was a close second. Situation normal: experimentations and explorations. For the most part, after that year of groping to fully define myself, I became a better person, more settled, albeit more politically radical.

My first car stolen—a Chevy you didn't need a key to start. My first play staged at the Free Southern Theater, actually a short story based on Civil Rights work that I transformed into a playscript. By the fall of '69, my first marriage and shortly thereafter my first child, a daughter—Asante lead off a team of five siblings. My first apartment, my first post-army job. All the usual transitions and endeavors we undertake when we become an adult.

four

I've been on the front lines of conscious political activity since I was sixteen years old. Sometimes our struggles were reformist; other times we were engaged in radical activities. I've been literally around the world, from the Lower Ninth Ward of New Orleans all the way to China and a bunch of places in between: arming nuclear warheads in South Korea while in the U.S. Army at the age of nineteen; over hills, up rivers, down streets in Nica Libre (Nicaragua) in support of the Sandinista revolution; opposing the Ku Klux Klan in Tupelo, Mississippi; on the main avenue, Canal Street, in my hometown of New Orleans, face-to-face with repulsing former self-avowed Klan leader David Duke; conferences in Africa and festivals all through the Caribbean island countries, sometimes as a producer, other times as a participant or reporter; plus posting field notes from exotic places such as Suriname and Zanzibar.

I've witnessed and been an operative in a distinctive and sometimes dizzying array of events, some of them hard, others of them heartening, all of them serious even when we were having fun. From dancing in the streets of Rio and the plazas in Havana to avant-garde theater in Munich and whistle-stopping in London and across the midlands of England, it's all been a major learning experience. Now, in 2018, I can honestly and confidently say I've seen and learned a thing or two.

Through it all, the one thing I really knew, the one thing I was absolutely certain about, is that I wanted to write. Even when I didn't know why I felt the way I did or how to effectively jot down my thoughts and feelings, I would write anyway. Broken lines. Half-formed, half-baked literary disasters. Eventually a few gems. I'd write my life and vow to get better at expressing myself, better at addressing my peers and whomever else might read my work. Ultimately, long after I'm dead and gone, I want to leave behind literature that communicates with future audiences.

My first work was journalism, my junior high school newspaper. Mrs. Nelson was the advisor, and we won a second place in a national contest from Columbia University in New York City. Poetry and fiction followed quickly in high school. In tenth grade, I got kicked off the school paper for writing a glowing review of James Baldwin's play, *Blues For Mr. Charlie*. Essays and epistles were the norm when I moved through the army. I used to type long letters, staple the pages together, fold them over in thirds and write the address and return address on the back of the last page, stamp that, and then send the self-contained missive off without an envelope. Eventually dramatic scripts developed when I joined the Free Southern Theater after the army. I stayed in school at Southern University in New Orleans long enough to get kicked out for being a leader of student demonstrations, but that school year, 1968-1969, was also the fodder for my early plays, along with public confessions and political analyses. All of these efforts, everything I wrote was toward making concrete my chosen profession: I was a writer. Regardless of where I was and what I was doing, I was always writing.

This book contains selected writings from between the summer of 1968, which was when I consciously crossed over into adulthood, up through May 2018, right after March 24th, when I celebrated seventy-one cycles of circling the sun.

These words are mine, define and express me. But more than just poems, essays, and autobiography collected and edited, this gathering contains reflections of many, many different places, times, and experiences I've encountered, and the many, many people with whom I have interacted. My world is a world of words, a testimony concerning diverse critical connections and a few decisive disruptions. Hopefully, these words live up to my credo, my commitment to be about beauty.

Be About Beauty

be about beauty
as strong as a flower is
yet as soft too
as an open petal
receiving the mist
of a midnight raindrop,
be about beauty
no matter life's dirt
be about beauty

Kalamu ya Salaam
New Orleans - June 2018

Pilgrim Journey

I MET MYSELF

I met myself coming around the corner one day, and I almost didn't recognize me.

We so seldom see ourselves as we actually are. Even in a mirror we often see what we hope to be or what we fear we are, exaggerating both flaws and beauty. But when we see ourselves in the faces of others, then we really see.

Would you know yourself if you saw yourself the way others see you?

Of course, when we are young—or at least when I was first moving beyond my teen years—it never occurred to me that the past had anything deep to do with me personally. My father was from the country. I was from the city. I didn't really see how his life was shaping my life. One African proverb says you can't truly judge the man until the man has reared a child. So when can you truly judge the child?

Somehow, in the way most of us in America have been acculturated, I thought of myself as distinct from my parents. I did not consciously know their ideas about life except by inference in terms of what they encouraged and/ or discouraged in me, and therefore I was blissfully unaware that much of my own ideas were shaped and influenced, if not outright determined, by the ideas my parents held.

When my mother was battling Hodgkin's disease, she had her three sons take turns driving her across the city to a hospital that was located in the parish to the west of New Orleans for chemotherapy treatment. During these long drives, she would talk to each of us, not about anything in particular, but many years later I realized she was consciously spending her last days conversing with her sons.

I'll never forget how well she knew us; how after Hurricane Betsy hit, my mother had written a long letter to her youngest sister, my aunt Narvalee, who was by then living out in California, a single mother with one child, my first cousin Frieda. My mother was a college graduate and a third-grade school teacher. I knew she could write, but she opened her letter saying if she could write like Paul in the Bible or like me, Lil Val—wow, I realized: My mother admired me as a writer.

That was in 1965, three years before I joined the Free Southern Theater and became a professional writer. By 1973 she was dead. If she saw me now, would she still admire me, would I remind her of the young man she loved— or would I be so strangely changed that she would know who I was but not know the me who came to be over the intervening years between now and when she last saw me? I wish I could see me the way she would see me if she looked at me today, she who knew me before I knew me.

Have you ever had a long talk with someone who knew you well, but had not seen you in over ten years? Say you're having a quick drink with Gilbert after seeing him at Walgreen's; he was picking up a prescription for diabetes medication and you were getting a refill of blood pressure medicine. Gilbert was your best friend from elementary school with whom you used to share lunch. You and Gilbert had even planned and literally started to run away together just for the romanticized adventure of two adolescents exploring the world away from the dictates of parents.

Or maybe you are hugging Eric and laughing with your arm still around his shoulder, and he is playfully punching you in the chest the way y'all used to do while playing sand-lot football games on the crisp autumns of weekends decades ago, and Eric would laugh at something you said and retort, "Boy, you still talking all that shit."

Or maybe it was Woodrow you encountered. He was coming out of Picadilly's, and you were going in planning to meet your wife for dinner. Woodrow was someone you used to laugh with pulling pranks in high school, and now, even though he walks with a cane and has only half a head of hair, Woodrow gains your admiration as he tells you about the business venture he's started. His enthusiasm is contagious as he speaks to all the wonderful skills and information he's learning. His eyes are animated as he leans into you, one hand familiarly resting on your right shoulder as he describes the joys of getting into a whole new area and keeping up with thirty-year-old guys who are not even half his age.

Or you see Sandra in some office hallway, she who could outrun a cheetah back in eighth grade. She is still slim and vivacious. She greets you not only with a girlish giggle and bubbly "hello" but waves a well-manicured hand at you while balancing a cup of steaming coffee in her other hand; she's married and has a beautiful diamond ring that literally shoots off a flashing rainbow of refracted lights when she waves good-bye. Seeing her brisk walk and the swing of her lithe hips makes you self-conscious about all the weight you've gained.

I temporarily quieten some of my concerns about who really knows me by insisting people who have not seen me in years cannot really know me. The two questions—who knows me, and do I know me the way other people know me—take turns as the focus of my mind. Then I wonder how much of me today is the old me that friends knew decades ago.

The old folks say it's easy to change your mind but hard to change your ways. Is the way I am today more or less the way I was way back when, and if so, where did that constant part of me come from? Was I born the way I am, or are all of us shaped by our interactions with and responses to our nurturing environment? Over a lifetime do we remain essentially the same or is it possible to fundamentally transform ourselves?

The things we think about can surprise us. Where did that come from? we ask ourselves while looking around to see if anybody saw us thinking these crazy ideas.

I remember riding a subway in Manhattan. I hallucinated for a minute and thought I saw my mother and father at a train stop, standing close to each other. My old man handsome, with a dimpled smile and a seriousness dripping from his eyes, his dark head held high; my short mother looking up, her eyes shining. He had one hand lightly on her waist, and she was leaning into him, two hands caressing his chest. I had never seen my mother touching my father like that, never thought of them as head-over-heels infatuated with each other. But there they were.

Suddenly I started wondering about what Momma and Daddy were thinking and feeling, how it was to be young and black in the late forties. How did fighting in two wars affect him: once in the Pacific and later in Korea? Before she died, my mother's younger sister told me why we used to alternate going by the Robinsons on Mardi Gras one year and the Robinsons coming by us the next. Frank Robinson and my father were best friends, and Daddy had asked Mr. Robinson to look out for Mama while Daddy was in the war. I wonder now how it was to be a pregnant woman with two small children and her man returning to war abroad after surviving World War II.

I can't believe how dumb I was to ignore them. How could I be so uninterested in the roots of myself? Even though in my early manhood years I served in Korea on a missile base located on a remote mountaintop, I never really discussed Korea with my father. Like most youth, I was too self-absorbed to want to learn anything about my origins, or any of me that wasn't actually embodied in my physical person.

When I was still in elementary school, I gave a speech by Frederick Douglass and won a prize in a church contest, and later in junior high school, playing Crispus Attucks, I jumped out of a closet—well, actually from behind a curtain—hoisting a sword fashioned from a coat hanger and proclaiming: "I'm a proud Black man who is willing to fight and die for my freedom."

I liked that kind of Black history but ignored my father's fight to be hired as a laboratory technician at the Veterans Administration Hospital. He wrote letters all the way to Washington, D.C., kept arguing his rights, and finally a directive came down to hire him. They did, but they wouldn't promote him, even though he was the best lab tech they had, so good that he was the one training the college interns, some of whom were hired after his training and even promoted because they had a degree. Meanwhile, Daddy languished in lower grade positions because he had no sheepskin. I never heard him complain about mistreatment—was I deaf or did he just silently suffer, nobly carrying on despite the slights heaped on him?

Now that I'm old as history, now that my teenage years are on page five hundred-and-something in an American history textbook thrown on the floor in the corner of the classroom; now that what I went through does not seem relevant to what teenagers today are going through—now I want to know my father's history, I want to embrace my mother's hardships.

There they were again and again, at each train stop. That must have been me my mother was carrying in two arms, gently bouncing up and down. I had on a funny, green knit hat swallowing my big head. I am the eldest of their three sons. Should I get off and at least walk close to them, hear what they are saying to each other? Look, my mother is talking to me. What's she saying? Before I can muster the courage to stand up and go eavesdrop on my parents, the train pulls off. I am strangely more anxious about bungling the chance to get to know my parents while they were standing at the last stop than I am curious about what I will see at the next one.

But the next stop is my stop. I get up and wait at the door as the train jerks to a stop. The door abruptly opens. People pour in and out of the train simultaneously. As I push through the throng, I look up and down the platform. They are not there. My parents are gone, or more likely, never were here. I feel alone, making my way in the world.

I promise I will never forget my parents as young lovers. I was so fortunate that they were my fate: Inola and Big Val. My mother, a school teacher who never forced me to do homework, who did not even try to dissuade me from taking an F in high school one trimester because I didn't want to do an assignment a teacher forced on me. My father, forcing us to grow food in the city and pick up all the trash on our block to keep it clean, but who never once tried to discourage us from picking up the gun in the sixties—that was my brother on the cover of *Life* magazine brandishing a shotgun during the take over at Cornell University. Big Val and Inola always encouraged us to fight, and they never made us conform to anything.

It is obvious to me now, but I have not always recognized this truth: I cannot fully know myself if I don't intimately know my past, intimately know the forces that shaped and influenced me, the people who gave birth to me, and especially the culture and eras within which I've lived. My head was spinning as my mental fingers tapped the codes of past experiences into the calculator of my consciousness. I was literally engrossed in my own world.

So there I was coming around the corner thinking all these thoughts, totally unaware that I was about to really peep who I was; suddenly I see someone I grew up with. That person looks old as they hug me, greet me, and playfully say, Heyyyy man, long time no see. They enfold me in a long, warm embrace, holding the me they remember. At the same time, underscoring my own self-absorption, I am struggling to remember their name.

In that moment I see their obvious joy and also see how much they have changed, how they have aged. I wonder what they are doing, what is their life like, what part of the city they live in, what kind of work they do, all the personal profile sort of information.

That's when I have this weird desire: I wanted to be able to fully embrace myself and know myself the way this old friend thinks they know me, and I was really curious to know myself from the perspective that my parents knew me.

I wanted to know all of me, and that's the moment when I had a news flash: now that your life is almost over, who are you really?

Am I only who I think I am, or am I really the complex summation of all that I have also been in relation to others and in response to the world within which I have lived?

As I walked to my car, I had a funny thought: my mind is not me. My mind may in fact be the biggest impediment to me getting to know me. Maybe my mind is the least reliable map of who I have been, a distorting lens when it comes to recognizing the self.

All personal intentions aside, all individual desires sublimated, all intellectual self-reflections and second guesses ignored, is it possible for any of us to truly know ourselves without the help and input of others who know us? Is it possible to move beyond letting our minds judge who we are? Would it be too overwhelming to consider letting the world we live in judge who we are? Can we shed the shackles of our own mind and be both free and fortunate to see ourselves the way others see us? And if that portrait was actually presented to us, would we recognize ourselves?

ALABAMA

one

it is late in december 1998; the weather is uncharacteristical-
ly warm. there is much that is wrong. an old man has killed
himself.

if he had been an airplane and fallen from the sky, the
forensic engineers might have diagnosed metal fatigue—the
quality of structural breakdown when the weariness caused
by the ravages of time destroys an object's physical ability
to bear the weight of existence. but this fellow was not a
passenger jet. he was just a chestnut-colored, elderly african
american who everyone said looked remarkably good for his
age.

his eyesight was fit enough—without glasses he could
drive day or night. and he would step two flights of steps
rather than wait on a slow elevator. he was sensible about his
diet and walked two miles every morning to keep his weight
down. plus, any day of the week, he could out-bowl his son.
no, his age was not a problem.

so what was so disastrous in his life that the permanent
solution of suicide was the action of choice to deal with
whatever temporary problem he was confronting?

we are not sure what exactly was wrong, but we do know
that when he resolved to end it, he was watching television.

got up and said something to his wife, who was in the kitch-
en. shortly thereafter went into his back yard with a gun in
his hand—no one in the house saw him go outside. but what
if they had? could they have stopped him? probably not. at
best they may have been able to momentarily postpone the
inevitable, but eventually life turns cold. or we are deluged
with the dreariness of chilly rains. and we die.

what did the slow-moving man think as he descended
the steps into the back yard? indeed, did he think, or was his
mind blank with certainty?

his body died there, but was he already dead in spirit?
does it matter what happens to the body, once the spirit has
been broken? this is a story about death.

two

i have often thought about those stark black and white
photographs of lynching scenes. we know what happened to
the lynchee, but what happened to all the lynchers? the ones
standing around. some smiling into an unhidden camera—
look, you can see that these people know that a photograph
is documenting them. a number of them are looking at the
camera full-on, challenging the lens to capture something
human in the grisly scene. a significant number are children,
young boys and girls, leering.

i have heard stories of whites who were repulsed by those
death scenes. those who were changed forever by witnessing
a lynching, hearing about a lynching, backing away from
their parents who come back home chatting about the nigger
who got what he deserved. ok. but what i want to know is
what happened to the lynchers who did not back away. those
who took in the murder scene as acceptable. later on in life,
how did they raise their children? do they have flashbacks of
lynchings—occasionally? often? never?

does watching a man or woman die a violent death
diminish the person who enjoys the spectacle? can one revel

in the fascinating flame of a human on fire and afterwards remain emotionally balanced? and what about memory: does the extreme violence of mob murder involuntarily replay years later triggered by scenes such as oj maintaining he did not slice nicole's throat, or wesley snipes on the silver screen bigger than life, kissing a white woman who favors irma singletary, your daughter's friend who divorced a black man after he beat her one night and she refused to press charges against him the next morning?

in many of those garish photographs there are a lot of people standing around. i wonder how many among those audiences are alive today, driving america's streets and buying christmas gifts?

three

richard hammonds was a handsome man. he was moderately intelligent. could work hard but really didn't like to exert his body to the point of sweating. believe it or not, what he was really good at was leather work. give him a piece of leather and his tools and he could make anything from shoes to hats and everything in between. and he would do it well, so well that a number of people have been buried wearing shoes richard had made—their family knew how proud the deceased had been of richard's handicraft, so that's what the corpse wore at the funeral.

for example, brother james sweet—his name was actually james anthony johnson but, with a twinkle in his eye, he would raise his left hand, flashing his ruby and diamond pinkie ring, graciously tip his every present gray stetson, and, in his trademark rumbling baritone, request that you call him "james sweet, bra-thaaa jaaaames sweee-eat, cause i'm always good to womens, treats children with kindness and is a friend to the end with all my brothers"—well, brother sweet had instructed everyone of concern in his immediate family to bury him in his favorite oxblood loafers that richard had hooked up especially for sweet. there were no shoes more comfortable anywhere in the world, and he, sweets, which was the acceptable short form of brother sweet, certainly didn't want to be stepping around heaven with anything uncomfortable on his bunioned feet (nor, likewise, running through hell, if it came to that—and he would wink to let you know that he didn't think it would come to that). of course, at a funeral you don't usually see the feet of the recently departed, but that was not the point.

the point is that people were really pleased with richard hammonds' handiwork. unfortunately, in terms of a stable income, although richard hammonds excelled at making leather goods, what he actually loved to do was watch and wager on the ponies. and since he lived in new orleans and the fair grounds racetrack was convenient, well, during racing season, which seemed to be almost year-round, richard spent many an afternoon cheering on a two year-old filly while his workbench went unused.

fortunately, richard hammonds seldom wagered more than he could afford to lose and on occasion won much more than he had gambled for the month. however, winning at the racetrack was uncertain. no matter what betting system he used, richard could never accurately predict when he would win big or how long a losing streak would maintain its grip on his wallet.

routinely, richard would do enough leather work to pay the house note and give eileen an allotment to buy food and then it was off to the races. needless to say, had eileen not worked as a seamstress at haspel's factory in the seventh ward, this would have been an unworkable arrangement.

but richard hammonds didn't drink more than a beer now and then, went to mass every sunday morning, and was moderately faithful, so what could have been a precarious and intemperate social situation settled into a predictable and manageable state of affairs until richard was wobbling home one october evening—he had had a very good day and had indulged in a few drinks at mule's; in fact, he had even bought a round for the guys and stashed a small bundle in his hip pocket for eileen and still had in his inside jacket pocket enough money to pay for every bill he could think of.

when the police stopped richard, his explanations of who he was, where he had come from, where he was going and how he came to have so much cash, weren't sufficient to please the two officers who were looking for a middle-aged colored man who had robbed and raped a woman over in mid-city.

we do not have to go into any details. the focus of this story is not on the beating, the injustice of his subsequent death, or even the condemning of the two police officers. remember, we are concerned with death, and the question is: when, if ever, did richard know he was going to die and what was his reaction, or more precisely, what were his thoughts about that awful fact, if indeed he ever realized the imminence of his demise?

four

everybody, sooner or later, thinks about dying. for many african americans there is even a morbid twist on this universal reflection on the inevitability of mortality. for us, it is not just a question of when we will die but also a more thorny question, a question we seldom would admit publicly but one that at some occasion or another consumes us in private: would i be better off dead? if you had been reared black in pre-sixties white america, sooner or later, you probably looked that thought in the eye.

however, the universality of death thoughts notwithstanding, there is a big difference between abstract speculation about the eventuality of death and the far more difficult task of confronting the stale breath of death as it fouls the air in front your nose. death is nothing to fuck with.

indeed, actually facing certain death can make you shit on yourself, particularly if death not only surprises you but also perversely gives you a moment to think about crossing the great divide. like when a lover, in the throes of getting it on, sincerely announces through clenched teeth that they are about to come, you respond as any sensible person would by doing harder, or faster, or stronger, or more tenderly, more intensely, more whatever; you increase the pressure and help usher that moment. Well, when it's death coming, what do we do: do we rush to it or do we withdraw from it? don't answer too soon. think of all the people you have heard of who died as a result of being some place they really shouldn't have been, being involved in some situation they should never have encountered, at the hands of someone whom they should never have been near. think about how often we die other than a natural death—and then again, what death is not natural, because isn't it part of human nature to die, and to kill?

richard never expected to die on that day, especially since he had just experienced the good fortune of a twenty-to-one long shot paying up on a fifty dollar bet. even when the tandem took turns trying to beat a confession out of him, even after his jaw was broken and he could only moan and shake his head, even then richard still didn't think of death. he was too busy dealing with pain. when they put the gun in his mouth, he perversely thought, "go 'head, pull the trigger, that would be better than getting beat like this," but even then, richard didn't really expect to die. he just wanted the beating to be over, and if it took death to end it, well, he was feeling so bad he thought that death might be preferable. yet, richard didn't really think he was going to die. in fact, as is the case with so many of us, richard died before he realized they were going to kill him.

we blacks wonder about fate and destiny, justice and karma. sometimes there seems that there is no god, or rather if there is a god then he is capricious with a macabre sense of humor—we grant him humor because to think of god without humor would be to concede that we are at the mercy of a monster who enjoys literally tormenting us to death.

which brings up another question: would we procreate if it were not so pleasurable? if sex didn't feel good, would we bother with conceiving children? for many of us the answer is obvious; of course, we wouldn't. that's why birth control was created—to protect us from disease and children, to make it possible for us to enjoy the pleasure of sexual procreation with none of the responsibilities of child-rearing. which means that the drive to have children may in fact not be as strong as we have been led to believe, or maybe, it's simply that in modern times we have been conditioned to think only of ourselves—the personal pleasures. but the question i really want to raise is this: what if death were pleasurable? would we end ourselves? what if it felt really good to die—not just calming, but totally pleasurable?

of course, richard was not thinking any of these sorts of questions as the two officers smashed in his face. formal philosophy is a task engaged in by those for whom survival is not a pressing issue.

five

every age, every people, every society has an ethos—a defining spirit. and this spirit expresses itself in sometimes odd and fascinating ways. for much of the 20th century the ethos of african americans was one of contemplating the future with a certain optimism. why else march through the streets of birmingham, alabama, and sing "we shall overcome" to bull connor, a man who was not known for any appreciation of music?

the birmingham of bull connor was just about half a century ago. during that period when bombs regularly sounded throughout birmingham and the deep south, if you go back and look at the pictures of black people of that era when they posed for a portrait, especially if they were college-educated, you will invariable spy among the men what i call the classic negro pose of hand to chin in contemplation. a variation is one temple of a pair of glasses held close to or between the lips; then there is the pipe firmly grasped, not to mention the college diploma held to the side of the head like a sweetheart—these are iconic images of optimistic negroes, images that capture the ethos of their era.

today, the hand has moved from the chin. we no longer pose in contemplative ways; what is cropping up more and more is the hand to the crown of the head, not in a woe is me posture, but more like: damn, this is some deep shit we're in.

unconsciously, during a recent photo shoot, i ended up in that pose. when the picture was published i was mildly surprised; i did not remember adopting that look of serious concern. but just because i don't remember it does not mean that it didn't happen. clearly it happened. there is my unsmiling portrait. and i see that pose more and more, particularly when i look at the publicity shots of writers. we are children of production—we are shaped and influenced, even when unconscious of it, by the prevailing ethos. a lot of us look like we are gravely weighing the upsides and downsides of both life and death.

and when people tell you how much they like that photo, then that tells you just how much the photo reflects our current contemplation of death. in those photographs rarely are we smiling. our eyes are wide open. we are not dreamy-eyed romantics. we are not lost in meditation. we are looking at death. the disintegration of our communities, the fissure of our social structures, the absence of lasting interpersonal relationships, the proliferation of age and gender alienation. the death of a people.

and when i took my photo it was supposed to be a happy occasion. but obviously the myth of the happy negro is long gone.

six

i wonder when the old man put the gun to his head did he hold his head with his free hand?

seven

richard couldn't put his hands to his head because his hands were handcuffed behind him.

eight

which story seems more plausible: the old man or richard? is it not odd that by piling up details and framing the story in a believable context, it is relatively easy to believe that richard hammonds actually died as a result of a police beating and shooting in the late fifties in new orleans? and that the old man seems to be a metaphor. but an old man (whose name i don't want to reveal because it would add nothing to our story) actually killed himself during the christmas holidays (of course i speculate and fictionalize a lot of the old man's story, but the suicide actually happened), and the story of richard hammonds is totally fictitious except for the cops who killed him—cops did kill negroes in new orleans.

nine

the old man and richard hammonds had gone to high school together, and gone to bars together, making merry, drinking and acting mindlessly stupid on a couple of occasions. they had double-dated a couple of times, and had once even engaged in sex with the same woman. (at different times, months apart, but the same woman nonetheless—she remembers the old man as the better lover because he was more tender, seemed more sincere.

(there had been this untalked about but often expressed rivalry between richard and the old man. close friends are often bound by both love and jealousy, so there was nothing unusual about them being attracted to the same woman. but remember richard was the handsome one. he was also glib, perhaps because he learned how to hold back his feelings. he could talk a woman into bed, or more likely the back of a studebaker—richard's father worked as a pullman porter and made nice money for a colored man and had bought a car but was often not in town to enjoy the car, and richard, though he didn't personally have much money, did have access to the car. anyway, richard never thought about what the women he bedded in the back seat thought about before, during, or after he bedded them. after all it was just a moment's pleasure.

(but the old man, well, he was a young man then, he thought about how others felt about him a lot, and though he fucked mildred, it was not because she was available, but because he was really, really moved by mildred and told her so. told her, "girl you moves me."

("i do?" she was used to men wanting to sex her, but not to men admitting that they were deeply affected by her.

("yes, you does," and he twirled her at that moment— they were dancing and he was whispering in her ear, dancing in a little new orleans nite club, to a song on the juke box—he twirled her. and smiled. and she had never been twirled quite like this gracefully dancing young man twirled her. and when she reversed the twirl and spun back into his arms, he momentarily paused and said, "i wish i could dance with you all night.")

the old man had not been angling to get her in bed; he was just genuinely enjoying her company. he liked to dance. she liked to dance. they were having a good time.

and when somehow they ended up making love on the sofa in her front room that night while her sister and her sister's children soundly (he hoped) slept two rooms away, he had been a little nervous at first.

her softness felt so good, before he knew it, a little cry caught in his throat. he was trying to be quiet, but goodness and quiet sometimes do not go together. i mean, you know how good it hurts to hold it in? well the possibility that the sound of your lovemaking will disturb and awaken others nearby, that anxiety about discovery adds to the covert enjoyment. so, instead of surfacing upward through his throat, the cry was redirected down into his chest, but it bounced back and was about to pop audibly out of his mouth. mildred felt that sound about to pour forth like a coo-coo clock gone haywire, and with the mischief that only a woman can summon she cupped one hand tightly over his mouth and with her other hand reached down and gently squeezed his testicles.

ya boy liked to died. he shuddered. he couldn't breath. her hand tightly covered his mouth and partially blocked his nose. and he was coming like mad. and he moaned a stifled moan, air yo-yoing back in forth between the back of his mouth atop his throat and the near bursting constriction of his chest. finally, he wheezed gusts of exhales out of his distended nostrils, which flared like those of a race horse heaving after a superfast lap. and then he cried out and tried to call back the sound all at the same time. and that was followed with another terrible quake. in a semi-conscious state, he lay helpless, wrapped up in the murmured laughter of mildred's playful passion.

but he didn't hear her soft, soft laughter. he didn't hear anything. he was totally out of it. he was struggling to catch his breath, in fact had almost slipped off the large couch—if her legs had not clamped around him so firmly, he would have tumbled to the floor. after that he didn't distinctly remember anything until he woke up the next morning, at home in his own bed, and didn't know how he got there. he must have walked home or something, but all he could remember was her softness, her touch, his lengthy orgasm (he had never come that long before), and the way her legs held him when he almost fell over. you can easily forget a short walk home, but there are some experiences that are so sharply etched in the memory of your flesh, those encounters you never forget.

a couple of days later when richard asked the old man about mildred, whether they had done it, the old man had said, "no, we just had a good time dancing and i took her home. then i went home." richard had replied, "you should have got it, she likes you. i got her drunk and got it once, but she never would let me get no mo. but she likes you. you should get it." the old man had said nothing further, merely looked away, certain that richard would not understand that what the old man felt for mildred, although initiated by the sharpness of their sexual encounter, was, nonetheless, a feeling deeper than a good fuck.

many years later, when the old man was watching the house of representatives vote to impeach bill clinton for lying to the american people about the monica lewinsky affair, something terrible took hold of him. although he continued to see mildred for over twenty years and even had a kid with her, the old man had never told his wife. and he felt intensely guilty. intensely.

he felt horrible. felt like he had felt at richard's funeral. sitting in the catholic church before a closed casket. the body had been too brutalized to have a public viewing. the police had shot his good friend richard, shot him in the head.

while he sat between his wife and two daughters on one side and his young son on the other side, the old man was thinking about his dead friend when he looked up and saw mildred looking over at him with those large, limpid brown eyes. nearly every time he stole a glance her way, she seemed to be looking directly at him. he could not read her eyes.

but his friend richard was dead. and the old man's wife and legitimate children were at his side and his woman was across the aisle staring at him, and the old man felt really guilty about how he was living his life, and he put his head in his hands and just wanted to ball up and die. and he didn't realize he was crying until his wife dabbed his face with her handkerchief.

ten

a murder is a crime against society. we look at pictures of murderers and wonder about them. wonder what led them to do it. wonder do they have feelings like the rest of us.

what motivates one human to lynch another?

in the case of a suicide, everyone who survives wonders not only what led to the murder but also, particularly for those who were close to the victim, we wonder what could we have done, what "should" we have done to prevent the murder.

murder is a crime condemning society and suicide is particularly damning of those who were close to the murderer (who is also the murderee). if you think about someone close to you committing suicide, you have to ask yourself, what did i fail to do that would have prevented that person from committing self-murder? while sometimes we ask that question of a mass murderer—what could have been done to prevent them from acting the way they did—we always ask that question of a suicide. and why? if we cannot stop people from committing large and impersonal murders, how can we hope to stop small murders, the most personal of murders: the suicide? the question is perplexing.

after a while though, you come to an awful realization: maybe it is impossible to stop people from killing each other and themselves. indeed, is it not a certainty that it is impossible to stop suicide?

eleven

if you are shot in the head with a large handgun, it can be messy.

twelve

if you shoot yourself in the head with a large handgun, it can be messy.

thirteen

the old man's casket was sealed before the funeral mass just like richard's had been. a closed casket is a terrible death, for it is a death which suggests that this death is much more worse than ordinary death. this is a death you can not look in the face. and what can be more horrible than imagining how horrible death looks when the corpse is too horrible to look at?

fourteen

mildred was at the old man's funeral. so was their son who favored his mother but had his father's skin color. mildred had not talked with the old man in over two months, and then it was only briefly over the phone. he had said something about being sorry he had never been brave enough to marry her. and hung up. mildred had waited in vain for him to call back. as anxious as she had been, she had never once broken their agreement. she knew where he lived, knew his phone number, but she never called. never. and now he was dead, gone. life is so cruel, especially when much of your life is lived cloistered in a box of arrangements shut off from what passes for normal life. to everyone, mildred looked like the statistic of single mother with one child: a son, father unknown. but what she felt like was a widow, a widow who had never been married, but a true widow nevertheless, her de facto husband's corpse sequestered in a closed box, not unlike her whole life, lived unrecognized, outside of sight. issac (mildred and the old man's son) used to ask who his father was, but he stopped asking after weathering junior high school taunts. and once he was married and had children of his own, he understood that what was important was not who his father had been but what kind of father he would be for his children. when his mother called and asked him to accompany her to the old man's funeral, issac at last knew the answer without ever having to rephrase the question. mildred and issac both remained dry-eyed throughout the service, even though inside both of them were crying like crazy.

you can not gauge the depths simply by looking at the surface. printed on the program was a smiling snapshot of the old man. next to the closed casket there was an enlargement of this same posed photograph. but what picture of the old man was in various people's mind?

moreover, what does a self murderer look like whose death has left the corpse too gruesome to witness? certainly not like the smiling headshot on the easel surrounded by flowers.

was the look in the old man's eye as he pulled the trigger anything like that wild look in the eyes of white people staring at a lynched negro—of course not. but what did he look like, looking at his own death?

fifteen

have you ever seen a picture of the man who was convicted of bombing the baptist church in birmingham, alabama, and killing those four little girls? he looks like a white man. and once you get beyond the racial aspect of the murderer, he looks like a man. and once you get beyond the gender aspect of the murderer—a grown man killing four little girls—well, then, he looks like a human being. murderers are human beings. they look like what they are. it is a conceit to think that murderers look different from "ordinary" human beings. what does a killer look like? look at the nearest human being.

sixteen

while i admit i have not seen a lot of pictures of white people—and then again, i have undoubtedly seen more pictures of white people than of black people when you consider how the image of whiteness surrounds us and bombards us in school, in commerce, in television, in entertainment, in advertisements, everywhere—but anyway, i don't remember seeing many white persons in the classic negro pose of yore, nor in the contemporary iconic hand-to-the-crown-of-the-head pose.

in examining the photos of lynchings, i see none of the concern for the future that the hand to the head would indicate. that hand to the head indicates that a person has a heart. that a person is feeling life, and though the life that is felt may not be pleasant, at least we are still feeling.

but when you watch and listen to and smell a person dying, and when you cut off your feelings for the fate of another human being, well... and you know it is not biological. have you read about the civil wars in africa typified by the hutu vs. tutsi conflict? how literally thousands of people are hacked to death. it is one thing to fire a gun or drop a bomb; it is another thing to whack, whack, whack with a machete, slaughtering a human being as though assailing a dangerous beast or a tree that was in the way of progress. when any of us, be we white, black, or whatever, when we sever our feelings to the point that not only do we methodically and unfeelingly commit acts of mass murder or acts of ritual murder, but we can watch murder and not feel revulsion, then obviously we have moved to the point that death gives us pleasure.

when i first raised the issue about death and pleasure, you may have thought, "oh, how absurd." but the next time you are chomping your popcorn and sipping your artificially flavored sugar water while watching thrilling scenes of mayhem, murder and mass destruction on the silver screen (perhaps i should add that you have paid for the privilege of this pleasure)—but the next time the bodies fly through the air, the bullets rip apart a young man in slow-mo, the very next time you watch an image of death and get pleasure from it, see if you can remember to say "oh, how absurd."

i think you won't be able to, any more than at the moment of orgasm you would holler "oh, how absurd." for you see pleasure in and of itself is never absurd—perverse perhaps, but never absurd. and taking pleasure in someone else's death: oh, how...what? how do we describe that pleasure? what is human about enjoying death? or perhaps, since deriving pleasure from someone else's demise seems to be a norm today, maybe i should ask, what is inhuman about enjoying death?

there is much that is wrong.

WHAT I SAW WHEN I SAW *SELMA*

If, in 2014, we're still making 'white savior movies' then it's just lazy and unfortunate... We've grown up as a country and cinema should be able to reflect what's true. And what's true is that black people are the center of their own lives and should tell their own stories from their own perspectives.

—Ava DuVernay

one

Spring 1963 (or thereabout). I was in the 11th grade at St. Augustine High School, New Orleans, when I first got arrested. Sitting-in at Woolworth's lunch corner, corner of Canal and Rampart Streets. We were the young soldiers of the Civil Rights Movement, the optimistic naïveté of youth meeting the stubborn earnestness with which we non-violently attacked Jim Crow, whose sanctioned agents replied with billy clubs and rough arrests, or else turned a blind eye as rabid thugs were let loose on us. Jeers, slaps, and worse crowned our heads.

I was not prepared for how the scene of the Pettus Bridge beat-down would affect me. Both times the brutality stunned me: I saw the movie twice, first with my wife, then the following day with my grandson. All I could do was fight back the painful memory tears of being maced by New Orleans' boys in blue when we demonstrated at Southern University in New Orleans, the spring of 1969. The pain of the chemical sprayed directly on your face, into your eyes, nose, and mouth, was not just the peppered burning but the gasping for air: you can't breathe. I could stand the clubbings and drubbings, but I couldn't breathe. Couldn't breathe.

I had forgotten how much I couldn't breathe. *Selma* reminded me.

two

Selma is only a half a page in the multi-volume tome of our historic struggle. Smudged and tattered, difficult to read for facts, but brimming over with emotional nuggets of truth.

Did you see those preachers digging in at the dinner table? You may think I concentrate on a minor message, but King and cohorts were often feted by people who could barely afford to eat; poor people prepared banquets for the royalty of the Civil Rights Movement. For many of us, these preachers represented messengers of deliverance, and Lord knows we needed someone to lead us out of the wilderness of the Jim Crow South. To others of us, these ministers were honorable misleaders trooping us deeper into the abyss of capitalism, consumerism, and devilish wanna-beism. Or as our mighty mouth of honor, our prophetic wailer who returned to the wilderness time and time again when he could have easily stayed gone—I'm speaking of a man named Jimmy, aka James Baldwin—presciently warned: the sixties was on fyah, and we should not want to be integrated into a burning house.

Our two-pronged struggle: one side advocating that we salute an all-American vision and the other advocating self-determination. *Selma* reminded me how much

Black&White together feared Black power. Which is why Malcolm was presented as a broken, solitary figure; SNCC as impetuous hot heads; SCLC as master negotiators and tacticians.

I understand that this was King's story, SCLC's vision. Hence this was a movie true to the Christian belief in the redemptive power of righteous suffering. But that beautiful moment when Annie Lee Cooper went Muhammad Ali on heavyweight Sheriff Jim Clark, flat-out socked him dead in his bulldog jowls, thereby striking a mighty blow for self-defense--compare that to King's stoic acceptance of a fisted greeting from a redneck upon his arrival in Selma. The mules of the world were tired of pulling other people's plows, of accepting horse-hidings; we were not farm animals any longer. We were in full-out revolt. *Selma* showed all of that, sometimes staring you dead in your face, un-miss-able, other times in micro details that you might not have noticed if you didn't know the context.

Did you know that when they mentioned Lowndes County, that Lowndes was a SNCC stronghold, and that their movement's challenging slogan was "move on over or we'll move on over you"? Did you know what the Lowndes County movement symbol was? The Black Panther. The same Black Panther that inspired Bobby, Huey, and Eldridge. Yes, Lowndes was the harbinger and inspiration for a soon to arrive, game-changing Black political movement.

three

Coretta confronted King about his infidelities. Oh, how wonderfully and deeply done was that scene. King immediately did a St. Peter and depressedly went into denial. Coretta calmly replied, I know what you sound like. I know. What you. Sound like. This was not reality television. No cursing, fussing, and fighting. I know (and you know I know) what you sound like, who you really are. "Do you love me?"

she jabbed, setting up her knock-out punch. And then as Martin struggled to find words of deliverance or extrication from this cul-de-sac, Coretta delivered the roundhouse KO: she asked did he love the others. The man of elegant words was clobbered mute and dumbfounded.

Time and time again, at crucial moments director Ava DuVernay took a Miles Davis approach, using silence and space to increase the tension rather than bombast and effusiveness. Silence. Empty space, eye shifts. Moments when we hold our breaths waiting for a response so we can exhale. Yes. No. Did you love them? Not, Did you do it? Not, I believe you. Nor the accusation: You're lying. No. Did you love them? Because certainly there were a number of thems. I am not stupid.

In that moment Coretta quietly had the last word.

She spoke for so many women: I am not stupid.

four

Unless you have been a leader in a mass movement, it is difficult to appreciate how lonely it is at the front. The fawning throngs that include attractive people who more than admire and adore you; their willing availability magnifies how lonely you are in the few quiet moments you have. Far away from home.

Temporary easement eagerly awaits outside your hotel door, or in some secluded room, maybe even the backseat of a nondescript sedan parked on the dark end of a discrete, unnamed street. Someone soft and warm approaches, offering the release of their embrace. And not just one someone. Some two, some three, some four and more. And you are so lonely. So tired of being strong. Even your Jesus asked for the bitter cup of lonely suffering to be gone from him.

In *Selma,* King is shown seeking succor by calling Mahalia Jackson on the telephone and asking her to sing to him in the dead of night. Sing to him. Sing. Does not go to Coretta and ask for her voice. Calls Mahalia. I need to hear...

We all have needs; how we satisfy (or suffer the dissatisfaction) of those needs is our personal journey. I understand King's dilemma. Howsoever we view the choices King made, one thing is clear: regardless of his dalliances, King rose in the morning and valiantly went to meet the man. That is the other important point: yes, sleeping around was a significant betrayal of his marriage vows, but the more important reality is that King went to meet the man. We remember King because of King confronting the man, not because of King coupling with other women.

The FBI spies have noted that in terms of marital fidelity, Malcolm was a saint compared to King. But saint or sinner, what mattered is that they both went to meet the man. And that they both were assassinated for their efforts. America deals violently with its opponents. It takes great courage to oppose American racism as the leader of a movement rather than simply as a lone voice in the wilderness. They will ignore you if you are a lone voice; they will kill you if you are an effective leader. That is why so much of our history is hidden from us. Our history reveals both our bravery as well as the ruthlessness of our oppressors.

Selma shows us the bravery and, with the use of FBI reports overlaid in type on certain scenes, hints at the ruthlessness of our oppressors.

five

King in jail. Coretta visits and tells him of her meeting with Malcolm. Martin accuses Coretta of being enamored. And immediately tries to call back his hurtful words. Perhaps he belatedly realized he was actually criticizing his own indiscretions rather than what he saw as Coretta's offense in meeting with brother Malcolm.

While SCLC was often at political odds over tactics with their youthful SNCC allies, SCLC actually feared Malcolm. Subconsciously—probably with a total lack of self-aware-ness—they feared that Malcolm, in his resolute advocacy of self-defense, would be perceived as more man than they were in their philosophical advocacy of non-violence as a response to White aggression and racism. King and the other preach-ers knew that the youth were closer in temperament to Malcolm than to King.

SNCC had invited Malcolm to speak in Selma. In the film, a decision was made to show SCLC's fear upon the arrival of Malcolm, but not to show Malcolm's Selma speech (part of which is preserved in a widely available YouTube video). Not to show Malcolm delivering his house negro/field negro analysis. Not to show Malcolm in action. A few weeks before he was assassinated. Malcolm standing tall, defiant, angry, but also full of sly humor that appealed to the youth's determination to bury Jim Crow.

The Malcolm shown in *Selma* was not the reality of the Malcolm who spoke in Selma in 1965; was not the Malcolm who met with Coretta and won her over, garnered her admiration—the Malcolm whose sincerity led Coret-ta to confront King with more resolve than when she first responded to the FBI tapes of King moaning and groaning in another woman's arms.

six

King turning around on the bridge. Again I understand. When we led a student movement and took over Southern University in New Orleans (SUNO) in the spring of 1969, our inner circle included a number of Vietnam era veterans. I had done a year in Korea, electronic maintenance of the Nike Hercules nuclear missile (my job included arming the nuclear warhead). We were fearless, some would say foolhar-dy, if not outright stupid. Surely impetuous.

The governor of Louisiana had vowed he would never come to meet with us in New Orleans as long as our demonstrations were going on, as long as we commandeered the running of the school and defiantly nullified the administration's rule. So we decided to caravan to Baton Rouge, the state capitol. I was under a court order, on bond awaiting trial for some of our activities. I was restricted to New Orleans. But I could not be a leader if I stayed behind.

An unknown Black man came to visit us the day before our journey. He identified himself as a state trooper. He came to warn us that an unnamed "they" intended to kill us. He pleaded with us to call off our trip. He literally begged us not to go.

That some of us always carried guns when we ventured forth in our struggle was an open secret. He said that our being armed was going to be used as an excuse to cut us down. Don't go. Don't do it. They going to kill you.

It wasn't the first time I had to face a high noon moment. I was not personally afraid of dying, but I thought about the students in our movement. Seventeen, eighteen years old. They were not volunteering to die. Most of them were not armed.

Our inner circle deliberated. For sure I was told it was too dangerous for me to go. I would probably be arrested as soon as we got to Baton Rouge, if not before on the highway. To go or not to go, that was my question.

I was prepared to be arrested, but not prepared for anyone to be hurt or killed while I remained behind in New Orleans because of some trifling court order. We all drove to Baton Rouge. But we decided to leave our guns behind.

The governor, of course, was not there when we arrived. I did not go inside the capitol building, stayed outside next to one of our vehicles. When the students entered the capitol building, some of the brothers smuggled our red, black, and green liberation flag into the building, took the elevator to the top, and waved the flag from the observation deck.

What a beautiful sight. From around the corner I spied a phalanx of state troopers in full riot gear marching toward us. Gas masks affixed, some had shields. None carried batons, rather they gripped assault rifles at the ready. Our shotguns, carbines, and hunting rifles would have been no match for the troopers' armaments. We immediately hustled the students out of the building, got in our cars, and returned to New Orleans before we could be attacked. It was a close call.

That scene on the bridge when King turned around. It wasn't personal cowardice or personal fear. He was thinking about others. Thinking about the ass whipping the marchers had suffered a few days earlier on their first attempt at the march from Selma to Montgomery.

I probably would have marched on, but I understand him turning around. Another great wordless scene in a movie filled with such poignant moments. Some have suggested that King had cut a deal with LBJ and was awaiting promised federal protection. Others point out that King decided not to defy a court injunction against the march because King feared doing so would have resulted not only in mass arrests and beatings but also might have ruptured his White House negotiations. Who really knows the whole story?

I have seen people beaten and bloodied while participating in a demonstration I led at SUNO when we took down the American flag and hoisted the red, black, and green flag of Black liberation. Thrown into the back of a paddy wagon, I could only beat on the side of the wagon as I heard fellow students screaming and crying beneath the police assault going down while we leaders were immediately arrested and locked up in the back of a van. Later that day, television news reports and the newspaper the next day had pictures of Sandra Marcelin, blood streaming down her face from a billy club blow to her head. We were fortunate that day. Many were brutalized, but none suffered broken bones or worse.

If you've never been caught up in a police riot; never seen young women beaten bloody by grown-ass men who had taken an oath to protect; never been responsible for leading a demonstration that put so many defenseless people in harm's way; if you have never been there, it is improbable, if not impossible, to fully understand why King turned around.

seven

Although she was mostly shown as silent in the movie, Diane Nash was a major leader of the Civil Rights Movement in general, and along with her then husband James Bevel (who was responsible for SCLC's direct action activities), the two of them were the major architects of SCLC's activities in Selma. Indeed, the Selma to Montgomery march is credited as Bevel's idea in response to the police killing of Jimmie Lee Jackson.

Ms. Nash had been the singular force responsible for continuing the Freedom Rides when CORE withdrew after the Greyhound bus was bombed near Anniston, Alabama. Diane Nash and the Nashville contingent of Civil Rights freedom fighters said, naw, if we stop now, segregation wins. The Diane Nash-led Nashville contingent, along with like-minded CORE workers from New Orleans, made sure that the Freedom Rides went on, but, oh, that's another movie.

"Forward ever, backward never" was her emotional and tactical calling card. At first glance, Diane Nash looked like a young, attractive, respectable, middle-class woman. But she was far more than mere eye-candy. Diane Nash was a field marshal held in the highest regard within movement circles. Hence in the film, she is correctly portrayed as present at the movement strategy sessions, and speaking up in favor of collective decision-making, rather than letting one man decide what should be done.

Diane Nash, who was one of the founders of SNCC, had elected to join her husband in SCLC—their romance is subtly shown: Bevel's hand lovingly on Diane's shoulder, the two of them exchanging eye contact. It's there but not writ large; if you don't know what to look for, you missed its depiction in the movie. But make no mistake: Diane Nash was no token woman in a movement too often dominated by male egos.

Diane Nash was Coretta's analogue in terms of her education and breeding and in terms of being married to a major leader of the movement. The difference between the two, however, was that Diane was a front liner in the struggle rather than a rear guard support activist. She was in the lineage of Daisy Bates of the Little Rock 9; Gloria Richardson of Cambridge, Maryland; and Fannie Lou Hamer of Mississippi—that same line that extends back through Harriet Tubman and Sojourner Truth during the era of enslavement, and Ida B. Wells during the post-Reconstruction period, a period second only to slavery in its brutality. Indeed, Diane Nash is an activist descendant of ancient warrior queens Nzinga of Angola, Yaa Asantewaa of Ghana, Xica de Silva of Brazil, and Nanny of Jamaica.

Our history is distinctive in that we have so many women who were famous warriors literally leading us in battle. As Diane Nash exemplifies, women warriors are our calling card: scour world history, you will not find among other people as many courageous women as we have, women who led as fighters and theorists of warfare.

The Chinese say that women hold up half the sky. In the seventies we said our women keep our skies from falling—but even that does not tell the whole story. As history makes clear, black women as both lovers and warriors healed us when wounded, enabled us when violently suppressed and gifted us with the strength to proudly walk this earth.

Black women.

Black warrior women. They ennobled all of us, which necessarily means they ennoble themselves as a critical and essential element of who we were, are, and can ever become.

Black women—all colors, all shades, all sizes, all generations.

Black women, they not only ennoble our people, at a critical level germane to all human beings, black women make better and more beautiful this terrible but wonderful world we inhabit.

eight

The moment in the morgue. Cager Lee identifying the body of his grandson Jimmie Lee Jackson, who was shot by a peace officer when Jimmie Lee stepped forward to defend his mother, Viola Lee Jackson, from a beating in a café after a demonstration the police brutally broke up.

Death is a heavy burden. Dealing with the death of people who paid the ultimate price for confronting intransigent oppression—well, what did Coretta call it? A fog. I would call it the great white fog.

Dying in the movement is a particular death that brings immense survivor's guilt to those who do make it to the other side after plodding through the slaughter.

My maternal grandfather was a minister. Founded a church in the countryside of Violet, Louisiana, just below New Orleans, down from Chalmette and Arabi, snaking south along the Mississippi River; and founded another in the city, Greater Liberty Baptist Church, 1230 Desire Street, which is where I received spiritual teachings until I left at age 15. In fact, the hope of a number of older parishioners was that I was going to take up the ministerial mantle.

I disappointed a lot of people when I rejected the calling and subsequently rejected religion altogether. For a few, that disappointment turned bitter when my grandfather died as a result of a stroke he had while speaking at a meeting that the SUNO administration had called, inviting parents and community people to come out and help them regain control of us student demonstrators who were literally and effectively running SUNO in the spring of 1969.

Rev. Noah Copelin's funeral was the first time I wore a suit and tie after mustering out of the army in June of 1968; that was also the last time I wore the euro-centric costume. My grandmother asked me to dress up; given the situation, doing so was not a difficult decision. The demise of my grandfather while speaking out on behalf of our movement, speaking up for his grandson—at what price, freedom? I asked myself that question many a night, many a time.

Death makes you serious.

My grandfather was an old man when I was a young man full of fire. As I watch *Selma*, at age 67, I am an old man. Of course I knew my grandfather. But I also knew old man Cager Lee. I knew many Cager Lees.

I know what it takes to stand-up straight after nearly a century of being bent over and beat down. What it takes to refuse to back down after saying "yes sir" all your damned life. What great humanity it took for a peasant to follow a King into non-violent battle. Through beatings and bombings, mayhem and all kinds of torture at the hands of formal and informal KKK nightriders and the modern-day paddy rollers who are euphemistically called the police.

It's as hard as being right-handed your whole life and then suddenly, instantly switching over to your left hand, walking a new walk, looking the foe straight in the eye, refusing to bow down. For those old men, being an upright man was no easy task. Indeed, being an upright man was a dangerous undertaking that could, and too often did, get you or someone you loved killed.

That scene in the morgue caused droplets of clear water in my eyes. At what great cost did Cager Lee earn the opportunity to vote? Mr. Lee was played by Henry G. Sanders, who was the lead actor in Charles Burnett's *Killer of Sheep*, one of a handful of undisputed cinema classics produced during the sixties era of the Black Arts Movement. Burnett's tour de force is now enshrined as an American treasure in the Smithsonian.

Sanders as Cager Lee was not a simple case of typecasting. This was acting at the highest level. David Oyelowo as King gave a stellar turn projecting the gravitas and eloquence of King while also giving us his humanity and interior conflicts. But what Sanders did was on a whole other level of embodiment.

Sanders had a quiet part, not many words. He had to use his body, his face, his eyes, the way he moved his jaws, the set of his lips, a halting but determined gait. A marvel of powerful understatement. Less is more only when there's obviously so much more behind, underneath, and in the interior of what is outwardly revealed.

It's not easy to simultaneously express both deep grief and deep resolve to carry on. A man, no longer young, stares full on into the awful face of death and is no longer afraid. Pushing past the white fog of death, a fog that enveloped him and all his people for all the years he had survived.

Back then, just past mid-century, if you were deep in the Deep South, in every direction you looked, all you would see was encased in a deadly white fog. But somehow your determination was to walk through the density of that death. Your grandson: dead. Your future: gone. How can you possibly still believe in the beauty of tomorrow, Mr. Lee? Oh, Mr. Lee! Old Mr. Lee. And that is the true beauty, caught up in the depths and death of segregation's great white fog, somehow you keep the faith, you still believe in a beautiful tomorrow. Your humble determination to keep on keeping on. To have been in the storm sixty-some (or more) years long and still successfully struggle to unfurl the question mark of your bent back, that unfolding defiantly displaying the emphatic exclamation point of uprightness; to still be resolutely striding forward; to still be human, still be what you have not previously fully been able to be, still be more man, more woman, more human than a murderous society has murderously prohibited. That's beautiful. That's truly beautiful.

Was Sanders acting or was he channeling Cager Lee? All the Cager Lees, generations of old men who summoned up the fortitude to confront what seemed to be a mighty and irresistible evil: the evil of Deep South racial segregation. You don't see many beautiful old men pictured by Hollywood. You don't find many actors who project this depth of dignity and forbearance.

If *Selma* was robbed in the Academy Award nominations, ignoring Sanders' portrayal of Cager Lee was a back alley mugging and murder.

nine

LBJ. Long, tall, cussing and cajoling, a Texas cowpoke who blew his chance to be crowned a King—rather than being contemptuous of LBJ, *Selma* was actually too kind to him. Joseph A. Califano, Jr., a top assistant for domestic affairs from 1965 to 1969, has led the charges of foul play leveled at *Selma*. Indeed, in a *Washington Post* op-ed, Califano outright states: "In fact, Selma was LBJ's idea, he considered the Voting Rights Act his greatest legislative achievement, he viewed King as an essential partner in getting it enacted—and he didn't use the FBI to disparage him."

For people who do not intimately know the history of the sixties Civil Rights Movement, *Selma*'s presentation of LBJ's role might be a point of contention. Moreover, although King's leadership is projected as an uncontested fact, SNCC had already established a Selma project prior to King's arrival in 1965.

Furthermore, 1964 was actually the most pivotal year of the Civil Rights emphasis on voting. That year, Bob Moses led SNCC in establishing Freedom Summer in Mississippi. That campaign brought national attention not only to the overall Civil Rights struggle but placed a spotlight specifically on voting rights. That same year, the Mississippi Freedom Democratic Party (MFDP) journeyed to Atlantic City to challenge the seating of the segregationist Mississippi Democrats. MFDP was the result of a coalition of local and national movement organizations. MFDP had held mock elections in Mississippi that generated over 80,000 voters. Significantly, one of the leading MFDP spokespersons was Mrs. Fannie Lou Hamer, who testified that she was "sick and tired of being sick and tired."

The man who was vice president when Kennedy was assassinated in November of 1963, and who would become the Democratic Party's presidential nominee in 1964, was LBJ—Lyndon Baines Johnson, a consummate political operative: 12 years in the House and 12 years in the Senate, including six years as Senate majority leader. In terms of setting new directions for American society, LBJ became the most accomplished president since Franklin Delano Roosevelt. Although not as popular as either Eisenhower or Kennedy, Johnson signed into law major legislation, including the Civil Rights Act of 1964, the Voting Rights Act of 1965, and the Immigration and Nationality Act of 1965. He was the architect of the "Great Society" and The War on Poverty. Additionally, he secured the 1964 Gulf of Tonkin Resolution that gave him war powers in Vietnam without having to urge Congress to declare war.

Ironically, Vietnam proved to be Johnson's Waterloo. The war provoked a massive anti-war movement domestically, which in combination with the major Black rebellions, especially the summer 1965 Watts conflagration, majorly contributed to LBJ's political undoing. Although he legally could have run, Johnson chose not to seek a second elected term in 1968.

In hindsight, Selma 1965 may be viewed as the apogee of the liberal Civil Rights Movement. Indeed engaging in a bit of hyperbole as to the importance of SCLC-led activities, King summed up the major Civil Rights legislative milestones as the results of non-violent activities. In a report to the SCLC national convention, King wrote: "Montgomery led to the Civil Rights Act of 1957 and 1960; Birmingham inspired the Civil Rights Act of 1964, and Selma produced the voting rights legislation of 1965."

The importance of those campaigns notwithstanding, Freedom Summer of 1964 was the critical beginning of the end of the modern Civil Rights struggle's legislative aspect. Selma 1965 historically is paired with Watts summer 1965, which was a veritable explosion of Black rage. Less than a calendar year later, 1966 marks the ascendency of Black Power, as initially articulated by SNCC's newly elected chairperson, Stokley Carmichael, and by SNCC field secretary Willie Ricks. But spreading far beyond the Deep South, the struggle of Black people against oppression was hallmarked by the 1966 founding of the Black Panther Party in Oakland, California.

LBJ recognized that American society was undergoing both tremendous stress as well as momentous social changes. Were it not for the militancy of the Black community and the simultaneous social disruption engendered by the Vietnam War, Johnson might not have been able to push Congress to pass the 1964 Civil Rights bill, and certainly would not have been able to push through the 1965 Voting Rights bill, whose passage was aided by the deaths of White participants in the southern Civil Rights Movement, particularly the deaths of Rev. James Reeb, a Unitarian minister from Boston, and Viola Liuzzo, a volunteer from Michigan who went south specifically to participate in the Selma campaign. Reeb died as a result of a brutal attack by White thugs; Liuzzo died of gun shots from KKK attackers while she was driving marchers back to Selma from Montgomery. Those two deaths in particular galvanized broad American support for passage of the Voting Rights legislation. On signing the bill, LBJ specifically referenced Rev. Reeb's assassination.

Violent rebellions had begun to flare up across large cities in America, especially on the East Coast and in the northern industrial areas. These conflagrations offered an ominous alternative to the non-violent struggles in the segregated South. I believe that LBJ perceptively realized that the Black struggle could not be ignored and potentially could indeed tear the country apart if the issues of segregation and other forms of racism were not dealt with. LBJ knew he needed the participation of Black leaders if the roiling Black rage threatening to engulf American society was to be successfully assuaged.

However, as a result of Johnson's ill-fated attempts at compromise at the Democratic Party's 1964 national convention in Atlantic City, SNCC organizers were loath to deal with LBJ. Rather than recognize the integrated MFDP delegation and reject the hardline, segregated Mississippi delegation, Johnson had offered the MFDP two seats in the convention. The SNCC-led caucus proudly rejected the measly and insulting offer. Among the leaders of the Southern direct action activities, only SCLC and Dr. King were willing to openly negotiate with LBJ and the federal government.

King had received the Nobel Peace Prize in December of 1964 and resultantly was the most widely known and widely respected Black leader. Whereas SNCC was defiantly unwilling to compromise on issues they viewed as basic principles, King was willing to negotiate with LBJ.

By 1965, the direct action arm of Civil Rights Movement was perceived as the major force of social change in

American society. Direct action had eclipsed the NAACP-led legal struggles, which had resulted in the landmark 1954 Supreme Court ruling outlawing segregationist, so-called "separate but equal" social structures. Although technically illegal, Jim Crow continued for a decade to be the law of the land in the Deep South.

The 1964 Civil Rights legislation that LBJ signed into law was the legal basis for challenging and changing the Jim Crow social structures of the Deep South; however, what was technically illegal was nevertheless de facto in daily practice. Direct action confronted and challenged both local de jure Jim Crow structures as well as de facto Jim Crow traditions. Black people and our allies were no longer willing to wait for court mandates to produce change. Through direct action, the Civil Rights Movement was taking the confrontation of segregation to the streets. As a result, the sixties were a time of social turmoil.

The social upheavals produced by a militant Civil Rights Movement directly confronting entrenched and intransigent Jim Crow heightened the strain on the status quo. The subsequent anti-war movement ended up rupturing the social fabric and massively altering civil society at large. Although not usually acknowledged, SNCC was a major force in establishing and encouraging anti-war activities. Specifically, by 1966 SNCC pushed for Whites to work in their own communities rather than continue working in Black communities in the Deep South, and a significant number of Whites who were former SNCC workers took up the anti-war movement as their own civil rights struggle. Moreover, SNCC is credited with pushing Dr. King to an active anti-Vietnam War position.

In many ways, Selma proved to be a turning point. The legal victories were won, but rather than celebrations of victory, nationally the Black struggle exploded far beyond simple demands for equality. At the same time, the anti-war

movement took off. By the seventies, the Women's Movement was a third focus of social struggle, and again former
Civil Rights warriors were at the forefront of the movement
for gender empowerment and respect. Both at home as well
as abroad, America was engulfed in major social and political struggle.

ten

On a national level, the five major Civil Rights organizations
were NAACP, SCLC, SNCC, CORE, and the Urban League.
With the 1966 ascendency of Stokely Carmichael and Rap
Brown to positions of leadership, SNCC, in combination
with SCLC lead by Martin Luther King, Jr., were positioned
as the two preeminent direct action organizations. Neither
the NAACP nor the Urban League were known as direct
action-oriented. CORE, who had earlier led the Freedom
Riders movement, by the mid-sixties was partnering with
SNCC in the explosive Mississippi campaign.

Picturing the complexity of the interlocking theories and
actions of the "Big 5" Civil Rights organizations, and making
clear how the actions of each organization did or didn't impact
Selma, could not possibly be done within a one-and-a-half-
hour, or even a two- or three-hour, Hollywood movie framework. Understandably, many of the details of the internal
organizational rivalries were left out of the movie. Although
she did not focus on this complex, sometimes contentious
backstory, DuVernay did allude to it throughout the movie,
especially the SNCC/SCLC back and forth.

From 1963 until 1966, John Lewis was the chairman of
SNCC, yet his participation in the Selma marches was not
simply the work of one committed individual: the Selma
campaign actually comprised three different efforts to cross
the Pettus Bridge.

All three marches were co-led by SCLC and SNCC
together. As was demonstrated throughout Mississippi, Civil

Rights activities were going to happen whether or not King participated. Indeed, King was not even present at the first march that was led by SCLC Hosea Williams alongside John Lewis. However, because of the film's emphasis on King and SCLC tactics and strategies, the complexity of the SCLC/SNCC co-leadership is not made fully clear. King garners the lion's share of the credit for the marches, but neither King nor SCLC as organization could have successfully organized the marches at that time without the critical participation of SNCC. Even though she focused on Dr. King, to her credit, DuVernay did not disappear SNCC from *Selma*. And on the other hand, SNCC was not negotiating with the White House, nor did SNCC command the cache among national religious leaders that King brought to the efforts. When King issued the call to national clergy to join them in the Selma struggle, religious leaders from across the country journeyed to Selma. SNCC did not have that kind of reach.

Selma was indeed a mass movement, larger than any one individual, Dr. King included. Facing a massive Black tide of resistance to racist laws and a racist criminal justice system, LBJ rose to the challenge and chose to assert active leadership. During this turbulent era, in order to contain if not extinguish the fiery Civil Rights Movement, LBJ decided to work with King. Indeed, one could argue that in 1965, in order to control if not fully quell the social turmoil that was racking the entire society, Johnson actually needed King more than King needed Johnson.

Although he was not as popular as Kennedy, LBJ proved to be far more effective in changing America, especially in regards to issues of eradicating legal Jim Crow. Ironically, many Black households held pictures of King and Kennedy; I've never seen a picture of LBJ grace the walls of any Black household. Many, many American men wanted to be like President Kennedy: articulate, handsome, married to a trophy wife, wealthy and powerful. I've never heard anyone suggest they wanted to talk like LBJ or that they thought LBJ was good-looking, nor was anyone I know desirous of having a wife like Ladybird—nor, for that matter, do I know anyone who wanted to possess LBJ's bank account and social connections, even though both were considerable.

The fact is people such as Kennedy are admired for their appearance much more than for the reality of their social accomplishments. LBJ was the Rodney Dangerfield of U.S. presidents: his great accomplishments did not help his image.

The subtext of the accuracy arguments against *Selma* is precisely the perceived disrespect of LBJ, whom his defenders believe is a president who should be honored, especially by Blacks and activists. But regardless of the reality, *Selma* was not LBJ's story, and Ms. DuVernay had no intention of creating a white hero, even as she did give him his due by depicting LBJ's important Congressional address, widely known as LBJ's "we shall overcome" speech.

I wonder what *Selma* critics would have said if DuVernay had quoted LBJ's March 9, 1965 (available on American RadioWorks' website) taped conversation with Bill Moyers, who was then an aide and press secretary for Johnson. Here is LBJ telling Moyers what message should be delivered to King following a sit-in at the Justice Department that LBJ believes King could have prevented or stopped once the direct action was underway:

> Yeah, yeah, but I would take a much tougher line than we're going to with him. I think that it's absolutely disgraceful that they would get in the Justice Department building and have to be hauled out of there. And I don't care if we never serve another hour. They're going to respect the law while they do. He better get to behaving himself or all of them are going to be put in jail...I think that we really ought to be firm on it myself. I just think it's outrageous what's on TV. I've been watching it

here, and looks like that man's in charge of the country and taking it over. I just don't think we can afford to have that kind of character running. And I'd remind him what he had said and take a very firm line with him.

LBJ was an astute politician, a master of manipulation as well as a resolute leader with the finely tuned instincts of an expert poker player. LBJ knew when to hold 'em and when to fold 'em. On the one hand, he took a harder pro-Civil Rights stand than any of his predecessors; on the other hand, he knew that votes were necessary, knew that he would lose a bunch of White votes. And, I'm willing to bet LBJ also wagered that he would pick up an equally large, if not larger, block of Black votes.

These concerns and analyses are far beyond the purview of *Selma*. I don't think LBJ was a reluctant ally of the Civil Rights Movement; I think he was a careful, but not a cautious, politician with a plate full of considerations, and like all of us he had a complex and sometimes contradictory dialectic at work in terms of how he dealt with the issues of his time.

The hard reality is that LBJ did more to advance the conditions of Black folk than President Kennedy actually did. No question about that. The problem, however, is that what we needed and were fighting for was more than assimilation and/or accommodations. In the second half of the sixties, many of us, King included, began to understand that if we were to truly overcome, there was a need for thorough-going systemic, political, and economic change in America.

In 1965, most of the Civil Rights leaders and allies had not yet appreciated that raw racial discrimination was not in and of itself our most fundamental problem. In *Selma*, SNCC is characterized as wanting to change the consciousness of Black people in contradistinction to SCLC's approach of protest and negotiation. The differing points of view are acknowledged but not fleshed out.

Selma did not give us the depth and breadth of the historic context and only subtly referenced the fascinating backstory of the movement's struggles around the right to vote and around economic issues. *Selma* was not a documentary, nor was it a history lesson. *Selma* instead was a character study, a superbly drawn portrait of major and minor characters at a particular juncture of the Civil Rights Movement. That people argue about its accuracy is an indication of the movie's success as an artistic project provoking us to reexamine the sixties history of American race relations.

Although not formally a biopic about Martin Luther King, Jr., no other movie—and certainly no other Hollywood movie—has so successfully and succinctly projected the complexity of King's personality. Also, no other movie has highlighted the broad swath of human beings who made up both the leadership and the foot soldiers of the Civil Rights Movement.

Moreover, although the movie mainly focuses on King, women are shown as integral to the movement, especially King's wife Coretta, who rises beyond wifely helpmate. She meets with Malcolm X when the SCLC ministers were trembling at the thought of his arrival. She contradicts King in prison. And after the brutal beating on the bridge, she courageously goes to Selma to participate in the follow-up march.

While some have complained that the movie's portrayal of women was not forward enough, within the context of the time period, *Selma* actually presents the women as the most radical elements. A woman physically swings on racist police. Diane Nash and Coretta King firmly contradict the men and offer their own analyses. The women stand shoulder to shoulder with the men as they march against Jim Crow.

Selma would have had to be at least another hour in length to even begin to situate the historical moment that was Selma and present the complexity of that struggle to audiences that only know of, and revere, King the Dreamer.

eleven

I was eating dinner with my family. I forget the exact year and the specific details, but I distinctly remember receiving a phone call at home. I know it was during the seventies. The caller identified himself as an FBI agent. He said they had a warrant for my arrest, and rather than send out agents to pick me up, they were inviting me to come in the next morning and be arrested—I know this sounds insane and unbelievable, but that is what happened. The man gave me a number to call and verify that there was a warrant.

The next day I called. There indeed was a warrant. I went down to the police station to be arrested. I had no desire to go underground, and it was obvious that I was being spied on. Subsequently the charges were dropped, and I forgot about the incident. I had long been under surveillance, not to mention I had been harassed, beaten, maced, and who knows whatever else the FBI and/or other law enforcement officers surreptitiously did to me; that particular and peculiar arrest was no big deal.

Nearly a decade later, upon my first trip to Cuba, legal dirty tricks appeared again. Although I live in New Orleans, because of the U.S. embargo of Cuba, I had to go via Canada. At the border on the Canadian side, the customs agent asked had I ever been arrested. Yes, a number of times. What for? Civil Rights activity. What about drugs? No, why are you asking me that? The Canadian agent actually turned the terminal around so that I could see the screen. Along with a list of other specifics there was an arrest notice for cocaine distribution, although there were no convictions.

The agent said because I was just in transit, he'd let me go on to catch my flight to Cuba.

In the early eighties, I was talking with a friend who told me that some years back, her cousin had been busted on a marijuana charge. The authorities promised to release him if he would say that he bought drugs from me. He refused. She said he wouldn't cooperate because he agreed with our student demonstrations and subsequent community organizing. I never met my friend's cousin, never had the opportunity to thank him.

There are other FBI stories I could tell. My point is that *Selma*'s depiction of J. Edgar Hoover and the FBI dirty tricks was an understatement. Hoover did not operate in a vacuum or without LBJ's sometimes open, other times tacit, approval. In the upper reaches of government, operatives and executives understand that they are to do whatever is necessary to get their job done, and at the same time they understand the imperative to shield the president from culpability.

Resisting pressures to release J. Edgar Hoover from service, LBJ kept Hoover as the head of the FBI. In language typical of the private LBJ, the new president opined that he would rather keep Hoover in the administration and have him "inside pissing out rather than outside pissing in."

Significantly, LBJ kept Hoover as FBI chief even after Hoover had reached retirement age and could easily have been forced to retire. Hoover-led COINTELPRO activities were terribly effective in disrupting activists of the sixties and seventies. It is important to realize that Hoover was not only the founding director of the FBI in 1935, but that heserved as head of the bureau until his death in 1972. With tentacles of surveillance able to spy on everyone's public and private life, Hoover was the most powerful man in law enforcement. He was an untouchable king within his agency's castle and was both known and feared for his "dirty tricks."

Although I personally am under no illusions about the nature of the system, I think the vast majority of American citizens have no appreciation of the depth and range of government operations and are specifically unaware of the government's war against political dissidents. In 2014, Edward Snowden's revelations about government surveillance and spying on American citizens partially pulled back the curtain hiding government operations against the Black movement since the forties.

Various agencies of government, from the federal level down to the municipal, were working to disrupt our movement. And in some cases, indeed in far too many cases, they were aiming to actually kill us. COINTELPRO in particular was a very real and very active government offensive against Black political struggles in the sixties, the seventies, and beyond. The tapes of King's sexual involvement with other women that were subsequently sent to Coretta were real. *Selma* does not go into the detail of when and how they were obtained. While only hinting at the extensive negative impact of the FBI's extra-legal, as well as sometimes illegal, activities, the movie does make clear that the tapes were the work of the Hoover-led FBI.

Beyond the private contact with Coretta, the FBI also threatened King with public exposure of the damning information. These and other FBI activities are documented in *F.B. Eyes* by William J. Maxwell. The book details a high-level SCLC meeting (with Coretta present) at which the FBI tapes and threats were discussed, and also quotes from a tapped telephone conversation in which King reflects on the FBI activities, lamenting: "They are out to get me, harass me, break my spirit." Maxwell postulates that the bureau was attempting to induce King to commit suicide. Significantly, the FBI pounced with the illicit tapes prior to King's December 1964 reception of the Nobel Peace Prize.

Selma does not delve into the details of this FBI sabotage, but I find it difficult to believe that LBJ was not aware of Hoover's efforts. Hoover was a vicious pit bull in dealing with those whom he considered enemies. LBJ was willing to confront Congress, but he left Hoover unleashed.

DuVernay knew who Hoover was and how his FBI agents attacked King and numerous others. She also knew that LBJ chose not to restrain Hoover. Some critics argue that LBJ was unfairly maligned in *Selma*, not given enough credit for inspiring and encouraging the Selma demonstrations. Unsurprisingly, those same critics are not only silent about the nefarious activities of Hoover and his legions of FBI agents, but also completely and cravenly overlook the fact that LBJ kept Hoover employed when he could have immensely helped by constraining, if not actually curtailing, Hoover's undermining of the Civil Rights Movement.

Summing up our Civil Rights history is a complex task, but *Selma* does a better job than any previous film. Still, it ultimately is a commercial movie and not a detailed history book. Critics who confront *Selma* for getting the history of the King/LBJ relationship wrong, or for not giving LBJ his just due, ironically manage to do far worse in their assessment of history than they accuse DuVernay of doing.

When we look dispassionately at the evidence available to us, can we prove *Selma* is factually wrong on the major issues? There is a big difference between getting the facts wrong and disagreeing with a particular interpretation and presentation of the facts. American society in general chooses to reduce everything to black and white, when in reality, things are more often than not both black and white, most often a complex melding, i.e., various shades of gray.

Whether it's King or LBJ, those who want to put a white hat on their hero are bound to be disappointed by the spectrum and shadings that *Selma* presents. In a sense, we want fairy tales and cartoons rather than hard facts of life and complex human portraits—characters who, like all human beings, display contradictions and shortcomings as well as honor and bravery as they live their lives.

twelve

In June of 1968, I joined the Free Southern Theatre, which was founded in 1964 in Jackson, Mississippi, by three SNCC workers: Doris Derby, Gilbert Moses, and John O'Neal. I wanted to be a writer. In 1970 I became a founding editor of *The Black Collegian Magazine*, a nationally distributed journal. In 1984, along with Bill Rouselle, I co-founded Bright Moments, a public relations and advertising firm. In 1997 I started teaching digital media to high school students. Along with a plethora of shorts and documentaries, we made *Baby Love*, a 75-minute dramatic movie in the summer of 2001.

Movie-making is one of the things I do. I call it writing with light and theorize digital media as one third of my three-pronged neo-griot approach to writing: text (literature), sound (recordings), and light (video).

All of which is to contextualize my appreciation of Ava DuVernay and her great accomplishment in making *Selma*.

As a project, *Selma* had a long gestation period. For one reason or another, five different directors (Michael Mann, Stephen Frears, Paul Haggis, Spike Lee, and Lee Daniels) were considered before DuVernay. The initial script was by British writer Paul Webb, who stipulated in his contract that regardless of the final outcome, he would get sole screenwriting credit. Pathe UK, a British media company, was the start-up money source. After some years Paramount took up the cause, and eventually production duties were shared by a team that included Oprah Winfrey and Brad Pitt. It almost literally took a village to make this movie.

Notably, even though *Selma* focuses on the U.S. Civil Rights Movement, the four leading cast members are Brit-

ish actors, all of whom gave excellent performances. David
Oyelowo was stellar as King. He had previously worked
with DuVernay on her feature *The Middle Of Nowhere* and
with Winfrey on the Lee Daniels-directed movie *The Butler*.
Winfrey championed the Nigerian-rooted, London-born,
British-trained Oyelowo. Carmen Ejogo had previously
portrayed Coretta Scott King in the TV movie *Boycott*, in
preparation for which Carmen had met with King. Tom
Wilikson as LBJ demonstrated incredible range in resur-
recting the imposing and shrewd president. Tim Roth gave
us a wily George Wallace. Not one seasoned film critic has
suggested that any of these actors was either inappropriate
or ineffective.

One assumption is that the British actors were able to
approach their parts purely on a professional basis, without the cultural baggage that American-born actors would
bring to the project. I have a different theory. Most Hollywood movies are theoretically grounded in the Aristotelian
concept of verisimilitude, i.e., giving the appearance of being
true to life. This approach invariably leads to imitation and
mimicry. DuVernay works in a radically different way. She is
a storyteller who is interested in the emotional subtext and
employs an emphasis on sharp micro moments to effectively
make a major point.

The subtlety of DuVernay's approach would be under-
whelming if the work was not expertly paced by both the
director and the actors. Moreover, the cinematographer has
the potentially daunting task of visualizing intimate details
and giving substance to fleeting moments, an approach
that calls for illuminating the shadows and illustrating the
importance of seemingly slight or insignificant moments
and motions. In great contrast to the prevailing Hollywood
penchant for bombast and ostentatious special effects, *Selma*
excels at presenting to its viewers the human grandeur and
gravity inherent in the ordinary and the intimate.

Consider the pas de deux of the Kings' marital relations, for example: from putting out the trash, to dealing with betrayals, to stepping up to the front lines of struggle—Coretta arriving unannounced in Selma and climbing the steps, King's stunned look as he watches her literally rise to his level. Such subtlety is not accidental. Or the blocking of the King/LBJ confrontations/collaborations: LBJ's patronizing hand on King's shoulder, King standing as he declaims that he can't wait.

There are numerous other examples, almost always presented as a human exchange between two people at a particular moment: Annie Lee Cooper attempting to register to vote, the registrar asking detailed questions that would be impossible for her to answer (Ms. Cooper's stoic composure as she realizes that she will be denied her right to vote is a major, albeit brief, acting triumph for Oprah Winfrey); Hosea Williams and John Lewis on the bridge at the first march (Wendell Pierce as Williams offers a remarkable understatement while surveying the water below and the police in front of them; emblematic of the macabre sense of humor common among Civil Rights workers during that deadly era, Williams asks Lewis does he know how to swim); and of course, the aforementioned meeting in the morgue between King and Cager Lee.

Those moments, as well as other similar scenes, are no accident. DuVernay expertly shows us one-on-one human exchanges even as she is presenting the inner workings of a mass movement. This is the master stroke of her movie-making. Rather than relying on symbols and stereotypes, she chooses to show us individual human beings rising to meet the demands of a historical moment. If you watch *Selma* for a second or third time—and you really should—notice how often the camera focuses on a two-character exchange.

DuVernay's subject matter is a mass movement; however, she illustrates the depth and complexity of that move-

ment by highlighting specific individuals within the movement rather than simply showing a mass of people following
one man. She literally had a cast that included hundreds of
people. Although the movie features an ensemble of actors
with speaking parts, *Selma* achieves its emotional impact by
focusing on the intimate rather than reveling in the grandi-
ose.

Then there is the question of the soundscape. The audio
track of a movie is often more important than the words
and images because the underlying sound leads, and in some
cases even determines, how the audience views and inter-
prets what is seen. In an interview with NPR, DuVernay
testified to the exactitude and great attention to detail that
went into creating the soundscape:

> The sound design for that bridge sequence is something
> I'm very proud of. And it's just about this kind of senso-
> ry immersion putting you on the bridge throughout the
> film whenever a body is broken—a black body, a white
> body—whenever there's any kind of violence to the
> body, sound becomes critical.
>
>   We spent a lot of time, believe it or not…trying
> to perfect which sound I wanted to choose for when a
> baton hit the body. And there were different levels of
> that, different tenor and bass that we played with to
> construct something that really felt—you felt it in your
> heart when you heard it. Because I think what we were
> trying to do with this whole film is to just elevate it from
> a page in your history book and really just get it into
> your body—into your DNA.

Each person who experiences *Selma*, consciously and/
or subconsciously, will respond to and judge whether the
soundscape is effective. Additionally, DuVernay understands,
and more importantly demonstrates, that silence is often the

greatest sound: the silence of expectation ratcheting up the tenseness of a specific situation or confrontation, the silence of resignation as a person mutely surrenders to a physically or emotionally overwhelming situation, the silence of agreement when one is determined to confront and do battle, and of course the intimate silence of shame, of love, of pride; all of those silences abound in the movie.

What is crucial is not only how successful DuVernay is in employing sound (and silence). Rather, the real art of movie-making hinges on the project's conception—not just the intent and presentation, but using the whole theoretical construct as map and structure for the final product. DuVernay made a movie about mass public demonstration but chose to present the bulk of the movie as intimate exchanges. Some would call this understatement; others might cite this technique as a failure to capture the tumult of the times. I believe that DuVernay's greatest achievement was to emphasize the human element of the people whom this society too often only sees as stereotypes.

Both DuVernay's ideology and aesthetic were crucial ingredients in the making of *Selma*. On the one hand, DuVernay micromanages mood and atmosphere to achieve emotional and intellectual impact, but on the other hand, she is no slave to raw reality, going more for meaning than mere appearance.

For example, in a domestic scene between King and Coretta, King uses a plastic bag that Coretta has handed to him to take out the trash. I don't recall plastic trash bags being in common use in the sixties. Groceries were bagged in heavy brown paper bags that we recycled to line our garbage pails. Indeed, the common "single-use plastic shopping bag" was invented in Sweden in 1962 and popularized in the seventies by Mobil Oil, allegedly to develop the market for polyethylene, a petroleum product. The point of this scene was not the use of plastic but rather showing King doing domestic chores. Whether in 1965 the King household actually used plastic, as opposed to paper, is not the point of the scene: the veracity of plastic bags is irrelevant. Throughout *Selma*, DuVernay focuses on human interactions rather than slavish recreations of the appearance of things. *Selma* is emotionally authentic without being factually correct in material details.

Although King is unavoidably a central character, the movie is called *Selma* and not *King*. Thus there are numerous scenes not only without King in them, but more important, there are numerous scenes in which King is not even referenced. The scenes without King are visual analogs to the film's use of silence. Moreover, what is of ultimate interest is that Steven Spielberg had previously purchased the rights to King's speeches, and thus DuVernay had the unenviable task of presenting one of the most famous orators in American history without being able to use his actual words.

Which brings us to the script. *Selma* was not originally DuVernay's construct; she was working with a script that focused on the King/LBJ relationship and turned it into a movie that presented an intimate view of a movement. She had to rewrite the entire script, including adding in major sections and exchanges, all while knowing that she was not going to get professional scripting credit.

DuVernay's process of starting out with the words of others and then overlaying, i.e. improvising, her own interpretation of the script, harkens to the jazz aesthetic of the fifties and early sixties. Similar to the way Miles Davis, John Coltrane, and many, many others took American pop tunes and transformed songs such as "Green Dolphin Street" and "My Favorite Things" into major aesthetic statements, DuVernay interpreted a pop script focusing on the "great man" theory of history and innovatively turned the standard into a major statement of collective African-American history.

thirteen

To be clear, even as I admire what she did aesthetically, I have differences with the film's politics, especially the overemphasis on SCLC to the detriment of SNCC's role in Selma and in the whole Civil Rights struggle of the sixties; after all, King was not present for the first of the three attempts to cross the Pettus Bridge. Further, how were field workers able to convince community people to confront both police and rabid white bystanders in a period when violence against blacks was rife? After the first beat down on that fateful Sunday, how were people persuaded to assemble for a second attempt two days later? And then, after the great disappointment of King's retreat on the second attempt, how were people recruited for an ultimately successful third march of resistance? This is where the SNCC emphasis on changing and developing consciousness was critical to the ultimate success.

A major shortcoming of *Selma* from my perspective is its failure to show the door-to-door contact of organizers and field workers with a population that had been victims of violence not only their entire lives, but indeed for as far back as anyone could recall: White violence had been a constant used to cow the masses of Black people, forcing us into resignation and even acceptance of our inferior position. The SNCC workers were no drop-in superstars, showing up for a weekend march but skipping the ongoing daily organizing efforts. Rather, SNCC field workers moved into those communities, lived and suffered side by side with the populations that they were ultimately successful in convincing to confront state and extra-legal Jim Crow violence.

No one, King included, could just announce that there would be a march and expect hundreds of people to spontaneously respond. The hard work of one-on-one organizing was the sine qua non of the sixties Civil Rights Movement.

When people lost jobs, when their homes were assaulted, their cars and cattle violated; when people had to suffer unimaginable hardships to confront a system of segregation that, in the words of Alabama Governor George Wallace, would last "forever"—given the fear of such physical and economic reprisals that were certain to come from the White power structure in response to Black demands for freedom and equality, how were people convinced not only that change was going to come, but that they could be the agents of their own liberation?

From my perspective and from a SNCC perspective, figuring out how to persuade people to put their lives on the line and rebel, that was the heart of Selma, heart of Mississippi, the heart of the Deep South Civil Rights Movement.

The church meetings were shown, but in general the church meetings were the culmination and not the beginnings of convincing people to engage in mass resistance. Most of the ministers were cautious and hesitant precisely because they had so much to lose: their physical church buildings, the tithes from the parishioners, the social status of being a power broker between the Black community and the White community.

Because of both the popularity and fame of King and his SCLC cohorts, ministers and preachers in general are often thought of as the backbone of the Civil Rights Movement. While it is true that SCLC leaders (King, Ralph Abernathy, Andy Young, and others) are often the perceived heads and mouthpieces, the real backbone of the movement were the young organizers who elected to live with the people, and the literally thousands of women who actively encouraged and supported the movement.

Women marched, women sat-in, and in many cases women were the principal leaders. Although often overlooked in popular perception, for a number of the struggles, women were the actual icons and faces of the resistance: Montgom-

ery—Rosa Parks, Little Rock—Daisey Bates, Mississippi—
Fannie Lou Hamer, Nashville—Diane Nash, Cambridge—
Gloria Richardson. Moreover, at the local level, it was an
unheralded corps of women who did the majority of the
detailed, day-to-day support work that enabled mass movement to successfully function: from record-keeping and
informing contacts of meetings and assignments, to cooking
meals and chauffeuring visitors, among literally thousands
and thousands of other seemingly minor but really critical
tasks, women quietly and effectively made sure that the jobs
were well done.

I realize I am reiterating ground previously covered in
this essay. But the importance of women's participation has
been pervasively underplayed, even though female leadership
is both obvious when we look at the various battlefronts, and
critical when we consider where successful, long-term struggles were waged. If indeed the preachers were an important
constituency, and undoubtedly they were, those religious
leaders were only a tertiary element at the forefront of the
Civil Rights Movement, the other two elements being the
mainly college-aged field organizers who took up residence
in Deep South communities, and the Black women in those
communities who, although too often uncelebrated, were
the central glue of the Civil Rights Movement.

fourteen

Perhaps DuVernay's greatest achievement in *Selma* was
intrinsic to her person. She made the movie from a woman's
perspective. She focused on human relationships rather than
on power positions and posturing. Over and over again,
DuVernay zeroed in on intimate details that we men often
overlook in our authoritative overviews of what we consider
important in the big picture of human affairs. For example, on one of the opening scenes, the Birmingham church
bombing of the four little girls, DuVernay is explicit:

[I] was approaching it from my point of view as a woman filmmaker: The idea of showing a bombing, showing a blast, showing any kind of detonation might be different from that of a male director who might be more interested—and this is just based on what I've seen for many, many years—might be more interested in the physicality of the blast, the gusto of that violence.

I was much more interested in reverence for the girls. It was important to me that you hear their voices. You hear what their concerns are at that moment as four little black girls walking down a staircase in what should be a safe place, in their sanctuary, in their church. They're talking about hair. They're talking about Coretta Scott King's hairstyle. They're talking about what little black girls talk about—getting your hair wet and keeping it pressed and doing all that kind of thing. You start to come into their world just as they are taken out of the world. And so from there, what is the next thing to show? Is it shrapnel? Is it fire? For me it was the fabric of their dresses and their patent leather shoes, all of the things that remain from the souls that were lost.

While we know that "the personal is political," the deeper truth is that you can't truly understand the political if you don't grasp the personal contexts and connections at play. On the human stage of history, how and by whom a message is delivered is often equally important as, and sometimes even more important than, the message itself. In any social conflict, the least powerful, the disadvantaged, the marginalized, the other, the oppressed and exploited, are forced by the circumstances of our condition—indeed by the necessities of survival in the face of cold and calculating malevolent authorities, be we outsiders racial, gender, ethnic, religious, or whatever—to read and respond to the moods and feelings of the dominant authorities. *Selma* is replete with moments of asymmetrical conflict, where the less powerful rise to confront a powerful and callous status quo.

Consider Ms. Annie Lee Cooper, who silently suffers the one-on-one confrontation with the registrar but, when assaulted by the sheriff, famously fights back and actually knocks the man to the ground with a powerful punch to his jaw. While there were numerous eyewitnesses who verified the truthfulness of the incident, it was DuVernay who figured out how to contrast Ms. Cooper's passive, long-suffering reality with this moment of resistance. *Selma* is rich because DuVernay insisted on showing us that Selma was more than King, more than one man against a segregated world, and indeed that the struggle was valiantly waged by both men and women.

My point is that *Selma* is not simply the work of a woman director; DuVernay is a conscious woman, a determined woman, aware of her history and social context, and willing to do her job firmly rooted in her own personal perspective, which includes deeply intimate connections to the film's subject matter. Her father lived in Lowndes County and told her about seeing the marchers pass by when he was eleven years old. Her mother would cross the Pettus Bridge on her way to work. DuVernay included the bombing scene because while researching the movie, Diane Nash told her that the Birmingham incident inspired Nash to move to Alabama. Conversation on the bridge was drawn from John Lewis' autobiography; details of the strategy sessions were outlined by Andy Young. Over and over, DuVernay drew on the personal in bringing to light the reality and importance of the Civil Rights Movement.

Ava DuVernay not only knew what she was doing, she also understood that the mainstream critics would be unwelcoming, that they would pick minor details to argue about while ignoring the overall importance and success of the movie-making process. DuVernay was not surprised that Oscar did not come a-calling. Speaking truth to power is not a task for the weak of spirit.

Making a participant-oriented Hollywood movie about Black people confronting segregation requires challenging current mainstream assumptions about how our history was made, indeed about who did what, and about who and how we perceived our selves to be, as well who and how we identify our allies, as well as our enemies.

Additionally, on an aesthetic level, there is the whole question of literally how to light and picture Black people, who by the way exhibit a far, far greater spectrum of skin tones, shadings, and facial features than the Aryan hues of Hollywood's traditional palette. How do you shoot Black people in night scenes? How do you light shades of blackness when contrasted with pale faces? Indeed, how do you picture with dignity people whom the popular American imagination sees as savages or, at best, as the disadvantaged and under-privileged? What camera angles do you use?

Even as aesthetic question after question has to be dealt with, there are overarching assumptions not only that art is more important than politics, but that "Black art" is really message-driven and aesthetically weak. Most Americans have been brought up to believe that Euro-centric aesthetics are more accomplished, more beautiful, more desirable than traditional Africa-heritage artwork. This is a subconscious orientation inculcated by our education, by the media, and by overwhelming presentations of the status quo art world of museums, galleries, textbooks, advertising, and popular image making.

Most mainstream discussion of *Selma* has focused on the film's message and its accuracy of representation rather than on the considerable aesthetics of the movie. The sensitive photography, under the direction of cinematographer Bradford Young, goes unexamined in most critiques. Similarly, the use of sound, locations, and editing are all ignored as critics concentrate on how "accurately" Whites are portrayed. As with our music, the unvoiced assumption is that our aesthetics are not conscious decisions worthy of discussion, but rather that the way we craft our artwork results from some natural affinity we have for arts and entertainment.

Selma, like most artwork created by non-Whites that consciously confronts the status quo, is looked at mainly as a message movie. While it is true that *Selma* will be the only history lesson on the Civil Rights Movement that goes beyond Rosa Parks and the March on Washington for ninety percent of the young people who see it, it is also true that *Selma* is an artistic triumph.

I think of *Selma* as an assault on all the modern-day Pettus Bridges, i.e., the contemporary social contexts that facilitate not only a willful ignorance of our history and a continued, violent suppression of our rights, but also a willful denial of our artistry and the value of our aesthetics.

We can accept the truism that truth is beauty only if we are prepared to accept that truth is relative and that no one has a monopoly on truth, the dominant social order notwithstanding. *Selma* presents a spectrum of human truths from a Black and female perspective, and that's beautiful.

Getting over status quo Pettus Bridges requires us to try, and try, and try again. Thank you, Ava DuVernay, for stepping forward to continue the struggle. As the most militant of the sixties argued, let there be two, three, many Vietnams. Let there be two, three, many *Selma*s. A luta continua!

The Selma Backstory

May 17, 1954 — Brown v. Board of Education

December 1, 1955 — Montgomery Bus Boycott ran for 13 months

September 1957 — Little Rock school desegregation movement led by Daisy Bates

February 1, 1960 — Greensboro sit-ins

December 5, 1960 —Supreme Court hands down a 7-2 decision in the Boynton v. Virginia case, ruling that segregation on vehicles traveling between states is unlawful because it violates the Interstate Commerce Act.

1961 — Robert Williams goes into exile, publishes Negroes with Guns in 1962.

Fall 1961-Summer 1962 — Albany (Georgia) Movement

September 20, 1962 — After being admitted to the University of Mississippi (Ole Miss), James Meredith was blocked from entering by school officials backed by state officials.

The Supreme Court rules that the University of Mississippi must admit African-American student and veteran James Meredith. Between September 30 and October 1, riots erupt at over Meredith's enrollment. Two people were killed and hundreds wounded. On October 1, Meredith becomes the first African-American student at Ole Miss after President Kennedy orders U.S. Marshals to Mississippi to ensure his safety.

June 1963 — John Lewis elected chair of SNCC (Student Nonviolent Coordination Committee).

August 1963 — March on Washington. John Lewis speech censored. King gave historic "I Have A Dream" speech.

September 15, 1963 — Birmingham bombing

November 1963 — The SNCC-led "Freedom Vote" campaign (mock election) polled 80,000 Black voters across the state of Mississippi, effectively highlighting voting rather than public accommodations as the major focus of the Civil Rights Movement.

November 22, 1963 — Assassination of President Kennedy.

Summer 1964 — Mississippi Freedom Summer project encourages hundreds of White, college-aged youth to go to Mississippi and join the Civil Rights struggle.

August 4, 1964 — Murder of CORE Civil Rights workers James Earl Chaney, Michael Schwerner, and Andrew Goodman.

Summer 1964 — Mississippi Freedom Democratic Party (founded April 1964 as an outgrowth of SNCC/COFO voter registration efforts that started in 1961) galvanizes national attention at the Democratic National Convention, which nominates LBJ as their candidate against Republican Barry Goldwater. Founding members included Fannie Lou Hamer, Ella Baker, and Bob Moses. Challenged seating of southern Democrats at the national Democratic

Convention in Atlantic City. LBJ offered a 2-seat compromise and when that was declined, LBJ maneuvered to block MFDP from participating and protesting. John Lewis, who was then chairman of SNCC, would later write that this was the major turning point. The MFDP attracted major national attention, and put the issue of black voting rights at the top of the news and the political agenda by both supporters and opponents.

July 2, 1964 — Lyndon Johnson signs the Civil Rights Act.

February 21, 1965 — Malcolm X assassinated by Black Muslims. Police surveillance had been unaccountably withdrawn, even though Malcolm's home had been fire-bombed on February 14, 1965.

February 7-8, 1965 — LBJ commits in full to Vietnam War

January 1965 — King/SCLC joined SNCC, the Dallas County Voters League, and local activists in the Selma voting rights campaign.

February 18, 1965 — A night march in nearby Marion, Alabama was attacked by Alabama state troopers and Jimmie Lee Jackson was shot. He died eight days later in a Selma hospital. In response a march from Selma to Montgomery was called for on March 7, 1965. While crossing the Edmund Pettus Bridge the marchers were viciously attacked by state troopers and Selma police. The event, which was televised and widely reported, nationally and internationally, became known as "Bloody Sunday." That march was led by Hosea Williams and John Lewis. King was in Atlanta. A follow-up March was called for the following Tuesday, March 9, 1965. King led the march, while on the bridge, King knelt and led the marchers in prayer, and then turned around. That night Unitarian minister and march participant James Reeb was attacked and died two days later.

March 17, 1965 — LBJ addressed Congress and proclaimed his support for voting rights, and urged Congress and the entire nation to join in the Voting Rights struggle. LBJ ended his speech with the phrase "we shall overcome." That same day, LBJ submitted the Voting Rights legislation to Congress.

March 21, 1965 — A federally sanctioned and protected march began from Selma to Montgomery. Approximately 3,000 marchers leave Selma headed to Montgomery. During most of the march, the government limited the number of participants to 300 people. On March 25, 1965, the last day of the march into Montgomery and a rally at the capitol, march participation swelled to over 25,000 people. That night, Viola Liuzzo, a Michigan housewife, was shot and killed by the KKK while driving march participants back to Selma.

August 6, 1965 — LBJ signed the Voting Rights Act into law.

August 11, 1965 — Watts erupts, marking a new phase in the Black freedom struggle.

New Orleans Culture

JAZZ 101

buddy bolden's blues legacy

they said i'm crazy
but they still play my crazy
blue black shit today

we came from farm land, cane field and cotton country, outta rice paddies and satsuma groves, following the river both down and up to the city to try to set up home where a newly emancipated man could live at least halfway free and a woman didn't have to be some man's mule just to raise her family.

we brought with us the profound sense of betrayal when the retreat of federal troops was masked by the hoods of nightriders, fellows whose daylight faces we all knew. the hard hoofs of horses announcing the flaming torches flung through the paneless windows of our one-room rural homes. the no work for smart negroes and the very low pay if you were dumb enough to accept what little was offered.

we had fought the civil war. we had survived the bewilderment of emancipation and now, when we should be free, we woke in the mornings and found ourselves harvesting strange fruit. we were the blacks with the blues. the unlettered ex-slaves whose agrarian skills offered no protection in the hinterlands and no employment in the cities. but, caught between the busted rock of reconstruction's repeal and the hard space of being put back into a semi-slavery place, we had no choice but to move on down the line. thus we came to the crescent, seeking at least a shot.

everywhere we touched down we created settlements. st. rose, luling, boutte, kenner—the first mayor was a negro. carrollton—we built parks and celebrated with sunday picnics, and on into uptown new orleans creating all those neighborhoods: black pearl (aka "niggertown"), hollygrove, zion city, gerttown and what we now know as central city.

no matter how hard big easy bore down on us, urban exploitation was still a bunch better than constantly falling behind on the ledger at the general store, owing more and more every year, barely enough to get by. in the summertime chewing sugar cane for supper and maybe catching a catfish for sunday dinner. in the winter time making turtle soup to last the week if you could catch a turtle, and always beans and beans, and more beans. somehow, even though we still had beans and beans and more beans and rice, it just seemed that red beans and rice was nice, nicer in new orleans than it ever was in the country and besides, there was plenty fishing in new orleans too, in the canals, in the river, in the lake, in the bayou, in fact, more fishing here than in the country. so although the city never really rolled out a welcome mat, our people nevertheless still managed to make ourselves at home.

we found some work on the streets and in the quarter, but mostly made work cooking, carrying, and construct-ing shit. some of us groomed horses, a healthy portion of us worked the docks. we eked out a living, gradually doing better and better. and it was us country-born, farm-come-to-city black folk who indelibly changed the sound of new orleans, who brought the blues a-blowing: loud, hard, and without pretense, subtlety, or any genuflecting to high society, these blues that were just happy to have a good time and were equally unashamed to show the tears of pain those country years contained, how the hard times hurted we simple, unassuming people who both prayed and cursed as hard as we worked, we who were not afraid of a good fight, and never hesitant about enjoying a good time each and every chance we got to grab a feather or two out of the tail of that ever-elusive bird of paradise.

we were the fabled blues people who brought to the music a vision no one else was low enough to the ground to see. and no one should romanticize us. we were hungry, we were illiterate, disease-ridden, and totally unprepared for urban life. moreover often we were live-for-today-damn-to-morrow merciless in the matter-of-fact way we accepted and played the dirty, limited hands that life dealt us.

ours was a brutal beauty. a social order where no child remained innocent past the age of four. where the sweet bird of youth had flown, long gone well before twenty-five arrived. where somebody calling your mama a whore was just an accurate description of one of the major lines of work. where your daddy could have been any one of five men you saw for a couple of days through a keyhole when you were supposed to be sleep, but were up trying to peep what it was that grown folks did that kids were not supposed to do.

our people brought an unsophisticated, raw sound that cut through all pretensions and gutsily stripped time down to the naked function at the junction of hard-working folks careening into saturday nite let's get it on. and of course by any standard of social decorum, we were uncouth and so was our blues, but it was this blues produced by we blues people that turned-out the music floating around new orleans, tricked it into something the world would soon (or eventually) celebrate first as jass (with two "s's" as in "show your ass") and then as jazz (with two "z's" as in "razzle, dazzle" keep up with us if you can).

it was our don't give a shuck about which way is up as long as we have a moment to get down.

our red is my favorite color morning, noon, and night.

our play it loud motherfuckers let me know you deep up in there.

our this ain't no job and you ain't no boss so you can't tell me shit about when to start, when to stop, or how nasty i get.

our if i drop dead in the morning 'cause i done partied all nite then just go ahead and dance at my funeral pretty baby.

our i'd rather play it wrong my way than right the white way cause they way may be correct but it sure ain't right.

it was this attitude, these blues, that turned new orleans music into something worth spreading all over the world. and it was we who were the roux in the nouveau gumbo now celebrated as crescent city culture.

it was our crude but oh so potent elixir that raised the ante on the making of music, it was our brazen, red-hot, blue sound and the way the first creators acted when they screwed up their lips to produce the untutored, slightly tortured host of notes which made the cascade of ragtime rhythms sound tame. we simple but complex characters who have been consistently overlooked, undervalued, and our social background scarcely mentioned in all the books (where do they think we uptown blacks came from and what do they think we brought with us?); we who were persecuted by the authorities worse than negroes singing john brown's body lies a-smoldering in the grave at intermission during a klan rally; it was us black heartbeats and our defiant music that made the difference.

and, yes, we had to be more than a little crazy to challenge the aural status quo the way we did, so, it is no surprise that buddy bolden, the preeminent horn player cut from this cloth, was an insane black man whose ascendency to the throne just made it easier for the odorous forces of the "status crow" (as caribbean scholar/poet kamau braithwaite calls it) to pluck bolden from the top of the heap and heave him into a mental institution and keep him there for almost thirty years, wasting away until he died.

they may have silenced our first king, but they could never silence our sound. and regardless of what anyone says or does, nearly a hundred years later, no matter whether they admit it or not, know it or not, like it or not, it is the bold sound of black buddy conjuring some raw, funky blues in the night, layering his tone on whatever was a given song's ultimate source. this neo-african gris-gris is the sonic tattoo marking the beginning and making up the essence of the music we now call jazz.

jelly's boast (backed up in writing)

i started jass with
latin tinged, café colored
keyboard handicrafts

if buddy bolden—or someone black like that—started jazz, then how could ferdinand lementh "jelly roll" morton fix his mouth to boast that he "invented jazz in 1903"? simple, my man was the first to write it down, to figure out where and how the notes go when put on paper just so a musician trained in the reading of music but untutored in the ways of the raucous folk could play these wild new sounds, or at least a rough approximation, or at least play the heads, the melodies.

and while a lot of folks like to claim that jelly's skill was because of the creole in him, most of those same folks know nothing about the deep draughts jelly drank from the brackish bottom of the blues' most funky well. jelly had songs that could make a prostitute blush and a pimp hide his face in shame. storyville wasn't no conservatory and jass wasn't no waltz. jelly knew this. he knew about the blacks. he knew about the whites. and especially about everything that went down in between. like all good blues folk he also had a mean streak, that cut-you-if-you-stand-still and shoot-you-if-you-run temperament necessary to survive saturday nights in the roughest parts of town.

no doubt it was because of jelly that the story freely circulated that jazz was born in a brothel, specifically the cathouses of storyville. but all that's said ain't necessarily so. sure, jelly played jazz there, but just cause jelly played for tricks and whores that don't mean that's where his songs came from. the music was actually made outside elsewhere and later on brought inside those doors. which is not to take nothing away from jelly because figuring out how to write it down was no mean feat, especially those lusty sounds his brothers uptown would just let rip, day after day and night after night, pouring their sacred souls into the secular atmosphere. jelly would listen, and listen, and grin, and hold those sacred riffs inside his jaws and against the crown of his mouth and later spit out onto paper those notes that a bunch of others had written in the air. i'm not saying jelly wasn't original, i'm just saying a good scribe can always write more than he or she individually knows, especially when they are present at the creation and have the initial shot at drafting up tunes taken down from the motherlode.

given the mixed nature of jelly's pedigree and his back-a-town, alley-crawling cravings, he was able to create music for all occasions. music for right now if you were ready to get it on, and music for later after all the squares were gone. music colored by what jelly suggestively called the spanish tinge.

and what was this latin tinge that jelly so glowingly spoke of? was it african rhythms run through the backyard of the caribbean? one critic talks vociferously about the arab influence—what he maybe means is the moorish number that spain slyly claimed as an original contribution, or mali's twist on the islamic prayer chant—arab influence, huh? arab sounds altered by contact with african souls and soil, and rearranged caribbean stylee (which "stylee" is just africans in the west reinventing our ancient selves). that mambo, that rumba, merengue, clave, son and so forth. those pentatonic scales, modes, falsettoes and nasal drones. yeah, it's all arab straight from the heart of africa. jelly knew, that's why he said the tinge in the latin rather than the whole roman enchilada.

anyway, as much as he wrote and as important as his compositions are, in the final analysis we remember jelly because jelly didn't forget the import of what he heard, because jelly found a way to write without emasculating the music's swagger, without perfuming the funk, without covering the flesh in a veil of false modesty.

we remember jelly because jelly accurately remembered us. and lord, lord, lord even if he had never written a note, just one quick listen will confirm how marvelously potent his playing was. that mr. jelly, mr. jelly, he sure could play that shit.

the beauty of bechet

sax moans river strong
spurting song into the sea
of our aroused souls

the cornet and its first cousin the trumpet were the first solo instruments of jazz, the first horns to carry the tone of defiance, slicing the air with the gleaming sassiness of a straight razor wielded with expert precision on someone who was dead but didn't know it yet (the hit was so quick that the head fell off before the body knew it had been cut). these brass siblings were the hot horns that caught the feel of august in the sun, a hundred-pound sack shading the curve of your aching back. especially the trumpet with its ringing blare, which could be heard cross the river on a slow day when somebody in algiers was practicing while a bunch of other bodies was sweating, toting barrels and lifting bales on the eastbank riverfront.

the second brass voice was the nasty trombone. you stuck stuff up its filthy bell. it was not loud but was indeed very lewd. a toilet plunger its regular accessory. of course you had drums and some sort of harmony instrument, a string bass where available, a tuba, sousaphone, banjo or even a piano in certain joints.

now the reed of choice was the clarinet. long. slender. difficult to master. the snakelike black reed. and that was the basis of your early jass bands.

everybody had a part. bechet was a clarinetist. an excellent clarinetist. extraordinary even. but no matter how well he sucked on that licorice stick he could never get it up the way he wanted it. get it to make the sound inside bechet's head. until he heard the sound of the soprano saxophone. the fingering was similar so he was familiar with covering and uncovering the holes. familiar with the right stiffness of reed and the just tough enough strength of embouchure. what the soprano saxophone did was enable him to challenge the trumpet—just ask louie armstrong, or give a listen to clarence williams and his blue five when bechet and louie took turns walking them jazz babies on home.

this mytho-poetic orpheus sired by omer soaked his reeds in mississippi muck and washed down the horn's bell in bayou goo.

what bechet did was press the humidity of crescent city summers into every quivering note he played with a vibrato so pronounced it sounded like a foreign dialect.

what bechet did was alter the course of history. the clarinet faded after bechet switched and the saxophone became the great horn of jazz. sure there were a couple of great trumpets in years to come (little jazz, fats, dizzy, brownie, and, of course, miles) but none of them turned the music around like the saxophonists did, like bechet, like bird, like trane, not to mention hodges, hawkins and the prez, and the list can go on and on. the point here is that bechet was the one, the first, the progenitor of a royal succession that is all but synonymous with jazz as an instrumental music.

and what was even more incredible back in the twenties and thirties was bechet's sense of africa as source and blues people as the funnel through which the source sound was poured. bechet speaks of that specifically. in bechet's autobiography he goes on for pages (pgs. 6-44 out of 219 pages of text) talking about his grandfather who danced in congo square, overlaying the legendary bras coupe (a runaway, maroon warrior of the early 1800s) story onto the life story of his grandfather handed down to bechet through bechet's father, thereby ensuring that the statement of resistance was made, the resistance that fuels the internal integrity of our music.

bechet was an early african-american griot. one of the first to consciously understand the music he played so well. to articulate the ancestral worship implicit in the call and response. or as bechet describes the music: "It's the remembering song. There's so much to remember. There's so much wanting, and there's so much sorrow, and there's so much waiting for the sorrow to end. My people, all they want is a place where they can be people, a place where they can stand up and be part of that place, just being natural to the place without worrying how someone may be coming along to take that place away from them." in brasil they call this feeling "saudade," this longing to be whole again, this we know that we were whole once and with all our being quiver with an anxiety, an almost unbearable longing, to be whole again, this hope—dare i say this optimism, colored by the reality of the blues—that, yes, someday, someway, we will be whole in some soon come future.

like a mighty river that never ceases to flow and which has seen it all before, bechet's sound was an ever-unfurling cornucopia of lyric delight, its alluvial melodies inundating us, fertilizing our spirits, rendering us both funky and fecund.

bechet's music was brazen, was brilliant, was growling sun bold. startling in its intensity. powerful in its keening. knowing—he was a philosopher of sorrow, was intimate with hurt as well as on first-name terms with joy. while life had its ups and downs, bechet played it hard at both extremes and always with a sparkle of hope shining irrepressibly behind and through whatever tears temporarily clouded his eyes.

all of that, all of his life, his individual self and his people's birthright, all was played through the bell of bechet's horn, so strong and unmistakable. unmissable. one listen and you got it. the force hit you. you felt it. bechet. bechet. he seemed to be that special sound you had been waiting all your life to hear.

freddie keppard, (unfortunately) fooling his self

keeps a handkerchief
cross my horn / don't record a
lick—they won't steal me

freddie was not the first and certainly was far from the last to think he could avoid being used by opting not to belly up to the capitalist roulette wheel of commercialization, not to get bumped to the curb by the pick-and-roll of economic exploitation combined with technical innovation. every time the man comes up with a new machine, invariably the new machines end up being, among other things, another cash-generating tool—and all in the name of progress and progressiveness.

but paradoxically, beyond the obvious remunerative

inequities and the misplaced hosannas to pretenders posturing as kings, the real rough side of the mountain is the inevitable further behind we fall if we refuse to use what little
opportunity the new technology presents. when we decline
to play we are ignored; when we do play we are exploited.
but at least when you play you get a hearing, even if someone else's echo of your sound makes more dough than do
you, the originator.

moreover, it was the technology of being heard that
enabled jazz to spread its wings. the music could never have
flown worldwide were it not for recordings, were it not for
musicians everywhere being able to "hear" what these wild
new sounds sounded like. our music could not be explained
with words or written down with symbols, had to be eared
to be appreciated. contradictions abound. were it not for the
technology the music would not have spread, and simultaneously the technology was used to exploit—a nutshell synop-
sis of african-american relations to the modernist means of
production.

of course, some of us saw the downside coming so we
attempted to duck. working with the limited vision that we
oppressed people often manifest, somehow freddie thought
he could lessen the impact of cultural appropriation by
refusing to play the game. fat chance. which is why few jazz
fans know the name freddie keppard. don't even know what
instrument he played, when or where, or why he should be
known.

the lesson of brother keppard is a hard dose to swallow
but when you are on the black unskilled-labor end of america's 20th-century economy, you don't have many choices. you can throw a handkerchief up over your shit if you
want to, attempting to hide the specifics of your fingering,
how you do the things you do, you can petulantly sit in the
corner with your face to the wall while the parade marches
past, you can even bark out curses at the seemingly endless

procession of white rip-off artists, but as the poet said centuries ago, the dogs who hang in the camp may bark, but the caravan moves on.

and though freddie keppard was the uncrowned king of new orleans trumpet playing in the wake of buddy's incarceration and oliver's departure, nonetheless his name is seldom mentioned in the chronology of jazz trumpeting precisely because he was eclipsed by nick larocca and crew, who were wise enough not to pass up the opportunity to play their sincere but nonetheless insubstantial versions/revisions into a rca victor machine thus assuring themselves the "we-was-here-first claim"—the original dixieland jass band in 1917 was the first to record a jazz record while freddie keppard stood on the sidelines, smiling as he stuffed his handkerchief back in his pocket. you see, after one listen to the pale cacophony recorded by odjb, freddie was confident that they never were able to capture even an approximation of his sound. he won the authenticity battle, but loss the jazz war. pale though they be, we know what larocca sounded like. and keppard, well, he's just a footnote fanatics and academics point to. time and time again, the truth marches on: even when we can't win, even when the deck is stacked and our getting hustled is a foregone conclusion, even then, if we don't play, we're worse off than if we play and lose. in the long run, our only chance is to play, to keep on losing until we win, because if we don't play, for sure we will never win.

the singing of a king/ oliver's telegram

STOP—my horn so strong
i call louie to chi with
just a 8th note—START

the reason jim crow was so violent is that, after world war one, black folk refused to go silently back into what segregationists euphemistically called "their places." instead we preferred to believe that any space we wanted to inhabit was our own, territory we had a right to, and didn't really want to be up next to some cracker no way, just wanted a sweet spot we could inhabit in peace, but it was not to be. but by then we were fighting for our rights (or like when the sheriff tried to close down a garvey gathering in new orleans with the words that wasn't no mark-us gra-vee going to speak here tonight, he was silenced by the uprise of black folk, arms in hand who insisted on their right to hear marcus mosiah garvey—and mr. garvey did speak that hot night in new orleans, thank you).

it was in this atmosphere that the "idyllic" southern scene, which never really was as romantic as popular culture portrayed, revealed its true colors: red, white, black and blue, as in beatings, lynchings, and assorted mayhem, as in we black and were fire-driven by recalcitrant whites who by dint of terror herded us into tightly policed, economically exploited, physically oppressed, psychologically damaging, blues-hued, segregated communities under social siege— especially intelligent black men, most of whom had never seen the inside of anyone's school but who could figure, invent, innovate, create, construct, organize, rearrange, tend and grow with the best of anyone on the planet except they, these intelligent ex-slaves, were seldom allowed to demon-strate their innate capacities, thus geniuses were fated to empty spittoons, carry rice sacks, and spend three quarters of their lives behind the butt end of a mule or on the working end of a shovel. or, if they were women, the limited choices were: wet nurse, clean and cook for a pittance, or lie to some white john about how long his little was.

except if one could play music. in which case the music gave you wings, actually was a ticket to ride, a way out of jim crow's den of inequities. so people who might have been professionals of all sorts had they had the opportunity to pursue those professions, picked up horns or mastered drums, learned to do amazing feats with guitar string and a pocket knife, or literally rewrote piano literature, gave new meanings to musical entertainment and captivated the entire planet with a dazzling display of aural inventiveness that significantly upped the ante on what was considered quality entertainment, as well as what was possible in the realms of melody, harmony, and especially rhythm—i mean, how did armstrong play that horn like that, not to mention he sang an entire song without words. wild!

so the singers, dancers, and especially the musicians were the first african americans to routinely travel, thereby getting the then rare chance to check out the world scene. these men and a handful of women became the most famous people in their communities, unrivaled by any other profession— including doctors and college professors, plus, they were overwhelmingly working class, didn't need anybody's sheepskin to certify that they knew what they knew, only needed to be able to blow that thing, sing that swing, or step lively while kicking up their heels properly keeping time with their feet, only needed to be themselves.

yet, make no mistake, this self they were was not a simpleton who just happened to have a good voice or an ear for melodies. no, we are talking innovation at a level which no one previously conceived. (i mean, for example, nude dancing been around since there was human skin, but it took josephine to consider wrapping her black hips in the phallic curves of a couple of dozen yellow bananas and shaking that thing in such spherical sensuous ways that even the legendary lovers of gay paree tripped, flipped, and damn near fell head over heels in love with a brownskin cutie who, without so much as working up a sweat, coolly demonstrated two dozen more ways of playing with a yo-yo.)

looking in the rearview mirror we sometimes get a backwards view. we think louie was loved because he was a clown but if we only knew. wasn't a hornplayer no where around—especially not euro-trained—who could even so much as carry mr. armstrong's horn case to a rehearsal for a pickup gig, not to mention engage in no out-and-out cutting contest. we forget that louie taught america how to both swing and sing at the same time, how to scat on the one hand and go to the core of the lyrics on the other, not to mention how to jump bar lines with melodic phrasing whose trapeze-like gambits from note to note left others stumbling along like they had two left feet and had never experienced the thrill of trilling a g over high c.

the beautiful people called the twenties the jazz age because nothing else gave you the full feeling of being alive like black music did. and though they pretended paul whiteman was the king, beneath the skin everyone knew who the real creators of jazz were. worldwide these originators were in demand, and, as the history of america has always demonstrated, whenever and wherever there is a demand backed up by dinero, the supply shall definitely roll forth.

thus these colored troubadours swiftly moved from city to city, scoping out what was new and getting the down-low on the economic, political, and racial picture in every place to which they might go. soon musicians started coming back home wearing clothes no one there abouts had ever laid eyes on before, with tall tales recounting command performances regaling kings and things, or swinging round the clock on ocean liners crisscrossing the seven seas, and not to mention jamming in countless places where english wasn't even spoken. and of course these ambassadors of swing picked up on a variety of wild ideas about possible lifestyles. yes, they changed the world with their music, but they were also changed by their contact with worlds they had never imagined.

and while it is true that each frog is acclimated to the waters where he was born, still, given the jim crow realities of the twenties, our people were always ready to jump and, as a profession, the musicians were the first out the pot. indeed, that was one of the reasons for learning to play in the first place, i.e., to get the opportunity to blow town and get paid at the same time. nice work if you could get it, which is why when king oliver wired the invite to louie, there was no hesitation in armstrong's step as he packed his grip preparing to split. how else could a poor, uneducated, but highly intelligent black man get to see the world?

armstrong, and countless others, came from a call and response culture, and when opportunity knocked, these folk were wise enough to immediately answer the door, the same door beside which a packed travel bag was usually kept at the ready just in case such an unanticipated but nonetheless highly appreciated chance might roll by and allow an ambitious person with musical talent a chance to make a strategic exit.

given the realities of poverty, jim crow, and the general hard way to go handed out to people of color, it is easy to understand that jass didn't just slip reluctantly out of town, but rather cake-walked away singing a simple song: if you don't believe i'm leaving, count the days that i'm gone. in fact, leaving town was a sign of this music's intelligence.

nick larocca's secret diary

anglos give dagos
money and fame for playing
negro's music—wow

i'll make this short and sweet: back in the days, new orleans anglos didn't like "niggers" and wasn't too particular about "dagos." had italians living in the same neighborhoods

with negroes, thus the many corner stores with retail estab-
lishments at the front door and living quarters either just
behind or just above the one-room store. which is not to say
that italians and negroes were viewed as one and the same or
that the two got along fabulously with each other, but rather
which is to say that the gray space between black and white
was far broader than is often recognized, especially in retro-
spect when people now considered white are talked about as
though they were always considered white. in fact, in some
quarters, rather than the descendants of the romans, the italians were considered at best as "dirty whites" who had been
mixed with blacks via hannibal crossing the alps, and thus,
in the good old color struck usa, it took a couple of generations and unrefusable offers from the mafia for italians to be
integrated as whites into the segregated black/white duality
of american society.

in any case the reason there were so many italians and
jews involved in early jass is not simply because the music
was their creation but rather because the music was the music
of the outsider, and to a significant extent italians and jews
were outsiders, especially as far as the upper reaches of twenties american society was concerned. while the italians and
jews wanted to assimilate, they also celebrated difference,
hence the predominance of blackface among this sector of a
society which overall celebrated whiteness pure as the driven
snow. think about it. what would cause someone who is on
the periphery to risk access to the interior by going further
out and painting their face black or playing music blackly?

don't say i got the answer, but do say, at least i got the
question. in any case, the important point to consider is
that of all the branches of black music, jass was the one that
whites (both anglos and wannabes) were more comfortable
embracing. or should i say, jass was the form they were more
able to embrace. (max roach jokes that frank sinatra's first
claim to fame was that he could snap his fingers on the beat

and sing at the same time, just like black singers, and it didn't matter how he sounded he could do it and thus is lauded as one of the great singers of all time except of course if you compare him to the authentic sounders of his time. think of a sing-off between sinatra and nat king cole.)

the white embrace of jass was significant. unlike the other forms of black music which were less flexible, jass was so malleable that literally anyone could play it, not necessarily well and certainly not in innovative ways that moved the music forward, but anyone could play it nevertheless and thus, unlike blues which took several decades for most whites to emulate, or various forms of gospel which are yet to be mastered by whites, jass gladly made room for the whole of humanity within its sounding.

Q: how were we repaid for creating a form which every human could use to sound their existence?

A: with so-called scholars, a few musicians, and a bunch of fans claiming that whites created or co-created jass. thus, when the odjb cut those first victor jass sides, the question of creating and innovating was effectively conflated and confused with emulating and manufacturing. we provided the recipe, they made the bread. but then again this is america, and that was the jass age.

the grimace behind armstrong's grin

they turned my birth place
into jail space—don't bury
me in new orleans

new orleans can be an extreme case of domestic abuse. like they say, don't take it, leave, don't hesitate, ready or not pack your shit, don't even think about going back, cause they don't really love you, not them control freaks who think they are kings and you are a feudal peasant in blackface. folk are in denial about new orleans when you hear them say: it's bad but not that bad, like as if he's a good man and you know how hard they are to find, nephew just gets a little upset sometimes and smacks you around but he loves you, really, really do, really? don't believe the hype.

louie knew. from the front gate to the back door armstrong had it straight, he was hip. home was where the heartbreak was. he had seen his father disappear; could have played hamlet looking for a ghost. had seen his mother tricked. had witnessed the best sound of an earlier generation sent across the lake to be housed with the mentally deranged—an enraged black man circa the teens and twenties was not insane, anger was a healthy response to what was being laid down. but anger and seven cents still wouldn't get you on the front of the bus. behind a screen is where you sat if you were black. louis wasn't no tom which is why he refused to be their token even after his spirit was gone: "when i die don't bury my body in new orleans" is what he said and meant, and since louis has passed on and his wishes were fulfilled, i.e., he is buried elsewhere, since then there are some new faces in higher places, a darker hue holds the whip, plots the comings and goings of how the system systematically shits on the unstrong, the unknown, the poor without a pot to piss in and having to pay rent to a landlord for the window out of which they throw it. your eyes may roll, your teeth may grit, but none of the real power will you git. not in new orleans, not until there is some change for truth. it may sound like i'm preaching but i'm not macking, i'm just steady facting about the way she blows down round the gulf coast in a heavenly slice of hell some people call the most fun you can have anywhere in america you go to new orleans you ought to go see the mardi gras cause there ain't much else hanging heavy in the air except the exhaust of used red beans and ricely yours and mine twenty-four hours at a time, big easy be steady bumping shit to the curb as they hustle every harry, dick, and john out of whatever money they got cause the winners down here ain't no saints and sinning ain't no crime. and if you don't know what i mean you better ask somebody cause new orleans may be big and easy but if you want to get ahead you're better off leaving cause they're most glad when you're dead so a funeral they can hold, an image they can unhold uncontradicted by the reality of poverty and exploitation. the bayou is a cesspool and nobody comes through the slaughter without some stank clinging to their clothes.

new orleans may be the cradle of jazz but it's also the tomb, they bury musicians here. louie knew, that's why he flew to chi and vowed to be someplace else when he died. don't bury me in, shit here is so low they got to bury you above ground, even while you still walking around trying to figure out your next move, which is why they razed louie's pad, made the move to build a bigger jail, it's called public housing for negro males. and if it sounds like i'm bitter it only means you just got a little taste of the special sauce, stale bread, po-boy seasoning in louie's red hot wail. but then again, maybe it's the bitter that makes the sweet so strong. whatever. no matter how you slice it, there ain't but one way to do it and that's to do it as best you can. morning, noon, midnight and dawn, can't we all just get along? hell no, not in new o. where it's legal to gamble but the majority ain't got much to bet with or on, except the vicious ways we kicking our rolling songs, crazy cooking our deep-fat fried food, and trying to hit a home run with the slim end of a very short stick. just like in bid whist you got to play the hand you was dealt cause that's all you got to fan with. some folks have ways and means, other folk got songs and dreams. and that's the way it comes and goes way down yonder in new orleans. some of you might wonder what all this has to do with jazz, well, it's like louie armstrong says, if you have to ask, you'll never really know. why was we born so black and blue? well our mamas birthed us black and the white folks made us blue, what else is left but to do what you got to do. throw me something mister they beg in the streets, but if you know like i know you best get your ass in the ring and swing like louie. you'll never see the forest unless you climb down out of the trees, live your life the way you wanna, just don't get buried by new orleans.

GUARDING THE FLAME OF LIFE: THE FUNERAL OF BIG CHIEF DONALD HARRISON SR.

It was a summer day in December 1998. The sky was clear, high, an almost pastel blue dotted by mere wisps of clouds. The shine of the sun bounced beaming off the white of the church's facade. Coming around the corner, brother man pushed a blue shopping cart that held a yellow fifty-gallon trash can with an ice pick stuck on the top of the plastic container. Dude had a fist full of dollar bills in his left hand. I knew what he was doing. He was selling beer.

"Yeah. Probably that old cheap Budweiser," my good buddy and internationally-exhibited visual artist Willie Birch wisecracked. About three-quarters of an hour later, the vendor had acquired a couple of cases of Lowenbrau in the bottle and stashed them on the bottom rack of the grocery buggy, now improvised into a mobile beer kiosk.

I spied a man in brilliant yellow shirt—it does injustice to the shirt to call it yellow, just as it does injustice to the sun to call it hot. The man was standing still; no breeze was blowing, but his shirt looked like it was moving. The hue of the deeply mellow, vibrant fabric was so intense that it made gold dust jealous. Turned out, as we talked, the brother would remind me that we graduated from high school together.

Then Roger Lewis, a founding member of the Dirty Dozen Band, walked up holding his baritone sax. New Orleans musicians have a tradition of resplendent cleanliness—as in mean, clean, and beautifying the scene. Roger's sartorial eminence was such that just the hipness of his presence was musical. He stood on the sidewalk with a slight rearward lean, angled just enough to let you know he was hip, and not so much that he looked like he was posturing or calling undue attention to himself. I heard strange and wonderful melodies in his insouciant stance, a bluesy riff in the way he unhurriedly unfurled a smile when I congratulated him on maintaining impressively high standards of beauty, vis-a-vis male attire.

But before the praise song to Roger was fully out of my mouth, nightclub bouncer and renowned gospel singer Joe Cool strolled by in a righteously pressed walking suit. The trouser hems draped softly over the tops of a pair of mustard-colored, burnished, kid-glove leather kicks that looked so comfortable he could have worn them on his hands—as I dapped him, I bent down and commented, "Look at that," pointing with my chin at his lovely loafers. "Leave it to you to give them something to look at when they bow down." Joe Cool has a beautiful grin when he is pleased.

Moments earlier, across the street I had seen our consiglieri relaxing on the stoop next to one of Treme's most responsible business people (as they were incognito I will not divulge their 9-to-5 identities, but I will say they were not visiting, that this was their resident neighborhood, and everyone who passed them spoke and were spoken to). The three of us were passing pleasantries for a minute when up pops union organizer and environmental racism activist Pat Bryant dressed in a black suit, looking like a Baptist preacher. In response to my ribbing about his get-up, Pat joked he had a Bible in his back pocket. With a straight face I asked, "What caliber?" He just smiled and showed us neither Bible nor gun. After giving me a conspiratorial glance, Pat said

something to our mutual counselor-friend about the low
nature of lawyerly work. The attorney calmly parried, "Like
Booker T. said, it beats working in the sun." Yeah, that made
sense; we knowingly head nodded. Pat leaned toward the
counselor to discuss a personal matter; I bid them adieu and
re-crossed the street to the church.

Back standing next to Willie, I surveyed the scene.
Shimmering and shimmying down the street a block away,
you could see the feathered form and also hear the drums
of the new-style Mardi Gras Indian, Fi Yi Yi. The distant
but distinct sound cut through the cacophony of the crowd.
Seemed like there was a couple of hundred people milling
around St. Augustine's front entrance at the corner of Gov.
Nichols and St. Claude.

Fi Yi Yi, in all his Indian glory, had his headgear on. The
mask fitted over his head like a knight's helmet, or like one
of them old papier-mâché, black and white skeleton skulls
like, well, like the one community activist/professional agita-
tor Randy Mitchell wore. Randy was belligerently waving a
black, pirate-like flag and daring anyone to take a picture of
his copyrighted costume.

As I turned to take in Fi Yi Yi's arrival, another adver-
tisement for African-inspired, colorful splendor stepped
softly around the corner. A man whose face I recognized
from second line parades strode confidently through the
crowd, his head cocked upward like a rooster squinting at
the dawn sky. He had on a black pinstriped suit, a blood red
silk handkerchief gushed out of his breast pocket, and he
was crowned with a white Stetson hat. His spotless skypiece
featured a small feather stuck in its side that made peacock
feathers look dull. I ran up to him: "Man, ain't no use in
looking for the sun, cause you the only thing shining!" He
waved at me good-naturedly and laughed.

Earlier I had been inside the church for the musical tribute section, but when the mass portion kicked in, the Indian

drumming and chanting that was going on outside piqued my interest. Their sharp shouts and sounds, un-ignorable as spear stabs, periodically pierced the quiet of the church sanctuary. Seemed like the drums were calling me by name. And that's how I came to be outside, greeting a plethora of cultural stalwarts such as Greg Stafford, the Young Tuxedo Brass Band leader/trumpeter and founding member of the Black Men of Labor marching club. Greg was resplendent in white from head to toe, including a tall, conical, African-inspired headpiece.

While waiting for the body to be released from the church services, many of us passed the time by greeting and hugging each other while reminiscing about good times and other great second lines. We were patient. Regardless of what was or was not going on inside, we knew Donald Harrison, Sr., would be delivered over to us for a final procession to the burying ground.

(So far I have not talked about the women—there were a couple of sisters so fine that when they strolled through the crowd, men stopped talking and just stood with their mouths gaped open. A little later, when my wife Nia came outside and started hugging me as she leaned against my shoulder, Willie started babbling about how beautiful Nia was. With every syllable, Nia's smile got wider and wider. I know that the significance of this interlude of describing the beauty of the women is lost on some people, but at the risk of being misunderstood, I say to you that wherever there is no deep and profound appreciation of women and music, beauty and dance, in such absence you find a general pallor and dullness to existence, an existence that opulence and ostentatious sex only make more sad. In any case, as clean as all the men I described above were, apply the splendor of their appearance to the pulchritude of the women.)

Inside the church, Fr. LeDeaux had said, there is something in us that celebrates life, celebrates through "music and dancing." He said that: music and dancing. A Catholic priest conducting a mass lauds the centrality of "music and dancing"—obviously this priest is a Black man (and I don't mean biologically; I mean culturally).

The procession at St. Augustine was unlike Catholic funeral services anywhere on this continent. The presiding priest both sang and preached as legendary blind pianist Henry Butler played in accompaniment. A trio of women read scripture. The highpoint was Donald Harrison's instrumental rendition of "Amazing Grace." Predictably, this was truly a memorable New Orleans funeral.

Unlike most churches, which have the pulpit at one end of the church, St. Augustine's altar is in the middle of the congregational seating, and what had originally been the dais and choir area is now where the musicians performed.

The church is décored with the usual artifacts of Christianity, but closer inspection reveals banners proclaiming the Nguzo Saba (the seven principles of African Heritage). Moreover, high up in the balcony, taking up the top wall, there is what looks like a ten to fifteen-foot ankh instead of a traditional cross.

The ankh is a traditional African icon—for those who would want me to specify that the ankh is Egyptian, I suggest that you miss the point that Egypt is African, or at least originally was before Eurocentric scholars with cultural axes to grind kept trying to point to Greece to explain the science and culture of North Africa. Anyway, there, in St. Augustine Catholic Church, the largest religious icon was an ankh.

The ankh represents not simply life in the abstract, but also the male and female principle of life in balance. The shape of the ankh has the ovary over the phallus: the circle (actually an upside-down teardrop, the pear shape of the earth itself), or female, sits atop the rod, or male.

Need I tell you that this is a Black church? St. Augustine Catholic Church is one of the oldest churches in the city and was built with money raised by "gens libre de colouer"—free men of color—and by contributions from enslaved Africans who made money from trade and handicraft sales. Moreover, St. Augustine is located in Treme, which is the oldest continuously existing African-American neighborhood in the United States.

For an hour before the formal funeral mass, there had been jazz and Mardi Gras Indian drumming, dancing, and singing. Trap drummer Shannon Powell and djembe master Luther Gray traded funky pre-funeral licks. Bassist Chris Severin held down the bottom. Milton Batiste bested the younger trumpeters with some absolutely, hideously awe-inspiring trumpet flourishes that favored all the tones that hang around, and in-between, but never at the center of the tempered scale—although I must say that "Twelve" (aka James Andrews, bka Satchmo of the Ghetto) was right up under Milton with some trumpet wah-wah effects he made by sticking his hand in and over the bell of his horn as if his flesh were a mute. The two Willies (Willie Tee and Willie Metcalf) played the keyboards like balaphons, that uniquely African mixture of melody and percussion. And only son Donald Harrison, Jr., was out front with saxophone—he was on alto, his prettiest voice. And there were plenty more hornmen and drummers coming and going, including the ever effervescent vocalist/trumpeter Kermit Ruffins.

At the end of the musical tribute section, I was called on to deliver a poem. I recited "Spirit & Flame." Much of what I said was chanted, some was not even in English, but, nevertheless and unfailingly, most of the people understood every sound I uttered.

On one side of the church sat All For One Records founder and former musical director for Sonny & Cher, Harold Battiste, dressed in a formal-length black, white-embroidered top of African finery, his elderhood sagely complemented by the upside-down halo of his magnificent white wisdom-beard. No one has made as significant an all-around contribution to New Orleans music as has Battiste, who is a prolific producer, composer, and arranger in jazz, rhythm & blues, gospel, and pop music.

On the other side of the church, the Big Chief of the Yellow Pocahontas and man who has masked for over fifty years, Tootie Montana, sat side by side with his wife and chief sewing partner, Joyce Montana. They could wear sack-cloth and look regal. Throughout the services people walked up to Big Chief Tootie and paid almost as much respect to him as to the Harrison family. Though Donald Harrison, Sr., was widely acclaimed for his intellectual prowess and historical insight into the significance of Indian culture, Tootie Montana is considered the most accomplished Mardi Gras Indian suit designer.

After my threnody, members of Chief Harrison's gang shook tambourines and sang over the coffin, offering a last testament of fidelity to the principles and beliefs of their Big Chief. Also on hand to pay their respects were a number of other Indian chiefs, including some from rival uptown gangs.

A veritable who's who of Black street culture slow marched up and down the church aisle for the last viewing of a man who, perhaps more than any other, argued for full recognition of the cultural significance of Mardi Gras Indians —a calling which, significantly, his children and grandchildren have actively taken up: his oldest daughter Cherice Harrison-Nelson teaches Mardi Gras Indian culture in the public schools and community workshops; his son Donald Harrison, Jr., is a professional jazz musician who has constantly recorded Mardi Gras Indian music; and his grandson Brian Nelson has become a Mardi Gras Indian chief. Though, thankfully, his work continues on, undoubt-edly Donald Harrison, Sr., will be missed.

Unfortunately, but also predictably, there were too many cameras (a couple of photographers had been requested by the family, but most were uninvited). Used to be you would only see the small, hand-held deals; now there are camcorders and video crews with ungainly boom cranes and artificial lights. All of this despite two big signs posted on the church's front door: "No cameras inside."

Most of the picture taking was futile. No matter what they shot with, none of those pictures could show you the spirit swirling around this gathering for the sendoff of Big Chief Donald Harrison, the Guardian of the Flame. Only the human soul can appreciate the profoundness of the spirit. A machine at best captures but a pale reflection. If you really want to make a memento of such moments, you should go and osmose the spirit through your pores, inhale the bouquet of real emotions and deep sentiments.

After over an hour of church services, the second line finally began. For a block or so, I slipped inside the eye of the procession, pranced just behind the trombones, saxophones at my side and trumpets nappying up my kitchen with corkscrew tones blown at the back of my head. We proceeded up Ursulines past where James Black used to live (I believe it was his mama's house), where, when Brother Black had passed on, the hearse stopped in front of the door and the coffin was pulled out and literally thrown up in the air in ritual salute.

Earlier I had hovered at the heart of Indian drumming and chants as we prayed in our own secular way for Big Chief Donald Harrison's safe journey to the ancestor realm. I am not an Indian nor a musician, but these are my people. I was here to bear witness with the vibrancy of my being, with my tongue chanting and body dancing, with my soul intertwined in celebratory resistance, shouting with all the others of us in the street—no building, no structure, no coffin, nothing could contain us. This is why we don't die; we multiply. Every time the butcher cuts one of us down, the rest of us laugh and dance, defying death. It's our way of

saying "yes" to life, saying "fuck you" to death and his nefarious henchmen, poverty and racism.

The funeral of Big Chief Donald Harrison raised two
important questions. First, when does spectacle overtake
ritual; and second, in light of the significance of the transition of this particular Big Chief, where do we go from here?

From the beginning in Congo Square on down to the
jazz funeral of today, there have always been two kinds of
audiences: those of the culture who come to make ritual, to
affirm and renew; and those who come to witness (a few to
gawk) and be entertained. Both audiences understand something powerful to be going on, which is why they both were
there/are here.

The ritual participants came, some literally looking
like they wore whatever they had worn to work yesterday,
or maybe even whatever they were wearing when they fell
asleep slumped over a bar table at three o'clock that morning; or, then again, they came like that fierce sister who wore
a circular, feathered, multicolored hat—to say it looked like
a crown belittles the splendiferous figure she cut every time
she bobbed her head, and don't mention when she would
turn and smile.

The ritual participants were the beaters of wine bottles
and the bearers of babies on their hips. They were those who
raided deep into the hearts of their closets to come out with
their hippest threads, and they were those who just heard the
commotion, threw open their front doors, rose up off stoops
and porches, and ran to add to the assembly, because in the
marrow of their being they "feel to believe" they are "called"
to join in. These often nameless and generally uncelebrated (outside of their turf communities), these indispensable
spiritual emeralds, are the standard bearers of street culture.
They came.

These are the ones who would have been dancers and not
just onlookers in Congo Square—the musicians, the singers,

the hip swingers, hollering until hoarse, and then shouting some more. These are the people whose existence in and of itself affirms the dynamic of the African way of knowing and celebrating life.

The others, the onlookers, were there to be touched by the profundity of the ritual—and while they are welcome to watch, we must understand that no matter what they think of what they see (or what they write or how many pictures they print up and put in books), the onlookers are an appendage and ultimately not even necessary for the functioning of this culture.

Sometimes there are clashes between these two audiences; sometimes there are mergers. These two groups of people are connected in time and place but are separate in culture and condition. Harrison's funeral makes me pause and ask: When does the spectacle of it, when does the gathering of onlookers, gawkers (especially the wanna-be sly cultural vultures—and you know who you are)—when does this press of outsiders become so present that it colors, no, mars the beauty and integrity of the proceedings?

It wouldn't be so bad if the non-dancers would step to the rear and sit quietly, or move out the way and walk on the sidewalk, but no, some of them are so bold as to want to be up-close and personal. And please do not misunderstand this as a veiled reference exclusively to so-called "White" people. There are a number of Negroes who show through and come back into the hood only when someone dies, and then only for a moment—don't blink your eyes or you will miss them. Like Dorothy, sometimes I wish I could click my heels and make all of them go away. Forever.

African-American culture has always had to function under the scrutiny of outsiders; however, the mix is becoming so disproportionate that you can't hardly feel the heat of the Black fyah because of the damp of so much chilly water.

Sometimes Donald Harrison (both Donald the father

and Donald the son) and I would talk about these and other matters. In fact, more and more the nature and preservation of our culture is becoming one of the major topics of conversation wherever the culture bearers gather. Regardless of whether we are misunderstood, there are a significant number of us who will never liquidate our Blackness to indulge in indiscriminate integration, particularly integration of all things Black into any thing White. Donald Harrison, Sr., could hold court for days about this.

Big Chief Harrison was a studious man who read voraciously and thought deeply about being and the meaning of life. I shall not attempt to put words in his mouth, nor to project my own sentiments through him. We need only tell the truth about him. We need only note that he gave name to the "Guardian of the Flame."

What fyah was it that he wanted to keep burning?

The people outside the church were like flint stones sparking against the hard rocks of our place and time. Mayor Marc Morial was inside expressing condolences. Outside, Ferdinand Bigard had dressed his son in a Friday night, negroidal-red Indian suit. The senior Donald Harrison's body was resting in the coffin inside the church. Outside, Indians were scurrying back and forth, chanting in the street. The fire was outside—also inside to a significant degree, but mainly outside—in the hearts and soul of the people who sang and danced during the musical tribute, and retreated to the street to wait out the formal religious part of the funeral.

People do not want to talk about this cultural separation of church and street, especially since the street is the more celebrated. Perhaps such celebratory discourse seems sacrilegious. Most of us who write and publish in mainstream organs are either Christians or are very reluctant to do anything that might be construed as anti-Christian, but facts is facts: those who maintain the street culture of New

Orleans are mainly blues people who are often very spiritual, but who are not necessarily very religious.

Yet, the street folk don't deny the church its place in the community. A significant section of the Black community goes to church, and most Black people, be they Christian or not, believe in "God." But spiritual beliefs on one hand and strict adherence to Christian doctrine on the other are two different concepts. This African-based spirituality sans Christian religiosity is what demarcates the Black blues people from their fellow Blacks in the community. Moreover, the blues people are generally the marginals of society, the most impoverished materially, but, at the same time, they are the richest in terms of cultural creativity and integrity, and particularly in terms of African retentions (both conscious and unconscious).

New Orleans would be a piss poor place to live were it not for the presence and culture of the Black poor/blues people of New Orleans. The people who don't own a pot to urinate in nor a window to throw it out of (over sixty percent of them are renters!), these are the people whom Donald Harrison spoke of, with, and for. These were the people who marched with him on Mardi Gras Day. These, and another element: the conscious brothers and sisters, kin and kind, who might work at City Hall or for the school board, but who dress out at appropriate occasions and shake their backfields like a saucer of Jell-O in the hands of a four-year-old. It is the poor and the conscious individuals who align themselves with the poor that keep New Orleans Black culture alive—the ones who will dance at the drop of a hat and can't imagine life without music.

This is what Donald Harrison asked us to keep alive, and this mission speaks directly to the second question: where do we go from here?

The best way to preserve New Orleans culture is to support the people who make the culture. Open doors for them. If you live or work in the big house, then throw food and resources out the window, pass on strategic information. But do it as a religious offering, not as a material acquisition or purchase. Make your sacrifice and then go home. Let the spirit carry on. Let those who make music and dance, those who sing and chant, let them be and do what they gotta do without the interference of outsiders of whatever color who have a vested interest in becoming experts on what they have never and can never produce: a culture as vibrant and exultant as New Orleans street culture.

There is room for all at the table, but if you can't cook, get out the kitchen. Make whatever contribution you can, and where you can't, get out the way and give the dancers room to do their thing.

Whether onlooker or participant, the passing of Big Chief Donald Harrison Sr. speaks to us, encourages us, cajoles us—we must carry on: support New Orleans culture. Guard the Flame with the seriousness of your life because that is precisely what the flame is: life. The flame is all about the joy and celebration of life. Be a guardian of life. Regardless of how cold it does or does not get, let the fyah burn full up!

SPIRIT & FLAME
(for Big Chief Donald Harrison)

you think this a costume?
you think this a ball?
you think this a lark?
just for the fun of it all?

Hoo Nan Ney!

the ancestors are enriched / our lives had been made
stronger / the flame has purified us / if only / for a
moment / the moment / of his flashing / his flaming
/ his wit / his anger / his upholdance of the legacy / of
resistance / intelligence / seriousness / sun seriousness
/ hot pepper / cayenne colors / the shout of life in the
face of whatever / the cultural tourists are calling themselves today / they / will be at the funeral / but who
marched with him / when he was alive / who carried
the flame / in their mouths / stepped in the sun then /
when / no cameras were allowed / who waved hard high
/ the banner in their hearts / what men and women /
sons, daughters / & lovers / who manifested / the dance
walk of black shine / guarding the flame of our time /
beaconing bright / terrible / and badder than that / on
our good days / in our wild ways / when nobody can't
tell us nothing / not a goddamn thing / and we sing /
and we shout / and we act out / black & red / african
culture / of many colors / don't take no trail of tears to
his coffin / donald harrison does not need your pity /
your moans / about what we gon / do / now that he gone
/ the fire is not out / if you continue to carry the flame /
if you are guardian / if you are in the groove / conscious

of who / & what we are / & all we come from / don't
cry / don't you moan / stand tall / walk proud / let every
waist wind up / let every foot kick forward / let every
mouth shout / let every eye shine / don't bow down / go
forth unbended / don't bow down / in sorry sorrow / you
never saw him sad / as a negro / hoping to become white
/ by committing cultural suicide / he said feed the fire /
keep the burning / grab some knowledge / be a scholar
/ know yourselves / honor your mother / honor your
father / love your people / all they been / and had to be
/ while working through the slaughter / moving forward
/ keep on dancing / beat the drum / the drums of life
/ sing the songs / of who we are / follow his example /
don't bow down / stand up straight / and guard the flame
/ the dark flame / of black fire / black fyah i tell you /
fyah / & flame the spirit of struggle / spirit & flame / big
chief / donald harrison / fayh chief / guardian / guardian
of the flame / guardian of the flame / be a guardian / of
the flame / the flame of life / shine on

YOU CAN'T TOUCH THIS...

one

Some people study fish. Intently. At the microscopic level. They can tell you about feeding habits, mating habits, growth rates, swim speed. You name it. But those know-a-lot experts too often overlook what's troubling the waters. I believe if you really want to understand fish, you need to consider the source and quality of the water.

If possession is nine-tenths of the law, environment is a significant factor in social development and stability. So, if cultural practices such as SA&PC (social aid and pleasure clubs) and second lines are the fish, we should examine what is the nature of their water: is it fresh, salt, or brackish; is it pristine or polluted; what are the sources and who controls the flow; does it have major commercial use, or is it mainly recreational? And, of course, the ultimate question, especially for those of us who are waterborne: how you gon' be fish without water? That's a big-ass question.

Back in the eighties, I sat on the NEA literature and jazz panels. Before participating at a decision-making level, I had no idea specifically how much tax money was pumped into cultural activities. I had never thought about where the SOBs (our sarcastic term for the funds-dominating trio of symphony, opera, and ballet associations) got their money. If those institutions had to make it mainly on ticket sales, drinks, and merchandise tables, they would all be extinct.

After closer inspection, I began to realize that the severely limited amount of monies earmarked for cultural development was dominated by SOBs that had no popular base. The argument was that the SOBs were absolutely essential to metropolitan areas, and that it was our national duty to help ensure the availability of Bach, Verdi, and *The Nutcracker* in our major cities. Can you imagine jazz, Mardi Gras Indians, and social aid and pleasure clubs making a similar case for significant funding? Neither could the cultural czars who control the allocation of grants.

But there is an even worse twist of the knife when it comes to determining who even gets to get in the long line to request funding. Over and over, we heard the big money mantra: in order to get serious funding, arts organizations needed administrative controls, boards, and annual audits, in addition to competing in predetermined, mainstream categories.

Certainly it is true that individual excellence might get recognized, but that is not where the bulk of cultural funding goes. The SOBs are hungry beasts, and the mainstream is not shy about keeping them fed and fat. In this context, where Black cultural formations have to fight for scraps, the fact that consistent Black cultural production even exists is close to miraculous.

Year after year, the social aid and pleasure clubs present scintillating anniversary processions, all without any significant monetary support from the government or private philanthropy. (Although with the new millennium, Black cultural formations are now receiving some funds; the allocation is severely inequitable.) Do a cost/production comparison between the SOBs and our neighborhood organizations. Who is offering more bang for the buck? Indeed, in the Black community we produce big, culturally powerful "booms" even though we are working with nickel-and-dime mainstream support.

Moreover, the audiences for the majors are small, whereas entire communities turn out to see and participate when Black groups come out. When one compares the percentage of a given community that actually witnesses an event, the audience for Black cultural formations easily outpaces the SOBs. But there is more. The now eleven-year-long destruction of the predominately Black public school system in New Orleans marks and masks the near complete obliteration of a neighborhood support base for Black cultural productions.

The neighborhood schools offered more than simply opportunities to pass on cultural skills to Black and minority youth: those schools also offered employment opportunities for many of the major cultural movers and shakers. Often, that employment was found in non-cultural roles, such as assistant teachers, sports coaches, or kitchen and janitorial workers, but these posts enabled a cultural worker to financially support their private cultural productions. This support network has been shredded by a plethora of corporate-envisioned, for-profit charter schools.

And then there is the logistical hurdle that now exists since students are bussed to schools miles away from where they live. After-school activities are no longer easy to coordinate, and often the students with the greatest needs or those who could best benefit from school programs are hampered in their participation by lack of transportation; they cannot afford to miss their bus.

These and other not-so-obvious factors are usually not noted when we analyze cultural production, but they are significant impediments and must be dealt with in order to continue to effectuate first-class cultural production on the black-hand side. Obviously, the particulars of this analysis need further discussion, but there is one other not-so-obvious factor that must be appreciated if we are to understand Black cultural development in New Orleans.

Black cultural development has not simply been a case of racial segregation. We were not doing the same thing as the mainstream, just focused in our own, racially defined communities. Indeed, Black cultural production not only has its own standards and audiences, but further, all of the significant expressions of Black culture have been alternatives to, rather than variations on, mainstream cultural activities. In a number of cases, Black cultural activities were actually oppositional to those of the mainstream. If one had to choose between catching Tootie Montana on Mardi Gras Day versus going on St. Charles Avenue to see the Rex parade, there really was no contest. Or, like we used to say, Rex didn't sew his own suit, and old boy sure couldn't sing and dance like our big chief with his golden crown.

A final contextual note. Black cultural organizations and formations had an oppositional core to them precisely because the social environment within which they were created necessitated, at minimum, an element of militant self-defense against the Ku Klux Klan, police, and political terrorism that continues to bedevil the Black community to this day. We were not simply combating mainstream apathy and ignorance towards us. From day one, our culture had to fight the malevolence of the mainstream that has actively exploited and oppressed us from slavery times into the present.

The materials we used for whatever our cultural production was were dearly purchased. Often our cultural activities were extra-legal, if not outright deemed illegal by the mainstream. In case one thinks this an exaggeration, consider the current so-called noise abatement ordinances, or the costly parade permits that shut down impromptu second lines and have even led to musicians being arrested and jailed for parading in the streets without official sanction.

Without even having to say it directly in lyrics, every note of some second lines is a "fuck you" shouted at mainstream propriety, rules, and regulations. That is the secret sauce in Black cultural production: it may seem like we're doing it just for pleasure, but we're serious as a heart attack. Pleasure and heart attacks are both clichéd ways to describe our cultural production, but there is a truth at the center of those oft-rendered descriptions.

What would make a day laborer who earns less than $28,000 annually spend $7,848 and 56 cents to create a suit he is going to wear twice (Mardi Gras Day and St. Joseph's Night)—or maybe three times if he chooses to come out on Super Sunday? Is he stupid to spend that much money on shoes and feathers when he doesn't even own a car and rents the house he lives in?

The answer is both simple and serious: our culture is a representation not just of the artistic best of us; our culture is a statement of our will and determination to artfully express our humanness. Regardless of what others think of us, or try to do and not do to us, we will embrace and celebrate our own invaluable and essential human beauty and goodness. Our cultural existence is a positive statement or, as community members exclaim when they give a big thumbs-up to a particular expression: "They was some pretty, yeah." To which the only sensible reply is a note of agreement with the community assessment: "Yeah, you right."

You right, they was pretty and you right, they was right to be pretty. In fact, it is essential that we produce our culture regardless of the cost, regardless of what others think, regardless of whether anybody else cares or witnesses.

Rain or shine, the imperative is to get out in the streets and do what we wanna. Our culture is a declaration of independence, of life, of humanity. An expression of our freedom to be we. Whoever we are, wherever we are, howsoever we choose to be "we." Yeah, we right!

two

The kings, the chieftains nobly sat: resplendently robed in colorful Kente, surrounded by an entourage of attendants and kin, attentive to every royal wish, desire, gesture, need. Supplicants respectfully bowed, casual conversations were suspended until well past regal earshot. They had a court of musicians with magnificent instruments: long, intricately carved drums; horns of various kinds, both natural and man-made; a choir of mellifluous vocalists. And, of course, agile and entrancing dancers. As is their birthright, these people of high birth sported metallic accouterments fashioned from the finest of Ghanaian gold—literally, from the glitter dust on the cheeks of the women, to the nuggets, the size of a baby's fist, on the wrists of the wise ones.

They had arrived in a solemn procession carried in on palanquins, boat-like vessels shaped liked small canoes. The entire circumference of the massive stadium was rimmed by their majestic assemblages. I did not know the languages, nor the specifics of these traditions, but even an untrained ear or an untutored eye could easily recognize that this was a presentation far beyond ordinary.

And then at the end, there was this joyous din originating from an impromptu, rag-tag ensemble strutting like they were the highest of the high. Rather than drums, most of them had boxes and commercial containers now doubling as instruments to beat on. Sort of like a cross between an African cakewalk and an Ewe wobble, working their thing while sporting their finest "rags." Literally—to use an Afro-American colloquialism—literally their ragged clothing now doubled as "glad rags."

As I sat in the bleachers in some stadium in Cape Coast, Ghana, I immediately recognized myself, or more precisely, recognized a component of my own cultural identity. The way they danced and drummed, sang and shouted, bringing up the rear in an exuberant procession proclaiming not their wealth but their vitality. This potpourri may have been impoverished materially, but they were spiritually and culturally expressive of an artistic, irrepressible, and hence, inspiring and invigorating lifestyle.

If you practice in the privacy of your bedroom but are restrained on the street as the parade passes by, you are not a second liner. You may secretly love it and harbor a deep desire to be part of it but…but you can't be what you don't do. Yes, some of us are observers rather than participants, and yes, there is an undeniable value in culturally relevant studies and analysis, but the being and doing is the critical element—the sine qua non.

We can't all dance like Tee-Boy. Man, he could kick it up. He had been in St. Aug's Marching 100 band and had been trained to raise his legs high, his upper thigh parallel to the ground. One time he did a circular jig on one leg and then reversed his twirling; 360-degrees clockwise and then a full circle back counter-clockwise, all the time hopping to the beat of the music, and his left leg steady-stayed high.

Or maybe we didn't have as much rump to bump as did Sister Vee, i.e., Veronica Mae Jones, who could make her butt cheeks twine in time to the beat, right left, left right, enough to make a drummer throw down his drum sticks. And she was on the usher board down to the church. But on this particular Sunday she was rocking a siren red cotton dress and waving an over-sized, rose-colored bandana, switching it like a metronome behind her pulsating behind. Oh, my Lord, what she want to do that for?

Seem like everybody out there had a little "some-thing, some-thing" they did to distinguish themselves. Even Old Broke Joe, who must a been ninety-some years old, leaned on his cane and did some kind of movements with his head like as if he was a super-hip pigeon or something; wasn't nothing else moving, just his head twirling atop his neck, in a herky-jerky, pecking motion, but on the beat. Right. On. The. Beat!

I started laughing, and this lady saw me looking on and said to her little girl, who looked like she was maybe six years old: "Go on, second line." And you know, that little girl dropped down in a quick squat, put her hands on her hips, jumped up, did some kind of hopscotch motion, crossing and un-crossing her legs, twirled, hippity-hopped for about half a minute, her two long braids with green-balled barrettes flying around her head, and then she leaned back, her lithe, tan arms folded cross her chest, froze in that pose for five or six beats, and then, with her chin jutting out at a defiant angle, looked up sideways at her mama, not like to ask for approval or praise, but like she was some kind of goddamn exclamation point, like when you the onliest one in the class what scored an A-100 on the final algebra exam. Got all them hard-ass equations right. Except this girl had just finished doing a nasty lil juke-step like it wasn't nothing. If she could do math like she could dance, you could have been an astronaut and she would of guided your rocket ship to the moon and back.

Everywhere you looked, everybody was doing something with their body to let you know that they knew how to celebrate life, and how to inspire any onlooker to want to celebrate, too. Well, go head on with your bad self. Well. Well. There was no limit to the variations. No limit to the joy their movements evoked in every onlooker. These revelers, your people, made you feel glad to be alive regardless of how well you were: physically, spiritually, intellectually, financially, or in whatever way. In each and every which way, they made you feel good.

The celebratory movements of your people made you thankful to be alive even if you couldn't expertly dance such a much like some of them seem to so effortlessly do. Didn't matter. Whatever you could do, if it was no more than admire, no more than smile, throw your hand up over your wide-open mouth, and shake your head in awesome wonder as you witnessed the vibrancy of this gathering of the saints—and that's who they were: saints. The holy ones. The elegant celebrants of sweet life.

This was the best of us. Yes, a handful of us were royalty, and some select few of us even had a healthy portion of gold. But whether prince or pauper, life is always about how you move through the world, dancing to whatever beats energize and motivate you. Regardless of how fast, or how strong; how intelligent or how accomplished at this, that or the other, one way or another, we all could celebrate life. Who-so-ever you were. How-so-ever you stepped. Our music. Our dance. On any given sun day, this was the best of us—of each of us individually, of all of us collectively. And you can't touch that!

MAN MASTERING METAL

Art is more than adornment, deeper than entertainment. Martin Payton is an artist, a man who confronts life through mastering metal. Physically wrestling hard, inert matter into fluid forms reflecting the human spirit of transformation, i.e., the real alchemy of changing "what is" into a creatively imagined "what could be"—what we, in the temporal twentieth and twenty-first century of our human existence, make to say: we were here.

Martin Payton is a blacksmith. Literally. A Black man who wrestles with metal, and in so doing reflects not just the ethos of his Black southern time and condition, but also projects the human heart cry: I am. Moreover, his art easily exceeds sociology. Far beyond the assumed haughtiness of abstract intellectual theory or the cash register ring of raw commerce. Far beyond. His is a spirit given form that we can touch and be informed by, just by viewing his statues, merely being in their presence. His work exemplifies the essence of Black life in America: we were borne here as commercial objects but have transformed our captivity into a liberation of the spirit and an elevation of our environment. Always. Always. Embodying our ancestral essence: regardless of conditions, make life better. Prettier. He works with steel girders, wrought iron, fire. He is an artistic gandy-dancer, harkening back to his twentieth century ancestors who labored at laying railroad tracks. They didn't simply toil as manual laborers; they whistled and danced as they worked. Making music was integral to how they stepped through life, and Payton is of their lineage.

Payton's family includes jazz musicians: bassist Walter Payton and trumpeter/pianist Nicholas Payton. His mentor was MacArthur Fellowship awardee John Scott. After college, Payton and Scott became artistic Ibeji twins, and together they produced *Spirit House* (2002), one of New Orleans' most iconic public artworks. Payton and Scott's sculptural creations celebrated life filled with happiness, joy, abundance, and laughter. Spiritual metallurgy is what Payton has done. Continues to do. He forces us who view his work—who see how he has twisted metal—to imagine that we could be more than whatever we are. That is, after all, the secret wish of every individual: we desire to be more than we are. Even filled with diagonals, Payton's work stands upright. He's got what in the vernacular is called a "gansta lean," which is simply the negrodal penchant for the asymmetrical. Or, as Leopold Senghor presciently noted: the negro abhors the straight line. Even a quick glance at Payton's statuary will evidence how he uses repetition to create rhythm. Add to that a new world insistence of jazzy improvisation in his use of negative space—his statues are as much about what is not there as they are about what is shown. Every piece has open spaces, upward thrusts, and an off-center balance that makes the work seem to simultaneously be falling and rising. This art is a virtual philosophical encyclopedia of post-modern style and substance. Payton educates and helps us; his art encourages us to strive to achieve our cravings as well as accept the challenge to be our better selves. Even when we are not fully cognizant of our own thoughts and feelings—indeed, especially then—great art ennobles us.

Payton's work frees us, even as we and it remain rooted to the ground. His heavy metal statues enlighten us. Standing before his art, we image wings. What great paradox Payton achieves. He makes us feel like flying. Or, at the very least, feel that we are witnessing the work of someone who has flown to the heart of the sun and returned with knowledge far beyond ordinary knowing. Such is the magic of his art: he gives wings to our imaginations. After all, he is from the New Orleans region, the place where millions of us entered into the North American phase of African time. His is a tradition of the enslaved working with metal: wrought iron grillwork. (See: Marcus Christian: *Negro Iron Workers of Louisiana* and John Michael Vlatch: *The Afro-American Tradition In Decorative Arts*.) Payton makes flowers out of a ferrous fabric, heated, hammered, and given quotidian elegance.

What we think is undoubtedly important; however, what and how we do, how we actualize our thoughts, these are the critical processes. All great artists as they mature make what they do seem easy, almost effortless. The reality is that they have spent literally decades wrestling with their chosen craft to arrive at the point where they no longer have to physically or mentally wage war with their materials, or struggle mightily in order to articulate their ideas. Once one becomes expert, then one can simply do without having to think about doing. Very often, over the decades, the resulting work becomes more condense, compact; less showy; sometimes even diminutive rather than immense or ostentatious. Masters are always pithy in their articulation even as they are profound in their meaning: the complex is elegantly boiled down to a simple, albeit not simplistic, profundity.

We sometimes lose sight of the fact that artwork actually requires hard work. One does not become a master artist without an outlay of time and effort. As our folk wisdom counsels: you can see a man's fall but not know his struggles.

If we only judge by what we perceive in front of us, we inevitably miss what is behind the reality. And, of course, masters are adept at masking the arduous work of apprenticeship. In the African-American tradition, mastery was often a necessarily camouflaged survival skill for avoiding detection and destruction by the larger society. But beyond mere survival, we advocated an approach to life that emphasized being cool, which is a quality integral to the DNA of an African way of being. Particularly during the North American sojourn, Africans were prohibited from producing a lasting materiality—our artwork was literally illegal.

In conscious contradistinction to the prohibitions of ancestral slavery and 20th century segregation, new world Africans conjured a vibrant spiritual and material culture. It is a major mistake that the artists who carried on this tradition are sometimes thought of as naïve, unschooled folk artists, as if they were not great thinkers, self-aware artisans. People such as Martin Payton are more than gifted prodigies or natural savants; they labor at developing their skills, often committing a lifetime to the arts. Born in 1948, Payton has spent over thirty years with anvil and kiln. No one can continuously work that long without thinking about what they are doing. Even if he seems to be simply placing found objects in a circle, what we are actually witnessing is a projection of the human spirit through a profound mise-en-scène constructed from whatever elements are available in a given circumstance.

When our elders talk about "making do," their thesis is an appropriate emphasis on action rather than reflection, or, as they are wont to preach: it ain't what you do, but the way that you do it. In a counterintuitive sense, an African sensibility goes beyond the basic formulation that substance is more important than style, that what a thing "is" is more important that what it looks like.

That seemingly obvious formulation is in fact turned on its head by African artists such as Payton, whose work suggests another worldview. Art is the vector that renders the process of stylization significant, more significant even than the material that is being acted upon. Payton sees scrap iron, and when he is finished, we see gods and spirits rising. The energy of art moves inert matter into the spiritual realm. Artistic stylization animates mute matter into something more than itself. In Payton's hands, the element of iron becomes more than what we see or touch.

Much like Einstein's relativity, Payton's artwork is at once simple in its existence and masterful in its formulation. It is only our philosophical ignorance, or our arrogance, that would allow us to view art—especially great art, although at one level or another, all art—as insignificant or lesser than. Implicit in sculpture is the axiom: how you be "is" (or becomes) what you be. Or, in more abstract terms: being is doing. In human terms, what we do with the world within which we live defines our humanity. Once I was touring a Ghanaian cultural official around New Orleans. While looking, he suddenly exclaimed, "Sankofa. Sankofa." I, of course, was mystified; I saw only a house with an iron railing on the front porch. I repeated the strange word and asked what he meant. He instructed that the design in the metal was an Adinkra symbol for going back and fetching what one has lost, one's past, one's ancestral patrimony. Over a decade later I would visit Ghana and run into literally thousands of people who looked just like individuals with whom I had grown up; no surprise there. But I also learned of Ghana's cultural double consciousness. They had this artwork that was twined with designs that were both representational and deeply symbolic. That mysterious sankofa word could be evidenced as a bird or as a curved heart-like outline. Moreover, these symbols were philosophical tenets. A bird, a heart—they meant much more than what one saw.

Whether considering nail-infused Nkisi spirit statues from the Congo area or the exquisite majesty of Benin bronzes out of Nigeria, to the intricately entwined Makonde figures in Tanzania or the sensual Shona soapstone carvings from Zimbabwe, not to mention the example of ancient Egyptian funeral artifacts, African-American artists inevitably are influenced by the immense totality of African material artwork, and, as a result of this wide-ranging array of influences, artists such as Martin Payton are subconsciously, and in some cases overtly, de facto aesthetic Pan-Africanists. Even when those artists have no specific political focus, they are attracted to and advocates of what is sometimes called an African aesthetic, which is diverse in its details and at the same time unified in its essence.

The fact that some of them are not aware of the connection, and that the majority of African-American artists have not actually been to Africa or worked with continental African artists/communities, does not negate their authentic Africanity. While there is no denying the disruption between the diaspora and its ancestral homeland, nevertheless a basic emotional and expressive unity has been maintained. Yes, there are distinctive differences between African Americans and continental Africans. Yes, African Americans have physical and cultural attributes that continentals don't have, but the differences are ones of detail and not of essence. Payton's artwork exemplifies and celebrates this cultural essentiality even as his sculptural output is reflective of the particulars of Payton's time and place within the new world.

There is a philosophical underpinning expertly articulated by Cheikh Anta Diop in his book *The Cultural Unity of Black Africa: The Domains of Matriarchy & of Patriarchy in Classical Antiquity*. Diop posits an overarching and unifying outlook that not only connects the far-flung diaspora to its ancestral source, but also is grounded in a fundamental differentiation between African and European cultural realities and expressions. Indeed, as Diop indicates, those who were removed from the motherland nevertheless continue to contain and exemplify a connective philosophy. The Brazilians call this nexus "saudade"—a nostalgia, a longing for that which was lost. When Payton affixes titles such as "Nzinga," "Toussaint," "Fannie," "Oshun," "Sojourner," "Tyner," "Dolphy," "Chucho," "Icarus Africanus," and "Kilamanjaro" to his work, he is announcing a pan-African approach that, beyond the obvious political and social meanings, explicitly celebrates the commonality of an immense and diverse body of human realities. Payton's artwork is reflective of personalities and conditions shared by African people in both the old and new world, from pre-colonial times to the twenty-first century.

African retentions are real. And what is retained is a deeptitude, an African way of knowing, light years beyond primal human expressions and strivings. Western society proposes the progressive model of human development: each era is thought of as more knowledgeable than the previous time period. After all, electricity is hipper than firelight. But what our African ancestry teaches us is that regardless of what we learn, we are still human beings utilizing our abilities to facilitate being alive and struggling with whatever are the conditions in which we find ourselves.

Moreover, what we know is not enough to ensure survival. Thought alone is not our highest expression. Thought must be mated with feelings, and our individuality must be immersed within a specific human society. The precision of our artwork is not craft alone but is also the demi-divine, material expression of human emotion. In child-like wonder I remember touching one of Payton's massive steel sculptures. Built atop gigantic springs, the heavy metal structure rocked. "Danced" would be an even more telling description of its movement: Payton had created a sculpture that dances. Suddenly I understood—really understood, deeply understood— Mardi Gras Indians dancing in all their feathered finery;

African masks worn by humans in ritual movement. Think of traditional Africa and you will inevitably envision fierce masks, beings jumping around with drums and fire. That's the way we have been taught to think of human-kind's homeland. Given this context, consider the miracle of Black artists who deal with the hard art of sculpture. Our art is no accident. The miracle of jazz was born out of the baseness of captivity. We all recognize the grandeur of the music, embrace the cultural majesty of the food, but we should also get hip to the achievements of architecture and the plastic arts, which include an innovative use of rhythm and color in shaping the lived environment. And beyond literally shaping the way we live in the world, more importantly, we actually shape the world itself. That's it: beyond merely being born into this world, by using art, we actually co-create our birth space. Payton makes art that defiantly proclaims the beauty of his individual being, as well as his people's hopes and, indeed, the shared history of African humanity. Above all, his sculpture exemplifies the immense beauty of the human spirit. Payton declares that we can be artful. Filled with beauty. The metal of our living can be forged into both a testimony of ancestral spirit, as well as a guide and gift to progeny yet to come.

Students At The Center

THE DIALECTICS OF MOTION: PRAXIS MAKES REVOLUTION

"Man is a social animal. He cannot exist without a society. A society, in turn, depends on certain things, which everyone in that society takes for granted. Now, the crucial paradox that confronts us here is that the whole profession of education occurs within a social framework and is designed to perpetuate the aims of society. Thus, for example, the boys and girls who were born during the era of the Third Reich, when educated to the purposes of the Third Reich, became barbarians. The paradox of education is precisely this—that as one begins to become conscious one begins to examine the society in which he is being educated. The purpose of education, finally, is to create in a person the ability to look at the world for himself, to make his own decisions, to say to himself this is black or this is white, to decide for himself whether there is a God in heaven or not. To ask questions of the universe, and then learn to live with those questions, is the way he achieves his own identity. But no society is really anxious to have that kind of person around. What societies really, ideally, want is a citizenry which will simply obey the rules of society. If a society succeeds in this, that society is about to perish. The obligation of anyone who thinks of himself as responsible is to examine society is to try to change it and to fight it—at no matter what risk. This is the only hope society has. This is the only way societies change."

—James Baldwin, "A Talk To Teachers"

I am sixty-eight years old. I get up some mornings and wonder why am I still struggling to make change, still hopeful that my actions can contribute to creating the conditions that make revolution both inevitable and irresistible. Why do I continue to fight against oppression and exploitation, especially when my life could be made more comfortable and pleasurable if I would just give up fighting against the status quo? My joints ache, my physical health makes it difficult for me to continue on these long marches, getting up early to prepare for battles, going for long stretches in the trenches of militant actions, staying up late to evaluate the day's work, analyze the conditions, and plan out tomorrow's courses of action. Struggle is hard. But then I realize, it's not about me. My life is not about me as an individual but about me as a social creature. I realize if I am not working on behalf of others, then I cannot actualize who I individually might be/come.

My father, country bred, war tested (WW2 and the Korean conflict, plus the domestic struggle for his rights as a Black man in the forties, fifties, sixties and beyond), my father big Val Ferdinand, taught his three sons by both word and deed: "You don't get no credit for what you do for yourself, you are supposed to do that. You get credit for helping others."

I do what I do because I can not be the person I want to become if I don't work on behalf of my fellow human beings. Working for self actualization through working with and for others is a bedrock principle of both revolution and love, which ultimately exist within a symbiotic relationship. Revolution without love is barbaric cruelty, and love without revolution is self serving and empty hedonism.

Revolution is ultimately about overturning ourselves as products of a deformed society and hopefully creating a whole and healthy society within which we all can live, develop, and contribute to creating a better and more beautiful life. In fact that is the revolutionary's objective: to make the world better and more beautiful than when we were born into it.

Here is a basic two-part summation of what I understand to be our SAC (Students at the Center) operating guidelines.

ONE. Work with where you're at, or alternately work with where you choose to be.

Identifying the educational community is not always easy in a society that is both pluralistic in terms of the ethnic and economic cohorts that compose the communities and at the same time communities that are stratified along class and ethnic lines with deep fault lines of gender issues as well as glaring and growing income and wealth disparities between the haves and the have-nots in a given society both urban and rural; mega-metros contrasted to small town and rural areas. To be clear, especially in the context of public education, there is a major question of the social identity of our students and the goals of our pedagogy. Who are we educating and realistically what do we propose that our students become?

We in SAC identify our immediate overall field of operation as the working class Black community of New Orleans, and specifically the public high school students of that community along with all of their fellow students in the schools within which we work. At one of the schools we worked from 2006, right after Katrina, to 2015 when our founding instructor retired, the student population was approximately twenty percent Vietnamese, and by contrast from 2000 to Katrina in 2005, we were at a high school which was 95% Black with a very small percentage of Hispanic students. Among the Douglass students approximately 20% were identified as special needs students. The point is that in each of those cases our curriculum was developed to meet the specific needs of the student population.

Our watch words are simple.

Start with where you're at, to get to where you want to go. Start with what you already know, to learn what you want to know.

In practice this means as Amilcar Cabral teaches, literally beginning with the physical and social ground beneath our feet, grappling with the physical and social reality within which we live. We do not boil this down to some mechanical, intellectual exercise but instead make this a fundamental practice of our daily teaching. So much so, that the intellectual work of earlier students becomes a major part of the curriculum of today's students. We literally include the writings of previous students as integral aspects of the current curriculum.

In order to successfully value our students we must question ourselves and each other as we struggle to create a better world. Relationships mean more than possessions. If we have to die to get there, then there is ultimately no "there" there, no heaven there. We must struggle to make heaven here and now, and in order to successfully do that we must understand why and how we are in hell. Simply put, while we recognize that there are core skills all students should acquire regardless of who they are, we do not believe that this means that one curriculum works for all students. No, we must consider who we are and where we are and develop our curriculum to meet the specific needs of our students.

TWO. The classroom size must be reduced if we are to actually reach and transform ourselves. There can be no overlooking of this fundamental fact. When the classroom is over fifteen or so students, we cannot develop genuine and thoroughgoing relationships because we never get to know and value each other as individuals whose goal is to work as a team.

Additionally, whenever possible we sit in circles rather than in columns and rows. How is it possible to teach democracy but organize our classrooms along stratified lines? This is neither an easy process nor is using circles a panacea or magic formula. At SAC we strongly believe in social learning, in democracy, which includes students making an active input into both what we learn and also in how we learn.

We must teach ourselves to consider and value our specific social conditions. Teaching landlocked people to fish is not teaching revolution, it is teaching frustration. Consider your conditions and shape your pedagogy to respond to the physical and human conditions; what works in the forest, may be impossible in the desert and what is efficient on the land, may be futile on the sea. So carefully consider your physical and social environment.

Look at the social norms of the society you are trying to change. We develop our curriculum by considering what are our needs. What strengths can we build on, what weaknesses can we strengthen, what debilities can we eliminate, and what shortcomings do we have to tolerate as we go through our stages of development.

The fundamental principle is teach dialectics rather than essentialism. There is no one right way. Contradictions are healthy, the essence of life is found in motion not in static stability. That which is most solid is that which is in organized motion. Relationships cannot be static; they too must change as reality changes. Discussions we can have at thirteen and fourteen are not the same as those we need when we are twenty or thirty.

We ask our students to look at their lives. We consider who we are as we work to become who we want to be. This is how we created the book *Men We Love, Men We Hate*. We looked at our social reality. How many of us live under the same roof with a biological mother, biological father, and biological siblings? We discover that the nuclear family is not our social reality, and then rather than bemoaning or pathologizing our social conditions, without either shame or discouragement, we recognize reality and chart a course to change or transcend that reality in order to achieve our self-defined goals. This gives us a healthy basis to analyze sexism and other ism conditions of our personal lives without wallowing in self-pity. To consistently and successfully change a negative reality into a positive requires unsentimental criticism and self-criticism. We as teachers who are also students must model the dynamic of examining the particulars of both our social and personal lives.

We must know both the soil and the trees from which we come as well our own specific particulars as both the fruit of our environments and the seed potential creators of and within our given environments. Beware, no environment is singular. All environments have multiple physical and social forces and levels.

This dynamic—and make no mistake, our praxis must be dynamic rather than static, flexible rather than formulaic— this process of first recognizing reality, second developing a response or a plan, third putting that response or plan into practice, and fourth evaluating the results, which actually is repeating the first step of recognizing reality although now we are recognizing the reality that has resulted not just from a given set of outside forces but a reality that now is partially a result of our attempts to transform our lives—this is the dynamic of our praxis. Truth is what is, not what was, nor what we wish and hope it to be, but rather in all its ever changing complexity, truth is what is.

Particularly for high school students, truth is a period of rapid and often bewildering change, a transition between being a child directed by others and an adult charged with the opportunity and responsibility of being self-directed. As a human being going through puberty and grappling with fluid social cross-currents of becoming an adult, these students navigate through a complex whirl of clashing conditions and expectations; an unpredictable and volatile set of social and personal circumstances, at the high school level confronting all these challenges and opportunities is a difficult task. At SAC we believe that part of the task of education is to actively assist the student in making the transition into adulthood. While such a task may seem obvious, successfully actualizing that task is neither easy nor guaranteed.

Our social realities are complex and too often include dealing with rape and other forms of sexual trauma and exploitation; dealing with self-mutilation and other forms of harming the self in reaction to untreated social trauma; and dealing with gender identification and other forms of personal development. These are not simple matters but nor are they so complex that they cannot be acknowledged and dealt with within the sanctuary of an SAC class.

This is one of the crucial roadblocks we face. The status quo does not want us to deal with our deformities. Many well-meaning individuals, particularly authority figures, are adamantly opposed to a revolutionary recognition of social reality, and thus, in order to deal with these social realities as part of our pedagogy, we must consider the conditions and not engage in futile battles with authority figures even as we engage in subversive work with our students. We must remember the battle is not really about fighting our oppressors and exploiters, although we know that such fights are often necessary; the real battle is to improve ourselves and to make the world a better place. Do not fall in love with fighting. Actualizing love of each other, that is the ultimate goal, the organizing principle, and the guide for when and how to fight.

Moreover, whenever and wherever fighting is necessary, our struggles should be revolutionary struggles precisely because only a revolutionary struggle fundamentally changes the shape and operation of a given society. It is critical that we understand there is nothing revolutionary about assimilating and/or uncritically integrating into the status quo. Indeed, whether subconscious, ill-informed, or opportunistic, assimilation and integration are actually and inevitably counter-revolutionary precisely because rather than over-throwing an oppressive and exploitative status quo, we end up overturning ourselves. To raise a fist while figuratively, metaphorically, or actually wearing a wig or a weave is a tragic moment of cognitive dissonance.

I use the word tragic in the classic Greek sense of a fatal internal flaw. We must recognize that weaves and wigs come in a plethora of shapes, sizes, and colors, but they all denote and connote self-negation. At its worse, the contradiction of engaging in militant struggle while simultaneously adopting self-negating behavior and aesthetics makes true revolution impossible, even as contradictory actions might be genuine expressions of desire and/or aspirations. To put this in blunt terms, we may fight against White supremacy while at the same time upholding, propagating and displaying negative self-images—and yes I am alluding to Beyoncé flashing Black power as she shakes her semi-blond weave.

A traditional American education instructs the student on how to function within their contemporary environment. A revolutionary pedagogy teaches not how to conform but rather how to change the status quo. In order to effectively teach revolution, i.e. the overthrowing of the status quo, we must first teach why an insurrection is necessary. To paraphrase Cabral, we are not militarists reveling in violence; we are revolutionaries struggling to create a better and more beautiful social and physical environment.

In the asymmetrical warfare of us against the establishment, as with any guerilla grouping, knowing when to advance and when to retreat is a very important weapon. In any social context, revolution is a matter of deeds not words. Slogans may motivate and inspire but only action can achieve our objectives. The more specific and accurate our deeds, the more successful will be our efforts to win each battle.

Moreover, the critical principle is to see and interact with students as agents of their own education rather than as objects of our educational work. Rather than the status quo truism that the teacher teaches and the student learns, SAC believes that the student learns and the student teaches. We are all students and we must all be teachers. We demonstrate democracy by practicing social learning, each one, teach one. We all can and should learn from each other.

This principle may initially seem counterintuitive. What can a mature adult learn from a teenager? What can an informed teacher learn from an ignorant student? If nothing else the teenager can teach the adult about social reality, the student can inform the teacher about what is working and what is not working in social life in general as well as in the particular lives of the student. This principle is important because societies are not just here and now, societies must also be concerned with the future—indeed, the whole purpose of education is to perpetuate a given society in the future.

A basic SAC truism is that teachers should seriously be concerned about the future and students should seriously be informed about the past. A thorough knowledge of our history is a necessary knowledge to use in transforming our present into a desired future. Need we add that most of today's teachers will not see the future a half-century from now, and in a similar way most of today's students were not even born a half-century earlier than now.

All human societies are a pendulum swinging between maintaining the past and creating the future. When we invest too much in either maintaining the past or in creating the future, we inevitably fail. Nothing will be as it was, nor will the future be like the present is. So then a basic task is to accurately grasp who we were, who we are, and who we want to become.

To articulate our goal of progressive social development we in SAC suggest our educational tasks should be based on concretizing three action steps: 1. we must seek to understand who we were, 2. we must critique (i.e. assess the negative and positives of) who we are, and 3. we must plan for and project who we want to become. Moreover, a dynamic understanding of society distinguishes four stages of development and recognizes the powers, problems, and potentials of each stage of development. Those four stages are: birth, maturity, decline, and death or regeneration.

As the Tunisian-born Arab scholar and philosopher Ibn Khaldun taught us, societies, like individual people, are born, grow to maturity, and then go into decline and death. This progression is inevitable unless disrupted by outside forces or re-started by conscious social actions of regeneration.

Once we have accurately assessed who we are and where we are, then we can begin to develop realistic goals and objectives as well as actually get in motion to successfully get to where we want to go.

This motion-oriented pedagogy means not only paying attention to who we are but also offering examples of who we want to become. In the classroom we must value diversity. Become a sanctuary within which it is possible to be oneself without stigmatizing the social periphery or falling into the cul-de-sac of overly emphasizing the social center (i.e. the status quo). Indeed we ought to embrace the other: the gender other, the ethnic other, the age other. We should promote next steps rather than vainly try to retrace past steps or impossibly attempt to stand still. Teachers should not be models of what we want students to become, but rather teachers should be guides assisting students to achieve what the students want to become. Neither the past nor the present are, or can ever be, the future.

Attaining self-consciousness is the first and critical step of a positive education. Rather than teaching obedience, we ought to be promoting self-awareness and skepticism. The best students are those who question. Students should question the world, question themselves, and question the society they live in, and, yes, students should also question their teachers. Rather than a negative, skepticism ought to be a core value encouraged in all students.

Second, after considering where we are, who we are, and who we want to become, we must heal our illnesses and fight for power, fight to actualize the principle of self-determination. We have all been wounded just by living here. We need to tend to our physical and social wounds. A sick soldier cannot effectively engage in the protracted struggle that is necessary to create a successful revolution. Emotional disabilities are much more crippling than physical disabilities.

We must pay particular attention to the gender dynamics. The devaluing and abuse of women is more prevalent and more pernicious than the racial White supremacist dynamic even as we are generally taught that the central problem is between Black and White. Our ultimate problem is in the devaluing of our humanity. In the opening decades of the 21st century this devaluing is most evident in the devaluing of the feminine within our society.

Our pedagogy is grounded in preparing students to be agents of change by raising consciousness and sharpening the skills of critical thinking. Critical thinking requires students to read and especially to write. Writing requires thinking. We can talk off the top of our heads without clearly thinking about what we are saying, but the discipline of writing requires that we not only think through what we want to write but also that we evaluate how well we write. Towards this end of developing writing skills, we start with easy assignments, but we also publish student writings and use them in the classroom as both curriculum as well as examples that we put on the walls of the classroom. We at SAC believe and practice the elevation and validation of student lives and ideas.

Of course in any classroom there will be deferring levels of literacy skills, but we go to the SAC watch-words: start with where we're at to get to where we want to go. Start with what we know to learn what we don't know. This principle necessarily requires us as educators to know, understand, and to a surprisingly large degree to empathize with our students.

Towards the end of knowing ourselves and our students, critiquing our environment and aspirations, a student innocently asked: You know what I really want to know? Where is the center. First we laughed and then we said: You and your fellow students are the center. The center is not a place but a relationship. You are the center. Your life and your wellbeing must become the center of our education.

Towards that end we teach our students about Paulo Freire and the negativity of the banking system of education. We teach them that memorizing is not intelligence. Critical thinking is the only right answer that matters. Critical thinking. There are no essentialities beyond change, beyond motion.

We teach Naomi Klein's *The Shock Doctrine*, especially because we in New Orleans are on the anvil of disaster capitalism. We teach that our conditions are no accident but rather the result of intentional exploitation and oppression.

We teach Vygotsky because understanding human development is fundamental. This development includes the use of tools and the understanding that language is one of the most important tools we have. We must learn to use language to help us identify who we are and what are our conditions, and use language to communicate with others that which we have learned, and more importantly to share our experiences with others. The use of language is necessary to teach what we know and to learn about what we don't know; language is necessary in order to tell the world who we are and learn from the world who they are.

We teach Jean Anyon because although the status quo espouses that America is a classless society, education has a definite class structure. Working class schools use a very different pedagogy from professional class schools, which in turn are different from the pedagogy used in ruling class schools. In order to teach about the class distinctions in the school room, we must also teach basic distinctions of class: those who survive by selling their labor, those who achieve levels of comfort by managing the labor, behavior and wellbeing of their fellow citizens, and those who thrive by owning the major means of production and by living off of unearned income, that is income generated by owning, essentially rent and profit. There is more, but we must start by teaching the basics of class structure so we can truly understand our conditions.

Obviously there is much more, but that is for another occasion and in small group sessions where we can address specifics. This is only an introduction to philosophical principles we employ in our SAC pedagogy.

A basic guideline: if we are to successfully recruit future revolutionaries, the messengers are equally as important as the message. Who articulates the word is equally important as the word itself. The goal is not abstract nor purely intellectual, the goal is found in the flesh and blood embodiment of our thoughts and emotions. We must be what we espouse. Moreover, we as educators are required to actualize our own capacity to become thinkers, leaders, and revolutionaries. We all can and should participate in making change internally on an individual basis, as well as externally on a social level.

We at SAC believe that revolutionary education is education for all and not simply for the best and the brightest, or for the cream of the crop, or for those who are good at taking tests, or any other exclusionary category. Revolutionary pedagogy insists on teaching and learning with and from each other. We must teach all and learn from all.

We also believe that creating the revolutionary pedagogy necessarily must include those who have been demonized and oppressed. Within our Black communities, that specifically means responding to the inhuman American criminal justice system. Again not simply in the abstract, but rather in the actual. We encourage exchanges and learning from those who are or have been incarcerated. Indeed, you can more often find a formerly convicted felon working with our students than a PhD expert. This is not to denigrate the PhD but instead is to elevate those who have been oppressed, those who have been exploited, and to understand we must learn from all levels of society. Moreover, they are we. They are our fathers, our brothers, our mothers, our sisters, our cousins, friends, and acquaintances. Do we or do we not believe in social rehabilitation?

The former prisoner who has thought about why they were imprisoned and struggled to understand how to change their conditions are among the best teachers in any society. We believe they ought to be and indeed must be included in our pedagogy. One of our next publications is *Go To Jail—Challenging A System Of Injustice*. If incarceration is a major aspect of our social reality, and it is, if incarceration is a major fact in our lives, and it is, if in 2015 more Black men today are incarcerated than the absolute number of Black men who were enslaved in 1815, then we have a responsibility to respond to this very real and pervasive social reality.

By a show of hands, how many of you have a family member or close friend who is or has been incarcerated? Within our New Orleans classroom the percentage of hands that are raised is well over sixty percent. Within our specific set of conditions, we have a revolutionary responsibility to transform the upraised hands to clenched fists who learn from our conditions and participate in the struggle to change ourselves and our world.

As I wrap up allow me to offer some thought provocations:

• When the bible tells us that God gave man dominion over the earth and all things that exist thereon, is this the basis for patriarchy and the physical conquest of others? Is this stolen land truly one nation under God; does the Christian God justify thievery and male-centered domination?

• What makes us human and how do we differentiate humans from other mammals? One of the texts I most enjoy sharing and discussing with our students is the *Epic of Gilgamesh* and particularly the discussion of domesticating Enkidu and Enkidu's challenging of Gilgamesh's kingly birthright. Is any individual or society born with the right to control others or do we have a responsibility to confront, resist, and possibly overthrow traditional society? *Gilgamesh* is full of these major philosophical questions and offers excellent opportunities to challenge traditional thinking, which is rampant and dominant among our students, without personally challenging an individual's particular beliefs.

• What principles are our ethics and aesthetics based on? How do we determine right and wrong, truth and beauty? Do we believe in eternal truths and principles? In SAC we believe that our job is not to offer answers but rather to ask questions. The Socratic method is more than simply part of our pedagogy. We don't have answers, we have questions.

• How do we successfully move from ideas to reality? I do not mean this in an abstract way, but rather in daily practice how do we shape ourselves to be agents of the ideas we say we believe? Moreover, in SAC we believe that nothing is ever finished; ideas and behavior must constantly be put into practice, evaluated, and redeveloped to keep up with both the times we live in as well as the changes we undergo. This question of how do we move from ideas (and ideals) to reality has two fundamental aspects: 1. how do we fund our programs and ongoing operations, and 2. as our individual social conditions (particularly interpersonal relationships) change over time, how do we accommodate those changes within the context of our ongoing work?

Of course there are many other questions and issues to be dealt with, but I just wanted to share a handful so that we can understand the SAC pedagogy is not a blueprint but instead is a particular praxis developed in an attempt to deal with major issues around challenging the status quo and working to help our students become agents of their own lives.

I am a born again pagan. A pagan is someone who does not believe in any organized religion. When I was born I did not believe in any religion. My parents sent me to church. Roughly when I was fifteen, I left the church and became born again. I am also a materialist. I believe in starting from the specifics of my physical and social reality, and that ideas and emotions shape our consciousness but that we can use our consciousness to reshape ourselves, our societies, and ultimately our world.

I get up every morning because I refuse to lay down to capitalism; I refuse to lay down to racism; I refuse to lay down to sexism and all the other oppressive and exploitative isms of our society. I get up because I want to be a better person and I understand that I can not become better if I do not help you become better. I get up so that I can go out in the world and meet you and together we can create a better and more beautiful world. Behold comrades, working together we are our future. Indeed, unless we work together, the only future we will have is one of continued oppression and exploitation.

No one can any longer deny that we are oppressed, that we are exploited, that our planet is being destroyed by global capitalism and unthinking physical and social explorations and dominations. The fundamental question we face is not what is wrong, but rather what are we going to do about it. Within SAC we believe in our own capacity to analyze our conditions and work to create better and more beautiful individuals, social organizations, and lifestyles.

Say it with me: I am me. And together with you. We can create a better world.

WE STAND BY OUR STUDENTS

start with what you know
to learn what you don't know
start with where you're at
to get to where you want to go

Our Students at the Center (SAC) class stood around in small clumps outside the school building. The weather was not welcoming, the temperature in the uncomfortable lower 50s, an annoying light rain falling. Tiesha stood unsmiling under a blue umbrella. I told her to hold that pose with her face booted-up and scurried over to my black leather brief-case to get the digital camera; I wanted to take her picture.

"You really going to take my picture?" she asked.

After taking four or five shots, I moved under the sparse cover of a tree, but it offered scant protection. The rain still fell on us. Tiesha smiled as she inspected the small screen on the back of SAC's digital camera.

Jim Randels, SAC's founder, pulled out the heavy African-American literature book from his backpack and proceeded to continue the discussion we'd been having before the fire alarm went off: What did Alice Walker mean about fruit awakening taste buds in the poem about her sister Molly?

Greta, the coordinator of the Smaller Learning Communities educational program, called on my cell and wanted to know where we were. She was on the St. Claude and Alvar street corner by the front of the school; we were on the Pauline and N. Rampart street corner at the rear of the school. Shortly she joined us and jokingly admired Jim's tenacity as chilly raindrops wet the book's pages. "Y'all really going to try and hold class amidst all this?"

"Yeah, why not?" Jim casually replied, pushing back his long, dark hair that helped earn him the semi-sarcastic nickname of "Jesus."

Three out of the eight or so students in class that day gamely struggled to answer the questions. We were outside because someone had set fire to the second floor bathroom. And eventually we were all called into the gym and dismissed for the day. A not-unusual, even if atypical, day at Frederick Douglass High School.

Every day working in the public school system, I battle the demons of despair; most times I eat that bear, but sometimes brother bear takes a deep bite out of my rear, and on such days, nursing my wounds, I retreat home to repair, often in the process questioning myself: why in the hell do I return to this day after day?

I love the youth, especially the students at Douglass, and I know that I, as an older Black male, make a major difference, especially as I do not represent authority, but rather an older version of the students themselves—or at least a version of who they can become once they achieve critical self-consciousness and commit themselves to life-long learning.

Any of us who work in a major American metro-area, inner-city public school intimately know Mr./Ms. Despair Bear, know the challenge of maintaining in the face of a system whose normal state is either chaos unreined, or else the even more sinister, terrifying silence of lockdown. But here is where we go every day, somehow nourishing the dream of teaching youth.

Some people have developed theories about teaching inner-city youth, and most of those theories are predicated on preparing these youth to participate in the mainstream, while never questioning the sanity of joining in a system that has systematically oppressed and exploited the very youth we are teaching. If preparing them to be productive citizens is the bottom line of what we do, then we might as well be teaching courses in suicide.

I do not apologize for my stance: I advocate education for liberation, not education for mainstream socialization.

I am interested in coaching youth to engage reality in two ways: 1. Knowing themselves and 2. Deciding for themselves what they wish to become. Those two simple objectives are the foundation for my praxis—the pedagogical theories I develop and/or adopt/adapt, and the day-to-day practice I use to engage with the reality of public education.

Like many professional artists, I became involved in this sphere because I was asked to participate in a specific program, not because I was seeking a way to work in the public school system, or even seeking a way to work with youth in a pedagogical dynamic. For most artists, teaching is simply a way to make the money we need to survive and enable us to do what we consider our real work, which is developing our art. In my case, although I have a long history of working with youth, it took over two years before I would consciously commit to teaching as a professional priority of my life work.

Contrary to what many non-teachers think, teaching in public schools is not easy money. Reaching our youth is hard, emotionally taxing, and intellectually challenging work, especially if the goal is education for liberation.

I teach at McDonogh #35 (a citywide school) and at Frederick Douglass (a district school). Citywide schools require students to meet specific academic requirements. District schools are based on residence in a specific geographic location. In New Orleans we have a three-layered school system: parochial (primarily Catholic), private, and public. The public sector is where the overwhelming majority of Black students are herded, although a significant number are in the parochial system. The New Orleans public school system is the largest in the state, with a $500-million budget that exceeds the budgets of every town and city in Louisiana.

Education is ground zero in the systemic exploitation of Black people in New Orleans—ground zero because public schools are the direct feeder for the necessary, albeit unskilled, labor needed for the tourism-oriented economy. I will not recite the alarming statistics; it is enough to note that in New Orleans, they are building more hotels every day—where will the bellhops and maids come from? For those not fortunate enough to work in a hotel, the public schools prepare them for the penitentiary. If you are reading this, I assume you are already aware of the statistical fact that more Black males are in prison than college.

Teachers who would educate Black youth but shy away from making (or else are incapable of making) a political-economic critique of the school system; such teachers are themselves impediments to, if not downright opponents of, education for liberation. If we are not prepared to at least intellectually confront the implicit racism of using test scores to fail students who school systems have systematically miseducated; if we are unwilling to recognize the utter under-preparedness of system administrators and the lameness of their solutions; if we are afraid to address the difficulties of middle-aged Whites trying to educate Black working class youth—in short, if we are unwilling to face what is really happening in public education, all of our "innovative" programs will fail because they are not addressing the real problems.

We are at war for the future of our students. In New Orleans, tourism is the number one (two, and three) industry. Our schools are the way they are because the economy continues to need drawers of water and hewers of wood, continues to require a labor force to clean, cook, and serve. And though they cannot articulate it in political language, our students know. The ones at the citywide schools, encased in a near zombie-like state of obedience, work to escape the neo-slavery of tourism via college and a "good job" somewhere else in America. Those at the district schools rebel or else go through the day in an alienated state of non-engagement with the curricula, which they generally (and too often not incorrectly) perceive as a waste of time.

This is the context within which Students at the Center works as a creative writing elective. Everyone who visits our classes, or looks at *Our Voice* (a student-run newspaper we publish), or reads the chapbooks and poetry collections we publish, or views one of our numerous videos, marvels at the work and wants to know how we do it; I smile. Although we employ specific techniques, there is no secret ingredient. It's the fruit of protracted struggle, the fruit of the hard work of encouraging the students to take their lives and their futures seriously.

Three of our basic principles: 1. No class larger than 15 students. 2. Sit in a circle. 3. Require each student to participate in discussions. We also encourage students to engage in peer-teaching with their fellow students who are not in a SAC class or with middle- or elementary-level students, including those in after-school programs. We strongly urge students to get involved with social change organizations and agencies, a number of which are active partners with SAC.

In addition to reading our work aloud and taking turns reading a wide variety of materials, we teach active listening skills by talking about how to ask meaningful questions and modeling this ourselves. Silence is death; no student is allowed to not participate. While we do not accept rote responses, at the same time we do not reject any honest response as "wrong" or "inappropriate." We are not working on what Paulo Freire calls the "banking" concept, wherein we as teachers have fed our students the "right" answer and are prodding them to give us back that specific, "right" answer.

Instead, the SAC methodology is to begin at the beginning. We begin with the experiences and real thoughts and reactions of our students. We begin by affirming the importance of their existence, their personalities, howsoever and whatsoever they may be. One particular tool in this affirmation process is the story circle, a technique developed by John O'Neal and others in the Free Southern Theater: we sit in a circle and take turns telling a story about a selected topic.

To be successful, we must actively listen to our students. This process is one of building community. It is not a one-way process of simplistically asking our students to spill their guts to us while we silently sit in judgment. Indeed, in SAC we all participate as equals; we teachers tell our stories when our turn comes. We all tell stories and we all listen to each other.

Whether a person intends to or not, if they honestly participate, they end up facilitating two things. One, we all learn more about each other, and we thereby become closer to each other. Two, we learn to articulate ideas and emotions that previously had never been publicly expressed. For many students, this is their first experience in an educational setting of being embraced for who they actually are rather than for how close they are able to come to some external standard that is set before them as a kind of holy grail.

We then encourage our students to write. Again, we do not require any one-to-one, write-the-story-you-told process.

Rather, we ask them to write about a variety of topics, and even encourage them to write on a topic of their own choosing if it is a topic they strongly want to express. When we combine the story circle technique with the prompts and inspiration that comes from the reading assignments, invariably students produce a richer body of literature than if they were simply asked to respond to abstract writing assignments. Here is an example from Maria Hernandez, a sophomore at Frederick Douglass who presents a brilliant social critique of the effects of violence that is also an unsparing and startling self-critique:

Just Like Him

They say when you're around someone for a long time, you start looking and acting like that person. The problem is that I didn't want to be like him in any way, but what can I say? I have his eyes, his hair, and recently I've acquired his personality. Lately I go crazy and snap. I bitch slap my little brother and on more than one occasion I've drawn blood from my little sister's lips. I didn't want to be like him, but I did it anyway. And something inside me is telling me that I let him win.

When you review student writing at this level, the work forces you to confront yourself. You cannot stand before this student and just go through a rote exercise.

What do you do? We publish the work and encourage her to do more. Maria's piece is included in a collection of Douglass writings called *From the Heart*. Just as our students learn from us, we as teachers learn from our students. The experience of liberatory education is necessarily a reciprocal relationship. We learn to know our students as fellow human beings with whom we share our lives and experiences, rather than seeing them solely as blank slates upon whom we teachers are trying to inscribe particular lessons.

When we say "start with where we are at," we are saying a mouth full. Our students have many, many problems. An upcoming SAC publication is called "men we love / men we hate"—recently, during a discussion of an excerpt on Black manhood from bell hooks' new book, a quick poll demonstrated that only one person of the 12 or so students lived in a two-parent family with a male as the head of the household. We were discussing patriarchy, which is a bit tricky when there are no patriarchs present in their day-to-day lives—and that was at the citywide school whose reputation is petite bourgeois (we pronounce it *boo-gie*). Many of these students are the children of first-generation professionals and lower-level managers.

Although functional enough to do their class work and pass standardized tests, even these students, the so-called best and brightest, suffer social stress and trauma at sometimes unimaginable levels. Sexual molestation, dysfunctional families, suicide, drug (especially alcohol and tobacco) abuse, STDs, and warped senses of self-esteem are endemic, indeed near pandemic, across economic strata. Without falling into the trap of either pitying or being repulsed by their problems, our task is to encourage the students to articulate the realities of their day-to-day existence. Unless and until they can honestly recognize and confront their own realities, they will never be able to truly transform themselves and their communities.

In this McDonogh #35 class, three seniors were working on projects. Angie Solomon was working on a two-character drama about a young woman trying to talk to her best friend about new feelings she is having that might be homoerotic, but might not be; she just needs to…to talk about it, and her friend is not wanting to listen. The brief piece illustrates the importance of being able to talk about life with a supportive friend. Asia Brumfield's piece is about her uncle, a high school student one year younger than Asia, who was murdered at a nearby school in a brazen hit in the school gym during the middle of the day. Rather than crafting a simple cry of sorrow, Asia was intent on examining the nexus of relationships in her family, which includes her father, who was imprisoned at the time of the school shooting, and a grandfather who had survived a barroom shooting. Marnika Farria explored the subject of rape, spurred by her own attempts to deal with her mother being raped when Marnika was 11 years old. As Marnika did her research, she discovered that her grandmother is also a rape survivor, although Marnika previously had no knowledge of that history of sexual violence in her own family.

These are not woe-is-me, feel-sorry-for-us-poor-down-trodden-negroes investigations; rather, these are honest explorations of complex social situations. For Angie, Asia, and Marnika, these investigations are brave and ultimately inspirational examples of self-transformation through confronting social issues at the personal level. Neither Jim nor I try to weigh these projects with overt political views. Our tack is to ask questions; we encourage them to dig deep within themselves and be as truthful as possible.

Because we are not a core curriculum class and because we are a "creative writing" class, we have more latitude with subject matter and lesson planning than do most of the classes. Although one might suppose this means that we are less rigorous in an academic sense, all of the students will tell you that, except for a handful of their other teachers, our SAC class requires them to work much harder than do their regular classes.

Even though they have to read more, write more, and think more, they come back, with some students taking our class two or three times during their high school matriculation. Last semester at Douglass we encountered the phenomenon of male students cutting their assigned classes to sit in on our writing class. One of them eventually persuaded his counselor to switch him into our class; another student, Bruce Lightell, got a note from his mother saying that it was okay for him to skip one class so he could be part of our SAC class.

Later in the semester, Bruce was selected as one of two students to represent Douglass at a statewide conference on an "agenda for children," where our SAC duo recited poetry. One of the counselors wanted to know how in the world could that happen, since Bruce was failing every class but ours.

Bruce has severe problems with text. His spelling is on an elementary level and his grammar is almost nonexistent, but he has a sharp mind and easily grasps concepts such as metaphorical consistency, which he calls "m-c." When it is time to publish Bruce's work, we patiently sit with him and correct each misspelled word. We question him about grammar. We do what editors have traditionally done for many, many highly rated writers whose manuscripts would be unpublishable without significant editorial help. One of my favorite images of Bruce is of his head buried deep in a dictionary, trying to find out the correct spelling of a word he wants to use. His academic shortcomings notwithstanding, Bruce has the fire and determination to improve himself, and his family supports SAC partially because they know the value of our work: one of Bruce's older cousins was previously an editor of the *Our Voice* newspaper.

We are not a one-shot project or a new approach trying to prove itself. We have made a long-term commitment to public education, long enough that we now have former SAC students who are currently undergraduates returning to work with SAC, along with alumni who are college graduates. Two of the more active of grads-turned-SAC staff attended Frederick Douglass—our staff is not just drawn from the academically better prepared students at McDonogh #35.

Indeed, at Frederick Douglass the situation is para-doxically both easier and more hopeless: easier because the students are more forthcoming; more hopeless because these students generally have only a modicum of reading, writing, and mathematical skills.

Steve Grant, a handsome football player, belies the stereotype of the jock who gets all the girls. In a moment of disarming honesty, Steve penned a short response to an Ishmael Reed poem. When he finished reciting his poem, there was a moment of stunned silence—we had never thought of Steve that way:

If I had a nickel ...

If I had a nickel for every time I had been rejected I would be poor because I've
Never really had the heart to approach a girl.

In one of his pieces, Steve gave us the title "From The Heart."

In a similar vein, I remember Darrow Reaux coming to class one day after being absent for two days. I asked him where he had been, why had he missed class. He dropped his arrest papers on the desk where I was sitting. I scanned the papers, gave them back to him, and simply said, "Welcome back." Turns out he was arrested because he was standing on the block outside his home when the police came through doing a sweep because of a fight that had happened nearby. I don't remember for sure, but it was probably after curfew. The next day, Darrow wrote a short piece which highlighted his arrest, but from a totally unexpected perspective:

I Told My Mother I Love Her

This girl in my writing class name is Anastasia and it seems like we're the same but we really don't know whose the blame. We both stay with aunt and uncle thinking that they were our real parents. My real mother name is Irita and my real father name is Darrow, but I don't called neither one of them mom and dad. I continue on calling my auntie Rose, mamma, and my uncle Junnie, papi.

The funny thing was I got arrested the other day and I haven't seen Irita for about three months and I ran into her in jail. I really didn't know how to feel when I saw her. I didn't even bother asking what she was doing here but she asked me, and I told her what I was in for. The police brought me in the back for booking. She came to the window and told me bye. In jail it is really crazy. Some old man was getting beat while the guards was feeding us cold luncheon meat. I went to court and the judge release me on ROR.

I went home to my mother Rose and told her I was in jail. They let me go without paying bail. My mother said she didn't know where I was because I left my cell phone. I left the radio on. The lights on and my writing everywhere. She told me don't go outside at night so I wouldn't have to fight with the police anymore. I told my mother I love her and good night.

The students at Douglass have no problem sharing their problems, whereas the better educated students at McDonogh #35 are also the more reticent and the least in touch with their true feelings. Often, they have repressed their thoughts and feelings for so long that their ability to express what is happening inside has atrophied. They have the words, in the intellectual sense, but lack the psychological ability to express themselves.

The Douglass students, conversely, are not hampered by self-censorship, but are rather limited in their language skills. By the measure of the LEAP tests (our state-mandated standardized tests), Douglass is the second-worst high school in the state. On a scale that ranges up to approximately 150, I believe we scored 11, and were surpassed in a negative direction only by our uptown sibling, Booker T. Washington, who scored in the single digits, a 9 out of the possible 150.

Their educational limitations not withstanding, our Douglass students produce creative writing that helps them cope with and begin to overcome the crippling effects of miseducation. There is a misconception that under-educated students are not ready to grasp philosophy, political-economy, the subtleties of high art, etc. However, just because the school system has failed to educate them, does not mean that our students are stupid and/or uneducable. That they score poorly does not mean they cannot think. Indeed, their environment forces them to develop very sharp analytical skills.

They are able to easily spot insincerity and incompetence. They know with the accuracy of a finely tuned Geiger counter which teachers are simply collecting a paycheck or impersonally teaching from a textbook without being concerned about the students as human beings. Students learn early how to dodge the bullies and con artists who daily confront and try to hustle them, both in and outside the classroom. They develop all sorts of evasive techniques to avoid physical harm and/or incarceration by police, guards, and other authority figures whose sole responsibility is to maintain law and order—a law and order that demands mindless obedience and compliance with arbitrary rules and regulations. In many, many ways, our students are far more realistic about their educational situation than are we who would teach them without taking the time to understand them or their world beyond the realm of abstraction or without a pejorative view.

A sure sign that many of us do not understand our students is our refusal to understand that even if students can't spell, they can reason; that even if students can't pronounce multisyllabic words, they can express themselves. How well a person does on a standardized test is no indication of that person's character or desire to learn. A test may measure what one knows, but it cannot accurately predict whether a person wants to or is capable of learning.

Thus, we read and discuss Plato's "Allegory of the Cave" or excerpts from Paulo Freire's *Pedagogy of the Oppressed*, alongside Toni Morrison and excerpts from the writing of Frederick Douglass; we read Sandra Cisneros and Birago Diop as well as Alice Walker and Langston Hughes. We not only read these authors, we discuss the relationship of the text to their lives and follow-up with assignments that ask the students to write, for example, about their own "cave" experiences. Here is high school sophomore Rodneka Shelbia's cave essay, written when she was 14 years old:

When I was 13 years old, I stumbled into a place with very little air and very little space. I was uncomfortable. I stumbled in this place not knowing what I was getting into, not knowing a way out. This place was a dark, confusing, messed up place. Being in this place was terrifying and painful, full of decisions. This place was a cave, a cave of many emotions.

This cave was a relationship between me, a boy named Tim, and a boy named Rodney. Tim was my boyfriend. Tim and I had a good relationship. We were known as the star couple. We had known each other for about three years, but we were together for about five months. Tim had what I look for in a boyfriend. He attracted me because he was himself. He did not try to be anyone else, and he accepted me for me. He was my 9-10, but we broke up. We broke up over a few words that were passed around and the pressure of Rodney.

Rodney was someone I would call a best friend. Tim, on the other hand, thought Rodney was not just a best friend. He saw Rodney as someone trying to get with someone else's girlfriend. After Tim and I stopped talking, Rodney and I started talking. Rodney was the type of nigga that would do anything to get what he wanted. He was good at his game, cause he got me. We were together for about two weeks, but after those two weeks he lost me. I had to leave him alone. I felt like I was cheating on him, cause I still had love for Tim, which meant Rodney wouldn't get all I had to offer, maybe not even half.

Now I was hurting, stuck in the middle of a four-wall cave, just confused. On each of the walls there was an engraving that somewhat frightened me. The first wall was engraved, "Rodney," next "love," then "Tim," and last "Decisions." On the ceiling and base of the cave there were little riddles and clues telling me where the answer lay. There was one in bold print that stood out like none other. It stated, "The answer lies where you stand." I sat thinking, "What does this mean?" What could I do to help myself, to strengthen myself, to free myself? I soon noticed two rocks next to me. Those rocks were nothing more than my feelings.

The first rock was soft and chalk-like. With this rock in my hands I looked around and repeated three of the clues to myself. 1) The answer lies where you stand. 2) Freedom is the key. 3) "X" out that that won't help. 1) The answer lies where you stand. 2) Freedom is the key. 3) "X" out.

I thought, "Freedom, freedom is the key. It can open the cave. The rock lies where I stand. The rock can "x" out the words on the cave. I can write freedom on the cave. It just might open." I was hoping and praying as I got up to try my plan. I got up to the wall, but the rock was so soft it crumbled up as I wrote. I found that the rock didn't engrave nor write, because the rock was soft and contained no strength, no power, only mixed emotions. It didn't help me at all.

I sat hopelessly thinking. "What am I going to do now?" I looked at the second rock and thought to myself, "Ain't no way in hell I'mma get that rock." So I just sat making excuses. "It's too far; I can't walk. It's too heavy; I'm too weak. It's in a pile of man-eating creatures; they'll eat me alive. That junk is gonna hurt. It'll probably make me look ugly." Then I thought to myself, "It's the only way out." So I walked over there to get the rock, but in the process I suffered. I bled and lost a lot, but I got the rock.

This rock gave me confidence. Every step I took with this rock felt like the hardest step in the world. When I got to the wall, I started to write freedom on it. That was very hard, because my hands were bloody, and the rock was heavy. I had to push the stone in the wall to make the engravings, but the good part about it was that as I engraved I grew stronger. I became more powerful, and my emotions came in line.

When I finished, the cave vanished. I became free. Rodney was gone. Tim was gone. Love was gone. And I was free, oh so free.

Although teaching writing is too complex and broad a subject than can be addressed in this short essay, one quick example will illustrate the difficulty, if not impossibility, of finding a working solution that addresses all the needs. Three of the students in our small class at McDonogh #35 are transfers from Douglass. This is a local example of the "brain drain" phenomenon that is common in under- and un-developed countries. While we struggle to meet the needs of all our students, including those who are intellectually gifted, a larger fact is undeniable: when the best students are relocated from the neighborhood schools to a citywide school, invariably the level of instruction goes down in the neighborhood school. The absence of "gifted" students in the classroom ensures that those who are left behind stay left behind.

We discuss these concepts with all of our students. Rodneka was considering leaving Douglass, and though there is no doubt that she would benefit from a better educational environment, there is also no doubt that were she to leave, Douglass would face a big loss. Our task as SAC teachers who recognize this dilemma is to provide ongoing educational stimulus and opportunities for all the Rodnekas we encounter, even as we recognize that schools such as Douglass do not provide a quality learning environment or instruction.

That is one small example of the complexities we face. I want to make sure no one romanticizes SAC and the struggle we wage. Students such as Rodneka deserve far more than we are able to give them, even though we, they, and their families recognize that SAC has given them far more than they would have normally received in their matriculation through the jungles of public education.

I am an experienced writer, sort of a writer-in-residence, but only "sort of." Although I have published books, have had my writings used as exam passages in the SAT test, and am an award-winning journalist in both print and broadcast, most of the students do not know me as a published writer. They simply know me as their teacher, the one who helps them write and shows them how to make movies. Additionally, I have spent years and years working as a community organizer at local, national, and international levels. I do not have to rely on teaching in this program to make a living, nor am I using this program as a stepping stone to get to another level in my writing career. Ultimately, education for liberation demands a commitment far beyond career development.

Moreover, I am not an "artiste." I am against an emphasis on the arts if the focus is on teaching technique and individualism. Our students need to focus first on their own realities rather than being seduced by the intellectual brilliance or the career bling-bling of some artist. In other words, it is not about me as the artist—the focus must remain on the students. Further, we have to model social commitment not by sloganizing and using clever rhymes to fight oppression, but rather by doing the hard work of helping others without requiring students to look up to us on our teacherly pedestals of wisdom, truth, and beauty. We must be serious about keeping students at the center of our work.

In our SAC classes we encourage students to critique the SAC educational process, including how we teach them. We ask them for opinions about what we should study, which programs we should do, and which we should pass up. Sometimes it is as simple as requesting they select a topic to write about for the week, or select the theme for a story circle; other times we lay out particular situations we are dealing with and ask for their input in the decision-making process that Jim and I ultimately conclude. The students quickly realize that they can help shape their education; they can help determine what they will learn. This engenders a sense of ownership and identification with the learning process that will never happen if one simply uses predetermined lesson plans and state-mandated educational objectives.

We realize that not every class can operate the way SAC does. However, we are certain that public education can be significantly improved by specifically focusing on the needs of the students, which, for us, means including the views of students. We believe another world is possible. We believe students are a resource and not just an object of education. We encourage the students to become agents of their own education, and we struggle with other teachers and administrators to make these changes widespread. Unavoidably, this is sometimes a contentious and even bitter struggle. There are teachers and administrators who actively fight against what we are doing, but, as the British are wont to say, "at the end of the day," the work our students generate stands out and speaks for itself.

Still, the attacks come. Some people say: SAC is successful because we work with only a handful of students; SAC is elitist because we pick only the "best" students.

At Douglass, there are racial antagonisms aimed at Jim Randels, a White teacher in a school that has only one or two White students, and none in any of the SAC classes. In the second semester of the 2003/2004 school year, a hostile counselor assigned us two special education students, plus one student who was a serious disciplinary challenge, plus three students who needed upper-level English to graduate and who also had to pass the LEAP test, but who had failed the English portion previously—all of this in addition to those who were assigned to us "just because," even though we are supposed to be an elective course, and even though the counselor did not include some students who requested our class.

Meanwhile we had a handful of students who wanted to learn how to write; two of who were intent on becoming writers.

So we circle the chairs and soldier on. And despite stumbles and setbacks, despite backbiting and resentments (the inevitable result of struggles to create change), despite having to deal with a wide range of student attitudes and capabilities, despite all of that, our students produce, and their work is both our defense and our offense. Their work is an answer to the question, Can public education be improved? We proudly stand by the work that our students do.

Marcus Garvey said, what man has done, man can do. Terence said, there is nothing human that is foreign to me. SAC says: start with what we know, in order to learn what we don't know. Start with where we're at, to get to where we want to go.

Five SAC publications are free to view or download (sacnola.com). They are:

1. WHO AM I? – Reflections on Culture & Identity
A book of insights and reflections.

2. The Long Ride
A collection of student writings based on events that are part of the long struggle for Civil Rights and social justice in New Orleans.

3. NEXT steps
Writings from Students at the Center Class of 2010

4. MEN WE LOVE—MEN WE HATE
An anthology on the topic of men and relationships with men.

5. WAYS OF LAUGHING
An anthology of young, Black, female voices.

Hard Times In Big Easy

HARD TIMES IN BIG EASY

I: What To Us Negroes Is Your "New" New Orleans?[1]

A system of thot

They are trying to kill us
We must survive
We must survive
Death to the system

FELLOW NEW ORLEANIANS, pardon me, and allow me to ask, why am I called upon to speak here today? What have I or those I represent to do with your "New" New Orleans? Are the great principles of political freedom and of natural justice, embodied in this celebration of a new metropolis rising from the ashes and debris of an old and inundated city, extended to us? And am I, therefore, called upon to bring our humble offering to this august celebration, and to express devout gratitude for the blessings resulting from your independence?

Would to God, both for your sakes and ours, that an affirmative answer could be truthfully returned to these

---

1 This speech was a keynote address for "After Katrina: Transnational Perspectives on the Futures of the Gulf South," a one-day conference held at Tulane University, New Orleans, 2013.

questions. Then would my task be light, and my burden easy and delightful—for who is there so cold that a famous city's sympathy could not warm him? Who so obdurate and dead that would not thankfully acknowledge such priceless benefits? Who so stolid and selfish that would not give his voice to swell the hallelujahs of New Orleans' forthcoming tricentennial jubilee in the year 2018?

I am not that man.

I say this with a sad sense of disparity between us. I am not included within the pale of this glorious celebration! Your high independence only reveals the immeasurable distance between us. The blessings in which you this day rejoice are not enjoyed in common. The rich inheritance of justice, liberty, prosperity, and independence bequeathed by your fathers is shared among you, not by me. The sunlight that brought life and healing to you has brought stripes and death to me. This pride and joy concerning the rejuvenation of our hometown is yours, not mine.

Here I am paraphrasing the 1852 words of Frederick Douglass: I opened by saying, "they are trying to kill us." I spoke plainly and without theatrical exaggeration or rhetorical flourish. I meant those words literally.

The advent of Hurricane Katrina is often used as a universal marker, separating the old and decrepit from the new and vigorous, separating corruption and incompetence from honor and expertise.

But for us, the arrival of the New New Orleans was a bloody birth. For you, James Brissette is just a name. For me, James Brissette is a name that conjures great sorrow. The unarmed 17-year-old who was gunned down on the Danzinger Bridge in New Orleans on September 4, 2005 was the future we sacrificed to the gods of industry and progress. He was not just another teenager who met an untimely death, not just another thug who suffered a justifiable demise, not just a quiet young man who was in the wrong place at the wrong time, which is how Laura Maggi described him in a June 20, 2011 *Times-Picayune* article: James Brissette was my student at Frederick Douglass High School. I feel his loss on a personal level.

I did not know Henry Glover, nor did the police officer who shot him and left him for dead. Two other police officers put his body in an abandoned automobile and burned both Glover's body and the vehicle in some pagan bloodlust rite. Did they dance around the macabre funeral pyre?

If only the bloodletting had stopped with those deaths—but it went on and on and on. And on still: added to the ongoing police murders are the insane killings we Blacks inflict on each other as we struggle to overcome poverty and decades of inequality and social destruction. Just this past Wednesday, on November 13, 2017, a seven-month-old baby boy named Deshawn Kinard was murdered, along with his twenty-five-year-old father who seemed to have been the intended target, and who died slumped over his son in a vain attempt to shield the baby from assassin bullets.

In this context of rampant shootings and killings, it is an insane society that does not provide for its own mental health. Why have those responsible for the collective wellbeing neglected mental health as a major issue? Why are hospitals closing rather than opening? Why are mental health services discontinued rather than expanded? Why do we assume we can ignore this need?

I believe we ignore the mental health needs of the Black and poor of New Orleans because we don't care about the Black and poor. Is it not true that we once called ourselves the city that care forgot? Now we are the city that forgot to care.

My purpose here today is simple: I will attempt to share some of the truths of my life. I was born and reared in New Orleans. I grew up in the Lower Ninth Ward. My mother was a third-grade school teacher. I attended Fisk Elementary

School through fourth grade, Phillis Wheatley Elementary for fifth and sixth grade, Rivers Frederick Junior High School for seventh through ninth grade, and St. Augustine High School for tenth through twelfth grade, from which I graduated in May of 1964.

I came of age during the Civil Rights Movement, and as a young man was an active participant in the Black Power Movement of the late sixties and early seventies. I have been a social justice activist, a writer and arts administrator, a health clinic administrator, an advertising executive, a radio personality and producer at WWOZ and WWNO, as well the executive director of the New Orleans Jazz & Heritage Foundation; the director of writing workshops, including a ten-year term at the head of the Nommo Literary Society; and currently am co-director of Students at the Center, an independent writing program that functions within New Orleans public schools. I know New Orleans in a multiplicity of ways, from diverse perspectives and with intimate access to information and experiences that cut across a wide swath of social, economic, educational, political, and racial lines of demarcation.

We suffered through Katrina, but most of us do not fully understand that experience even as most of us are still deeply affected by it. The majority of the flooding that happened was not because of levee failure. I repeat, for emphasis and because I want to make sure you fully hear me: the majority of the flooded areas of New Orleans were not caused by levee failure.

I ask you what levees failed in New Orleans East, which was the largest land and residential area that flooded? There was no levee failure in the East. The East was flooded as a result of Mr. GO, the Mississippi River Gulf Outlet Canal. Mr. GO was an economic scheme that had two disastrous, unintended consequences: first, Mr. GO was a major source of flooding in both New Orleans East and in St. Bernard

Parish; second, Mr. GO was an environmental disaster in the area between the Gulf of Mexico and the Industrial Canal in New Orleans.

The Industrial Canal was constructed in 1923 and connected the Mississippi River with Lake Pontchartrain to the north of the city. The Industrial Canal was built to rival the 1914 Houston Ship Channel as the two cities competed for commercial shipping. The Industrial Canal featured systems of locks that enabled large ships coming from the Gulf of Mexico to access the port of New Orleans along the Mississippi River. By the fifties, however, the Industrial Canal was limited by its inability to handle deep-draft maritime traffic. The business interests in this region successfully lobbied Congress to construct a deep-draft canal connecting the Gulf to the Industrial Canal. Mr. GO was completed in 1965 by the Army Corp of Engineers.

Unfortunately, the 76-mile canal was never utilized to the extent projected. Indeed, in a scathing 1997 report, David Barrett of the Competitive Enterprise Institute, a libertarian organization dedicated to "the principles of free enterprise and limited government," criticized the project in stark terms:

The MRGO project was completed 30 years ago to provide a shortcut to vessels travelling from the Gulf of Mexico to the port of New Orleans. The promised economic development along the 76 mile channel in poverty-stricken St. Bernard Parish has yet to materialize. What the MRGO has delivered is an $8-plus million yearly maintenance plan for commercial and recreational waterborne traffic. The nearly $1 billion price tag for the less than two large container ships a day that use the channel is baffling, especially considering that the channel only shaved 37 miles off the original route.

Worse, the MRGO has created numerous environmental problems. The rate of bank erosion is estimated at 15 feet per year. The increased salinity of the water is wiping out the brackish marshes and cypress forests—over 4,200 acres thus far—beyond the 27,000 acres of land lost during construction. Erosion threatens to break through into Lake Borgne and harm the oyster and marine fisheries. The Corps has estimated that in order to address some of the worst erosion problems it would cost $1.13-$3.19 million per mile.

So the motherfuckers who pushed this scheme through Congress not only ruined our wetlands and failed to develop the economy, they also have gone nameless in history and have never taken responsibility for the damage they caused, specifically for the flooding of New Orleans East and St. Bernard Parish, and for the devastation of the wetlands between New Orleans and the Gulf of Mexico.

As I said earlier, I grew up in the Lower Ninth Ward. We used to go hunting and fishing in the wetlands. After Katrina I went to the eastern end of Lower Nine, climbed the levee embankment, and looked over the concrete wall to the wet hell of the wasteland that stood where swamp flora and fauna, cypress trees and a diverse array of fish, fowl, and reptiles were once abundant. What I saw then instead resembled apocalypse. I literally nearly cried.

Worse yet, the Lower Ninth Ward was destroyed by a levee breach of the Industrial Canal caused by a large barge that was left in the canal. Over three stories tall, this barge broke through the concrete wall atop the levee. Whose responsibility was it to clear the canal, especially in light of the mandated evacuation of New Orleans? The levee didn't fail; it was busted open by a barge that was neglected.

In 2005 Lower 9 had over 70% home ownership and was overwhelmingly Black in its residential composition. If you go down there today, it is clear that there has been no serious redevelopment. This is a massive failure at all levels of government, from city to parish to state to federal—or is it? Perhaps this is not a failure, but instead the fruit of some very real intentions: the motherfuckers were trying to kill us.

And in case you think I exaggerate, I refer you to John M. Barry's book *Rising Tide: The Great Mississippi Flood of 1927 and How it Changed America.* Barry describes how the proud fathers of New Orleans blew up the levee in St. Bernard Parish in 1927, promising to compensate and make whole those who were affected by the flood. In his documentary about Katrina, director Spike Lee even includes footage of the officials actually igniting the dynamite to demolish the levee.

The people of St. Bernard never received what was promised. Worse yet, blowing up the levee was unnecessary, as the water levels had not reached flood levels and were subsiding prior to the government action.

We experienced Katrina, but did we understand what we experienced? Do we really know the causes of the damage that was done, and who was responsible? Have we undertaken real efforts to compensate those who were damaged and to redevelop the areas most affected? Isn't it ironic that the two areas most affected, most damaged, most destroyed as the result of human activity, and not simply the result of levee failure, have received the least attention, have had only a minuscule amount of redevelopment as compared to other areas of New Orleans? Is it any wonder that I do not celebrate the redevelopment of New Orleans? What do I, a child of Lower Nine, have to celebrate?

I return again to the words of Frederick Douglass.

New Orleans population - 2004: 484,674

2006: 181,400

July 2012: 370,138

Changes in race/ethnicity - According to the U.S.
Census Bureau's 2012 population estimates, there are
now 103,881 fewer African Americans living in Orleans Parish compared to 2000, but there are also 14,984
fewer Whites. Meanwhile, the number of Hispanics
grew by 4,830.

II: I don't want to live anywhere where they are killing me

one

it's crazy. most of us
kind of assume that where we are born
is home, where our first kiss was, learning to walk, literally,
throwing our first stone at someone in anger,
sitting at the table a mouth full of mother's meatloaf
or was it strawberry pie, or even monkey bread—
those twisted strings of dough that were a wonderful
combination of chewy cake and sweet stuffing—
catching the bus home from school with friends,
the first drink, wasn't it when uncle teddy
served you beer at thanksgiving, you were five?
like that, we think of that location in the mythic sense
the high drama that came later, the desperately sought
trysts, sneaking to liaison with someone you know you
ought to avoid, or the first time you got together
with someone whom you wanted the whole world
to know you were committed to being with for life,

or so you thought, how wonderful the world looked
as you lay dreaming on your back your head
secure in a special someone's lap, or how short
the walk after the dance from the club to the parking lot,
what you wouldn't have given for a reprise of that heaven
the way a lover looks when their whole face smiles
just because you came around the corner with
a yellow tulip in your hand and a pack of almond m&m's
secreted behind your back as you whispered
smokey's ooh baby baby into an eagerly awaiting ear
actually those were the preludes—the real high drama
came some years later, the first time calling someone,
anyone, to come and get you out of jail, which you were in
for doing something stupid, something really, really
stupid, and then there was the accident when you banged
up someone's new car, but those were just the breaks, not
the actual high drama of sitting sullen in some counselor's
waiting room, your head thrown back to the wall
avoiding the eyes of your better half who was now
the loyal opposition and whose eyes were the same eyes
only smaller in the head of the child for whom you
could not some how find the right words to make sense
of this mess that was formerly your marriage
where these scenes take place, the parlor in which
a cousin's camera has caught you crying, the foggy mirror
where you examined yourself, one flight up in a total
stranger's house and sheepishly you wonder what were you
doing in this blue tiled bathroom so very early in the morning
when you were supposed to be somewhere else—life is what
some people call this, and where you live your life, shouldn't
that be the place you call home?

two

the water. my god the water. the angry water
rain roaring sideways with the force of a freight train,

smashing your resolve to ride it out, or inching
down an interstate at two miles an hour so called evacuating
from the water. the dirty, angry water, running
if you were lucky enough to have wheels and a wallet
with plastic in it. the water. you will dream of
wet mountains falling on you and wake up gasping
for air as though you were drowning, oh the water
deeper than any pool you've ever swam in,
water more terrible than anything you can think
of, another middle passage, except this time
they don't even provide ships
I used to wonder how my ancestors survived
the Atlantic, Katrina has answered that question,
I wonder no more—there is a faith that is beyond
faith, a belief when there is nothing left to believe in,
no, not god, well, yes, god, for some, for many, it was
jesus, a few humduallahed, or whatever, but it was also
whatever that visited this terror upon us, and so
to keep believing in whatever, now takes something
the mind can not imagine, the realization that in order
to live you had to survive and in order to survive
you had to do whatever needed to be done, few
of us really, really know what we will do
when we've got nothing but have to find something
to keep us going, how you manage your sanity
in the water, corpses floating by, gas flames
bubbling up from some leaking underground line,
and you sitting on a roof and you just pissed
on yourself because, well, because there was
no where to go and do your business, five days
of filth, no water but flood water, no food but
hot sun, no sanitation but being careful where
you stepped, where you slept, where you turned
your back and eliminated, being careful to survive
twelve days later and you still don't know where

all your family is, if you've got faith, you're about to
use it all—is this some of what our ancestors saw?

three

it is over a month later and you still can't walk
on the land that used to be your backyard,
they treat you like a tourist, you can only
be driven down your street in a big bus,
you can only look out the window at what twisted,
funk encrusted little remains of all you ever owned
and some kid with a gun won't let you go
to get big mama's bible
this shit is fucked up, that's what it is,
fucked up and foul, the smell of a million
toilets overflowing, of food that been rotting
for days inside a refrigerator that became
an oven because the electricity was off and
the sun was beaming down ninety degrees or more
and the worse part is that none of what you
already went through is the worst part, the worst
is yet to come as government peoples with
boxes and things they stick into the ground
tell you that even if the water hadn't drowned
you, something called toxicity has made it
impossible for you to stay here, they are
telling you it is impossible for you to stay
in the house that been in your family
for over fifty years even though it's still standing
it's impossible to live here, and what shall
we call this? what shall we tell the children
when they ask: when are we going home?

four

I don't want to live anywhere where they have
tried to kill us even if it was once a place
I called home—but still and all, my bones
don't cotton to Boston, I can't breath
that thinness they call air in Colorado,
a Minnesota snow angel don't mean shit
to me, and still and all, even with all of that,
all the many complaints that taint my
appreciation of charity, help and shelter,
even though I know there is no turning back
to drier times, still, as still as a fan when
the man done cut the 'lectric off, still,
regardless of how much I hate the taste
of bland food, still, I may never go back,
not to live, maybe for a used to be
visit, like how every now and then you
go by a graveyard…I am not bitter, I am
just trying to answer the question:
what is life without a home?
what is life, without
a home? and how long does it take
to grow a new one?

III: Hard Times In Big Easy[2]

New Orleans is too Black to be so White.

From the obvious examples of food, music, and dance,
to less apparent realities such as rice cultivation, wrought
iron, and construction work—not to mention cultural
expressions from gospel and street processions for celebrations and funerals, to unique social organizations such as
the Mardi Gras Indians, the Baby Dolls, and bounce music
block parties: whenever one considers an element that is

2 Commissioned by the New Orleans Jazz Orchestra in 2016.

indigenous to New Orleans—i.e., born and bred here, rather than simply a variation of something imported to New Orleans (Mardi Gras, St. Louis Cathedral, and king cake are all imports)—one finds that whatever is both quintessential and unique to New Orleans is either created or fundamentally shaped by Black people. New Orleans is the Blackest city in the United States.

Yet Blacks have little political power, negligible economic clout, and, in the post-Katrina era, we Blacks have all but vanished as the public face of authentic New Orleans.

The pitifulness of Black political power in New Orleans is negatively impacted by the behavior of Black politicians themselves, who for some reason continue to demonstrate a penchant for mirroring their non-Black political peers. Ironically, corruption and venality seem to be the only areas in America within which racial equality has been achieved. To be clear, the majority of Black politicians aren't corrupt— although there is little doubt that they are part of a corrupt system and thus too often as much a part of the problem as they are potentially part of the solution. Nonetheless, with a regularity that is discouraging, Black politicians mirror White politicians: they cheat and lie just like their non-Black peers, except somehow, when Blacks do what Whites do, the behavior is deemed an indication of Black racial failure.

Thus, even within this dubious sphere of equality, there is discrimination. When a Black politician in New Orleans is caught breaking the law, that specific case is used to stigmatize an entire group of people, rather than to identify the failure of a specific official. On the other hand, in the context of public discourse among politicians, pundits, and the press, the exposure of wrongdoing by a White politician generally does not lead to any discussion of Whites being inherently criminal. The cause of culpability is not equally assessed.

The issue of color and criminality is so deep here in New Orleans that the 2014 conviction and incarceration of former mayor Ray Nagin, who is Black, effectively taints every prospective Black mayoral candidate. Even though there are far more White politicians in prison than Black ones, the general assumption is that every Black politician is corrupt until proven otherwise. This perception is one of the fundaments of the White domination of the social and political life of New Orleans: Blacks cannot be trusted in positions of leadership due to our alleged inherent criminality.

A follow-up punch to that way of thinking is that even when we are honest public servants, we are judged as incompetent. A particularly heinous example of this double whammy is the public firing and shamming of pre-Katrina Black educators and administrators, all of whom were summarily lumped into the category of ineffective at best and incompetent in general.

Within the economic sphere, our situation is worse. As if to emphatically underscore the erasure of any progress toward economic equality, the ILA Hall, located on South Claiborne Avenue a block off of Washington Avenue, has been razed to the ground to make way for the rebuilding of the new New Orleans. Other than Liberty Bank, which is now the only large-scale economic success story originating in the Black community, the International Longshoreman's Union was the major example of Black economic clout. The modernization of the riverfront, which included the move to container shipping, resulted in the destruction of the dock workers as an economic force. Two men can now do the work that formerly employed a crew of twenty or thirty.

Throughout the 20th century, laboring on the riverfront was an economic ladder out of poverty, as Black longshoremen were able to buy homes and finance college educations for their children. There are no ladders of similar social and economic mobility available to Blacks in 21st century new New Orleans. Individuals may escape the economic dead-ends of ghetto existence, but in order for groups to be delivered from the strictures and restrictions of poverty, there must be some systemic means of mobility. Especially within an economy driven by tourism, the minimum pay of available menial employment is not sufficient to lift large numbers of people out of poverty.

As puny as Black political and economic power is now, and seemingly will be for the foreseeable future, up until Katrina we could take some solace in the fact that New Orleans publicly had a Black cultural face, especially in terms of music and food. But all of that has changed. Increasingly, although Black at the core, the public façade of New Orleans culture is White.

In music, the current iconic New Orleanian is Dr. John and not someone such as Allen Toussaint, even though Toussaint has produced many more national hits and written more classic New Orleans songs. Nor is it Ellis Marsalis, the widely respected patriarch of jazz's most accomplished and famous family of musicians. Though he was born and bred here, and his advocacy of New Orleans jazz notwithstanding, New York-based Wynton Marsalis is not perceived as an icon of New Orleans music. Indeed, no Black group or individual is more touted as representative of New Orleans music than Dr. John. Dr. John even eclipses the Neville Brothers, who for over a decade were the traditional closing act of the internationally celebrated New Orleans Jazz & Heritage Festival.

Need I make the case for food? Ads featuring Black women as proud cooks are mere cosmetics on the fact that a quintessential soul food cuisine is dominated in the public mind by the Popeye's Chicken chain. Ditto for the visual arts: John Scott may have won a MacArthur genius grant as a visual artist, but the Cajun "Blue Dog" is better known and more readily identified with visual art in the greater New Orleans area, regardless of the fact that neither its creator, George Rodrigue, nor the Cajun culture the Blue Dog represents are native to New Orleans.

As significant as Black New Orleanians are in the arena of arts and culture, within their areas of expertise, not one of them represents the city as a whole. Non-Blacks are now identified as the faces of the city of New Orleans, and we Blacks are restricted to representing and/or "repping" de facto social and cultural ghettoes.

How can Whites so thoroughly dominate the public cityscape of New Orleans? While our population may be majority Black (60.2 percent, according to the United States Census Bureau), our political and economic structures are overwhelmingly White-controlled.

In the place where jazz was born—that great, Black-concocted amalgamate of cultures, instruments, styles, and genres of music, from ragtime to the avant garde and beyond—and in the place where the blues had their most accommodating down-south, urban home; in this cliché of a melting pot, a gumbo, a creole, an anything but mono-culture; here in post-Katrina New Orleans, the majority-White city council passed a noise abatement ordinance making it unlawful to publicly perform music on the streets after 8 PM.

No second line after dark. Shut up and go home, if you still have a home to go to. A single ordinance obliterates a centuries-old musical tradition in the newly gentrified, formerly Black neighborhoods of New Orleans. Rebirth Brass Band, a Grammy-winning ensemble, embodies the community's sentiments in a popular song whose chorus asks the pertinent question: "What bitch called the police?" While some may dismiss this as a non-event, the fact is that musicians have actually been arrested for parading without a permit. Is it really preferable to hear crickets in the dark of night rather than a rocking second line?

If your people were born here prior to the fifties, you have a different conception of what it means to be New Orleans. Prior to fast food troughs masquerading as neighborhood restaurants; prior to previously frozen foodstuffs fried or microwaved or both, mass-produced, artificially flavored and available in a plethora of garish colorings, under-spiced and over-priced, indeed sold at near usurious levels of profit; prior to plastic and paper replacing metal and china; prior to cell phones and charter schools, i.e., everybody has one; prior to all the new and improved that barely keeps a decrepit and inefficient infrastructure operable, in a previous century that now seems eons ago, New Orleans was obviously Black and would not recognize these fifty shades of Whiteness that blanket the city like a suffocating fog.

When contrasted against the bittersweet memories of what used to be, i.e., juxtaposing what we used to have against what we currently lack, this post-Katrina social reality makes me nauseous. It is not reductively the presence of Whites that is repulsive; it's the absence of Blacks—except, of course, in terms of incarceration. Moreover, consider this: the uptown areas where the most development and rebuilding have taken place are precisely the areas that were not flooded. Of the areas most affected by Katrina, only the predominantly White Lakeview neighborhood has been rebuilt and improved.

In further exhibition of the racial inequality, the Lower Ninth Ward and New Orleans East—the two areas that were devastated and for which the government is culpable at the very least for negligence—have received the least assistance; both were also majority Black. Lower Nine was inundated by a levee breach that was the result of a large, three-stories-tall barge left in the Industrial Canal even though there was an evacuation order. The East was flooded by MRGO (the Mississippi River Gulf Outlet Canal), which was constructed by the Army Corp of Engineers at the behest of economic interests. There was no levee failure that flooded Lower Nine, New Orleans East, and the adjacent St. Bernard Parish. The death and destruction was due to negligence in enforcing evacuation orders and hastily built business schemes.

Freret Street did not flood. Magazine Street did not flood. St. Charles Avenue did not flood. Yet literally millions have been spent improving those areas, while comparatively very little has been allocated to rebuilding downtown. The actual miracle of the new New Orleans is how successful the powers that be have been at ethnic alchemy, i.e., changing Black into White.

The rebuilding effort is not only wildly uneven from an ethnic perspective; from a perspective of physical infrastructure, massive issues are also apparent. Travel the recently repaired main thoroughfares and it is easy to believe it's clear sailing; take a side street and you better have a life preserver, a parachute, or some serious backup (you best keep your AAA membership paid up, at the very least). We don't just have pot holes: we've got bucket holes. The new New Orleans ain't nothing nice to drive through.

We still smile, and sometimes even laugh, but many of us are awfully bitter these post-Katrina days. Not bittersweet, no; we are rather just plain, un-sugared bitter, like a batch of beans gone bad. Somebody keeps issuing report after report that New Orleans is on the rebound, the recovery was a success, what was washed away was rebuilt. Ten years later, a hundred thousand Black people are not back—yes, the non-returnees are mainly poor, mostly without a college degree, and the majority of them women and children. Thousands of us are still here, but tens of thousands of us are also gone.

I fathered five children. Three of them now live in major port cities (San Diego, New York, and my Baltimore resident daughter works in D.C., another port city). Ironically the two who currently live in New Orleans both work government jobs, one with the city administration, the other with the Army Corp of Engineers. Although the three who live elsewhere are economically stable, their credentials and experience notwithstanding, they cannot move back to New Orleans mainly because they would not be able to find employment within their career areas, not to mention they could not even come close to matching their current salaries. Indeed, one of them was seriously considering taking a 40% pay cut, and even then she was way above the salaries available in New Orleans.

The very people we need—young, educated, socially conscious Black people—cannot afford to live in New Orleans even if they were born and bred here. They cannot thrive here the way they have the opportunity to do elsewhere. When you pull back and look at the larger context, the reality of the new New Orleans is replete with ironies.

In the midst of this recovery, the truth is that the wealth gap is growing wider. A 2015 Bloomberg report labeled New Orleans second-worst in the nation for income inequality. Atlanta was first; however, Atlanta's median household income was $46,466, which was more than $12,000 higher than the median income in New Orleans. If our median income is $35,000, then the poor families struggling below the median are trying to get by on less than $25,000 a year. The *Times-Picayune* article on the Bloomberg report goes on to detail that the bottom 40 percent of the population earns less than 7.5 percent of the total income.

Immediately after Katrina there was talk of a smaller footprint. Some argued that we were being extreme and alarmist when we said that a "smaller footprint" was code for "kick Black people out." Well, ten years later, the proof is in the residential reality. As the Times-Picayune article makes clear, not only is New Orleans at the bottom, but our trajectory towards total inequality is accelerating—referring to the index used to measure the wealth gap, the article states that "New Orleans' Gini coefficient rose 5.39 percent since 2008." Redevelopment has been brutal for Black people in New Orleans.

In a city where an estimated 64% of the population were renters pre-Katrina, post-Katrina rent prices have tripled, quadrupled, or been raised to even higher levels, thereby ensuring that poor Blacks will be unable to afford housing even if by some miracle they found a way to return and secure employment. Southern Louisiana was once touted as the "Sportsman's Paradise." This area is now lauded as a dream location for entrepreneurs and business start-ups; however, non-college educated Black people, who previously were the majority population, can no longer afford to live in the new New Orleans.

Even for the minority of Blacks who live in family-owned homes, the urban landscape is bleak, as we are generally non-competitive in terms of education. The post-Katrina firing of literally thousands of college-educated Blacks who worked in the school system created a massive economic hardship whose ripple effect contributed to the near total destruction of middle class and professional Blacks in New Orleans. Doctors, lawyers, accountants, and other Black professionals no longer had a client base that could afford to pay for professional services. The result has been that many professional Blacks have either not returned or have depart- ed after unsuccessfully attempting to rebuild their lives in the new New Orleans.

As bad as the social, political, and economic situation is, there is another aspect yet to be confronted: environmental destruction. Profit at all and any cost drives decision-making in both business and governance. Far too many politicians are in denial concerning environmental and ecological issues. Some critics have argued that we currently are, or soon will be, past the point of no return. With the unchecked erosion of the Louisiana coastline, we are fast approaching the end of the road. In fifty years there may not be a "here" here.

Having taught high school post-Katrina, I know many young people have given up on New Orleans and are electing to leave. At one point, while sitting in Houston watching Katrina waters reach above the Circle Food Store doorway and knowing that the rebuilding process would be un-equitable and skewed against us, I considered moving to Oakland. However, when I returned less than two months later, despite the massive, heartbreaking destruction I witnessed, and despite all the thoroughgoing, neo-apartheid social engineering that was enacted in the name of progress, I decided to stay.

Fortunately I live in the Algiers section of New Orleans on the West Bank, so I did not have flood waters to contend with, only roof damage and property loss that was minor compared to what the majority of my East Bank friends and family members suffered. Even though I was spared the major struggle of picking up and putting back together the physical pieces of my life, I was unprepared for the battles ahead. Although I tried mightily to keep a positive attitude, the truth is I was clinically and psychologically depressed. My depression was complicated by physical illness: I survived a serious blood clot that almost took me out.

Survival has not been easy. A number of close friends have died. Each loss weakens me—some mornings before I rise, I wonder when will be my great getting up morning, when I transition from this plane.

I am 68; I don't have the energy, the stamina necessary to make light work out of struggling with post-Katrina social conditions. My biggest battle is deflecting the bitterness that constantly threatens to engulf me. When I see Whites blithely jogging through Treme in the mornings or dancing weirdly in Congo Square; when my daughter tells me of the latest moves the city officials are making, such as requiring expensive parade permits for activities that pre-Katrina were either free or of only a nominal charge; or when I witness the inordinate levels of penal colony construction happening at the same time some new social engineering expert in a suit delivers a report about the education miracle that is making life better for needy New Orleanians, my rage approaches murderous levels: neither jails nor charter schools address the issues of poverty and systemic exploitation and oppression.

I can't keep writing this. It makes me too mad. It makes me too sad. It's not healthy. And yet, there is a deeper truth: like a number of my peers who are sixty and older, I love living here so much I'm willing to do whatever to hold on.

I will fight for my right to be respected as a human being. I may be censored, but I will not shut up. I may get taken out, but I will not bow down.

There is a fierce oppositional stance at the core of Black New Orleans culture. A colleague once told me, man, if you would move up here to New York, you could make a lot of money and get a lot of your work published. I knew my friend was right about the opportunities available in New York or elsewhere, but I'm stubborn. I don't do what I do simply to survive or to thrive within the status quo. I'd rather struggle in New Orleans than kick back in New York.

It is also true that wherever in the world I or anyone else might choose to go, the reality and repercussions of the wealth gap and the limitations of poverty (regardless of race or ethnicity) will have to be dealt with. I know that gentrification is radically altering the face of New Orleans, but I also know that gentrification is a worldwide phenomenon. Housing and business developments in formerly low-income inner city areas, resulting in the expulsion of low-income residences who are no longer able to afford the cost of living, is the new norm in urban lifestyles. Back in the seventies we said that urban renewal meant negro removal; gentrification is urban renewal on capitalistic steroids.

There may not be much of a future in being a die-hard Black New Orleanian, but to me the essence of life requires something beyond mere survival or creature comforts. In a nation that is increasingly culturally homogenized, New Orleans is a distinct and different flavor.

Because I'm addicted not only to freedom and self-expression, but also to red beans and dancing in the streets, because I'm totally hooked on celebrating a culturally oppositional way of life, and also because of the massive emotional inertia that personally anchors me in this rough and limited environment, I choose to stay. Although I seriously considered leaving and indeed, immediately after Katrina, had one foot out the door, I've weathered the leaving-home storm. I ain't going nowhere else within the United States. Although my hometown may never become what some of us dared dream it could be, I nonetheless believe the fight is worth the effort, whether we win, loose, or draw. I elect to continue to make New Orleans my home.

I know that New Orleans is changing, and that my personal resistance in the long run will be futile; nevertheless, being a proud, Black New Orleanian is my birthright. Regardless of what others may decide, for me living in New Orleans is a voluntary social commitment. Or like we used to say back in the day: I'm born, bred, and hope to die right here in Big Easy, no matter how hard it gets.

WHAT TO DO WITH THE NEGROES

one

There is a secret hidden in the heart of New Orleans, a secret hidden in plain sight but ignored by all but the secret citizens themselves. Before Bienville arrived in this area in 1718, Native American scouts informed the adventurous Frenchman that there were groups of Africans—they probably said "Blacks"—living over there in their own communities, and that these self-ruled women and men would not talk to Whites.

Although how the Native Americans knew that the Blacks would not talk to Whites remains unexplained, the report contained in Bienville's writings seems accurate on the face of it. After all, close to three centuries later in post-Katrina New Orleans, there remain a number of us who are reluctant to talk truthfully to outsiders—not out of fear of repercussions or because of an inability to speak English, but rather we remain reticent on the general principle that there's no future in such conversations.

Indeed, I am probably breaking ranks simply by writing this, although what I have to say should be obvious. Whether considering our 18th century ancestors who inhabited the swamps of the North American Southeast from Florida to Louisiana or unsuccessfully trying to question a handful of staunch holdouts among the Mardi Gras Indians, there have always been Blacks who were both proud of being Black and determined to be self-determining—not just constitutionally free as any other 21st century U.S. citizen, but independent of any higher authority, whether that authority be legal, religious, or cultural; whether that authority be other Blacks, wealthy Whites, politicians of any race or economic status, or whatever, none of that mattered. We recognized no higher earthly authority than ourselves.

Sometimes, when it looks like we are doing nothing but waiting on the corners, sitting quietly on a well-worn kitchen chair and sipping a beer in the early afternoon shade; when people pass us by as we hold court on one of the many neutral grounds, i.e., medians, separating the lanes of major streets in Central City; when you see those blank stares at a bus stop—sometimes what you are witnessing is not what you think it is.

We are not waiting for the arrival of a messiah or for a government handout. We expect nothing from our immediate future but more of the past.

Our talk will seem either fatalistic or farcical and certainly will not make sense to you. Not the weary blues etched into our cheeks nor the coal coloring the sagging flesh beneath our eyes; neither the mottled black, browns, grays, and streaks of blond or red on our woolly heads, nor the aroma of anger clinging to our clothes, have anything to do with our failures or our failed expectations. We never anticipated that we would be understood or loved in this land ruled by men with guns, money, and god complexes.

No, what you see when you look at us looking back at you is a resolve to keep on living until we die or until someone kills us.

two

The history of New Orleans is replete with the inexplicable in terms of how Black people lived here. In the late 1700s, before the Americans arrived as a governing force in 1804, a nominally-enslaved Black man could be seen walking to his home, which he owned, carrying a rifle, which he owned, with money of his own in his pockets—yes, I know it seems impossible, but the impossible is one of the roots of New Orleans culture.

Under the Spanish there were different laws and customs. We had been offered freedom in exchange for joining the Spanish in fighting the English. Join the army and get emancipated: all you had to do was shoot White men…and avoid getting shot yourself.

The Black Codes guaranteed Sundays were ours. All the food, handicrafts, services, or whatever we could sell, we could keep the proceeds. If you study the colonial administrative records, you will notice that our economy was so rich that the city merchants of that period petitioned the governor to be able to sell on Sundays (like the slaves did).

Prior to the Civil War, the Louisiana Supreme Court ruled that a man had to pay back money he borrowed from a slave. Not to mention, imagine for example Mrs. Latrobe, a Baltimore, Maryland, resident and the wife of an architect who designed and built New Orleans waterworks, and "…how shocked I was to see three Mulatto children and their mother call upon me and say they were the children of Henry." "Henry" was the dearly departed son of Mrs. Latrobe. He died of yellow fever and was buried in New Orleans in 1817, three years before his father also died of yellow fever and was buried next to his son in St. Louis Cemetery. Much like many, many people today, Mrs. Latrobe had no idea about what was really going on in New Orleans.

You can read the papers all day and sit in front of the TV all night and never get the news about a significant and shocking subculture in New Orleans—a subculture that not only is unknown to you, but moreover a subculture that really does not care to be known by most of you.

Our independently produced subculture is responsible for the roux that flavors New Orleans music, New Orleans cuisine, New Orleans idioms, New Orleans architecture, the way we walk down here and especially how we celebrate life even in the face of death. From the mythic African retentions of Voodoo spiritual observances to the historic musical extensions from Congo Square, this subculture has made New Orleans world-renowned.

I don't remember the Black sufferers ever receiving a thank you or a blessing. Instead of having our contributions recognized, the Black poor and those who identify with them have been demonized. When Katrina's waters came, those who were largely affected and eventually washed away were overwhelmingly Black. Our "saviors" gave us one-way tickets out of town. Four years later, there were no provisions to bring Blacks back here—I say "back here" instead of "back home" because back here is no longer back home. Post-Katrina New Orleans is not even a ghost of what our beloved city was.

What is gone is not just houses or pictures on the wall, not just the little neighborhood store we used to frequent, or the tavern where we hung out on warm nights; not just the small church in the middle of the block or even the flowerbed alongside the house; not just the old landmarks or some of the schools we used to attend, not just the jumble of overcrowded habitations or the storied stacks of bricks we called the 'jects (a.k.a. projects), housing schemes we knew by name and reputation. No, it is not just brick and wood that is missing from the landscape. What is gone, what we miss most of all, is us.

We the people are not here. What is left is an amputated city ignoring its stumps. Moreover, even if it were possible, our city does not desire to re-grow or replace what was "disappeared." Good riddance is what many of the new majority say.

"Good riddance" is sometimes proclaimed using the coded language of "a smaller footprint" (reductively, a smaller footprint means fewer Black butts). At other times, "good riddance" is spewed forth as the uncut racist cant of "lock all those savages up."

three

Although poor Blacks controlled none of the city's major resources, we were blamed for everything that was wrong: from a failing school system to rising crime; from ineffective and corrupt political leadership to an "immoral" street culture of drugs, sagging pants, and loud music; from a rise in sexually transmitted diseases to deteriorating neighborhoods. When responsible citizens wrote to the *Times-Picayune* daily newspaper suggesting what ought to be done to address these concerns, high on the list of panaceas was our incarceration, as if so many—indeed, far, far too many of us—were not already in prison.

How convenient to ignore the glaring statistic: the largest concentration of Black women in New Orleans is located at Xavier University and the largest concentration of their age-compatible male counterparts exists across the expressway in the city jail—dorms for the women, cells for the men. The truth is disorienting to most: what has been tried thus far, whether education or jail, has not worked.

The people who complain the most about crime in the city, or should I say the voices that we most often hear in the media complaining about crime, are from the people who are the least affected.

However, worse than the name-calling is the fact that New Orleans is now a city that forgot to care, in the aftermath of the greatest flood trauma ever suffered by a major American city—yes, the damage of Katrina surpassed the massive destruction of Houston in 2017, in terms of death and overall metro-area destruction, not to mention that New Orleans was impoverished compared to the relative wealth of Houston, America's fourth-largest city. On a comparative basis, for the majority of the city's poor people, New Orleans is devoid of public health in general and mental healthcare in particular.

In the entire Gulf South area that was directly affected by Katrina, only in New Orleans were 7,000 educators fired. The federal government guaranteed the salaries of teachers in all other areas and guaranteed the same for New Orleans teachers, but the state of Louisiana made a decision to decimate the largest bloc of college-educated Blacks, the largest bloc of regular voters, the largest bloc of Black homeowners.

The denouement was that the entire middle-class Black strata was disenfranchised. Black professionals, the majority of whom lived in flooded areas in New Orleans East, no longer had a client base, and most could not re-establish themselves in New Orleans. What was left of the Black New Orleans social infrastructure was nothing nice.

four

How does anyone explain why, in a "post-racial" America, economic inequality gaps are widening, not closing?

In a city that prior to Katrina had one of the highest rates of native residents, why are so many young adults leaving rather than staying?

Why is spending nearly twice as much per pupil to service half the pre-storm population called a success in educational innovation—especially when the current status quo is economically unsustainable, not to mention that comparable pre-storm healthcare and retirement benefits are no longer offered to teachers?

I don't even know how to identify what is happening to us without sounding like a cliché of class warfare, without sounding bitter about racial reconciliation, or ungrateful for all the charitable assistance New Orleans has received.

I know that my voice is a minority voice. I know I don't represent all Blacks, nor most Blacks, nor educated Blacks, nor your Black friend, nor Malia and Sasha, nor…I know it's just plain "stupid" to talk like I'm talking…

I know. I know we Blacks are not blameless. Indeed, we are often co-conspirators in our own debasement. Too often we act out in ways for which there is no sensible justification. Yes, I know about corrupt politicians and a seeming endless line of street-level drug dealers, about rampant gun violence and an always-for-pleasure, 24/7 party attitude.

But amidst all our acknowledged shortcomings, I ask one simple question: who else in this city has contributed so much for so long to this unique gumbo we call New Orleans culture?

Like the state of Texas finally admitting that "abstinence only" sex education has led to higher, not lower, rates of teen pregnancy, unless we materially address the realities of our social situation, we may find that the short-sighted solutions we have put in place will, in the long run, worsen rather than solve our problems.

five

Most days I am resolved to soldier on, to suck it up and keep on keeping on, but sometimes, sometimes I feel like Che Guevara facing a summary execution squad of counter-insurgency soldiers.

Sometimes, after working all day in the public schools or after hearing Recovery School District administrators refuse to allow us to teach an Advanced Placement English class because "we don't have any students capable of that kind of work"; or, after finding out that a teacher we worked with last year is no longer employed not because she was not a great teacher but rather because (as they told her without a note of shame or chagrin in their voices): you are being surplused (i.e., terminated) because we can get two, young, straight-out-of-college, Teach For America instructors for the same price we paid your old, experienced ass; or, when the city accidentally-on-purpose bulldozes a house for which that same city issued a building permit to the couple struggling to rehabilitate the now obliterated property, and meanwhile this insane city administration, four years after the flood, has yet to come up with a coherent plan to address the 40,000 or so blighted properties that dominate the Ninth Ward (Upper Nine, Lower Nine, and New Orleans East) landscape—sometimes, I just want to calmly recite Che's command: Go ahead, shoot!

Just kill us and get it over with.

six

But until then: *a luta continua* (the struggle continues)!

Coda

THAT OLD BLACK MAGIC

Black writers write White. This is inevitable for those of us of the African Diaspora who unavoidably use the language of our historic captivity as though it were our mother tongue when in actually English (Spanish, French, Portuguese or whatever European language) is our father tongue, the language of the alien patriarch who negated our mothers' tongues and mandated we use an other tongue; a white tongue in black mouths.

I believe our music is our mother tongue when it comes to representing the full and most honest spectrum of our thoughts and feelings, our responses and aspirations, our dreams and nightmares concerning who we are and the conditions with which we struggle. At the same time, the father tongue/imposed language is the lingua franca of our daily existence. This mother tongue/father tongue dichotomy represents the articulation of our classic double consciousness. When we make our music, we are our own authorities and our own creators and innovators. When we write the English language, the social authority of the language is vested in the dominant culture.

The language of our dominating step-father is a language that has not only historically degraded us but is also a language which demands conformity to alien values. Moreover, the words of the "King's English" are often incapable of expressing the complexities of our values and realities, especially those values of positive "otherness." For example, what English words are there that give a positive description for spiritual beliefs outside of the "great religions of the world" (all of which, incidentally, are male-centered, if not outright patriarchal—think of buddha, krisna, allah and his prophet muhammad, etc. not to mention jehovah and god the father, son and holy ghost)? In English, as well as most other European languages, all other religious terms, e.g. animism, ancestor worship, Vudun/voo-doo, traditional beliefs, all of them have a negative or "less than" connotation.

When we consider the specifics of our history in the western hemisphere, English becomes even less suitable for describing our reality. There are literally no English words for important segments of our lives. But beyond the negative articulations of our resistance to exploitation and oppression, significant aspects of our existence are "undefined" in standard English, either because analogous concepts do not exist or because our concepts are oppositional to dominant ideologies. In this regard, the Black tendency to coin new words is not just slang; creating words is a necessity if we are to reflect not simply our reality, but also our worldview and our aspirations.

At the same time, Black culture is by nature adoptive and adaptive. We can take anything and make use of it in our own unique way. Thus, the fact that English is a foreign language does not stop us from shaping and literally restructuring how we use the language to make it work for us. This adaptation of a language we have been forced to adopt is, however, for the most part an oral activity. When it comes to writing, there is less latitude in the restructuring process. If we wrote the way we talk, few people would be able to read it, sometimes not even the authors, partially because the standards for writing are much more rigidly enforced than the standards for talking, but also because although we can make sounds and use gestures when we talk to give specificity to our utterances, this specificity is lost in the translation to text.

Just as there is no way to accurately notate Black music using standard western notation, there is no way to accurately translate all aspects of Black life into text because, in the words of musician Charles Lloyd, "words don't go there." For technical and/or social reasons, writing the way we speak is then either impractical, impermissible, or just plain impossible.

Yet, this impossible dream—writing Black in a White language—is precisely the task of the Black writer. The limitations of language are merely that: limitations to be overcome. Indeed, although undeniable in their negativity, the limitations of language are actually the least of our problems with writing.

The more we learn about writing, the dumber we get about ourselves. Unless accompanied by a critical consciousness, the formal act of learning to write at the college and graduate levels alienates us from the majority of our people. An overwhelming percentage of the examples of great writing we are given inevitably comes from outside of our cultural realities; many of those examples are literally apologia for racism, sexism, and capitalism (or colonialism). The very process of learning to write well is a process of not simply studying others, but indeed a process of adopting the methodologies and values of an alien culture, a culture that has generally been antagonistic to Black existence. As a result, almost by definition, anyone the mainstream considers to be a good Black writer is either culturally schizophrenic or at the very least ambivalent about the values exhibited by the majority of Black people not only in the United States but indeed in the whole world.

If any of us spends six or more years intensely studying how to write in an alien language, then, to one degree or another, we cannot help but be alienated from our origins if our origins are outside of the culture that we have been taught to master as a writer. One sure indicator of this bipolar state would be the references we use in our work. In general, three groupings will stand out: 1. Greek mythology, 2. western canonical writers (from Shakespeare to Raymond Carver), and 3. western philosophy (with a notable emphasis on modernity in terms of Freudian psychology, existentialism, and postmodern individualism).

While I do not argue that any of these three groupings are irrelevant to our daily lives—after all, we are partially a social product of western culture even as we are marginalized and otherwise shunned by the American mainstream— I do argue that to elevate these cultural references to the major tropes, images, and structural devices of our writing implicitly alienates us from those aspects of our own existence that are based on other cultural values and realities. Indeed, at one level, to engage in intellectual argument via writing reductively requires us to drag into our text words of Latin origin. We cannot even restrict our word choice to simple Anglo-origin words, but are forced instead to use multisyllabic words whose origins are twice removed from our reality. (A quick perusal of the vocabulary used in this essay will illustrate that point.)

In any case, the upshot of all of this is that the more we master literacy, the more non-Black our expression becomes, because the formal mastery of literacy is synonymous with covert indoctrination in western views and values. This is the dilemma of academic study that all writers of color face.

So profound is this dilemma that many of us who have mastered writing become so alienated from our "native" selves that we are unable to move an audience of working class Black people, whether the audience members are reading our books or listening to us recite. How odd then, for example, to be a Black poet with an MFA in creative writing and be unable to rock a Black audience. But then, one of the purposes of our education was to teach us to act like and fit in with people who historically achieved their success by excluding and/or oppressing and exploiting us.

Please do not construe this as an argument against MFA writing programs or against studying writing in college. I strongly believe in the value of study, both formal and informal. The question is, do we go to school to learn how to do what we want to do, ever mindful of the institutional objective, which is to make us like them—or do we go to school to prepare ourselves simply to fit in, to get a good job, to be recognized by the mainstream as a good writer? Or, to put it in other terms (community to student): "We sent you there to bring back some fire, not to become mesmerized by the light show!"

This brings us face to face with a profound fact of the Black literary tradition: almost without exception, those Black writers who have made the greatest contribution to our national literature were either self-taught or were consciously oppositional to the mainstream in both their content and in their use of language. Think of the highly educated W. E. B. Du Bois, whose great body of work is a veritable arsenal of charges against the West, as well as a celebration of Black life and resistance to oppression. Think, conversely, of Paul Laurence Dunbar, despondent that he was never accepted for writing in straight English; other than dialect poems, his most lasting contribution are poems such as "The Caged Bird Sings" and "We Wear The Mask," which focus on the dilemma of alienation. Think of Langston Hughes, Richard Wright, James Baldwin, Amiri Baraka—all of them self-taught. Think of Francis Ellen Harper, an activist author; Ida B. Wells, an activist author; Toni Cade Bambara, an activist author—all of them autodidacts. Or if we want to consider those who were specifically educated as writers, think of Nobel Laureate Toni Morrison, Pulitzer

Prize winner Gwendolyn Brooks, or Dr. Margaret Walker Alexander, all of whom focused their magnificent and often iconoclastic work on the lives and struggles of working class Black people. These and many others are the great writers of our literary tradition.

Just as not one great musical innovator within the realms of blues, jazz, gospel, or Black popular music has become great primarily as the result of formal musical education, in a similar vein, not one major Black writer who has been college-educated has made a profound impact on our literature (or in American literature as a whole for that matter) unless that writer has consciously taken an oppositional stance. This is no accident. Indeed, throughout our history thus far in America, opposition to the mainstream has been a prerequisite of Black greatness in any social/cultural endeavor. Whether this will continue to be the case remains to be seen.

It is too soon to tell whether what is sometimes referred to as the "New Black Renaissance" in Black literature will produce major contributions to the historic continuum of Black literature. While it is true that popular production is at an all-time high, as the case of romance writer Frank Yerby demonstrates, there is a big difference between popularity and profundity, between bestsellers and seminal contributions to the tradition. Frank Yerby dominated the bestseller lists for romance in the fifties, yet his work is hardly read and seldom referred to today. Will many of today's bestsellers be subject to the same popularity vs. profundity syndrome?

Capitalism materially rewards commercial success and, in the process, emphasizes the entertainment value of a work while minimizing any political values. Art becomes a spectacle and/or product for distribution and sale, rather than a process and/or ritual for community uplift. Indeed, there are those who argue that an emphasis on political relevance is an artistic straightjacket. My response is that the diminution, if not total negation, of such relevance is a hallmark of commercialism, a philosophy that is best summed up in the adage: everything is for sale. I am not arguing against entertainment; I am arguing for political relevance and for the elevation of people before profits, community before commercialism. Or to borrow a phrase from Jamaica's Michael Manley: "We are not for sale."

When the Bible queries, "What profits it a man to win the world and lose his soul?" a fundamental truth is raised. Do we understand that the soul is a social concept, that our existence as individuals is directly dependent on social interaction? The writer who is alienated from the self invariably argues for the supremacy of the individual, the right to write and do whatever he or she wants to do without reference to one person's effect on or relationships with others. Whether pushed as good old American, rugged individualism or postmodern self-referentialism, the outcome remains the same: alienation from community and schizophrenia as to the personal self.

Unless we consciously deal with the question of alienation, we as writers will find ourselves unconsciously and subconsciously at odds not only within our individual psyches, but also with our native (i.e., childhood) and ethnic communities, howsoever they may be defined. This fundamental fact is not a problem peculiar or exclusive to Black writers; it is a problem for all writers in America.

Whom we are writing for determines what and how we write. Writing presupposes audience, assumes that the reader can understand or figure out the message or meaning of the text. Some writers write for the approval of other writers; others seek to impress critics; many attempt to capture a popular audience of book buyers. Those are but a few of the many audience segments that influence, if not outright determine, the nature of writing. In ways often not transparent to or consciously acknowledged by the writer, the tastes and interests of the presumed audience actually shape the writing. Choices of subject matter and vocabulary, style, and genre are all interconnected with the interpretative abilities and desires of the presumed audience.

The authority of the audience as auditor is particularly important for writers who are peripheral to or marginalized from whatever is the mainstream of the language that writer uses.

All writing also brings with it a tradition. Over time, standards of literacy develop. The writer then may seem to be a Janus figure: glancing in one direction at the audience and trying to shape the writing to appeal to or at least be understood by the assumed audience, and glancing in the opposite direction, trying to match or exceed the prevailing literary standards. For writers of color in the United States, the very act of writing alienates us from our native audience, most of whom are not readers grounded in the literary traditions of the English language.

I would argue that the truth is that every writer goes down to the crossroads—and not once or twice in a career, but each and every time we write, whether by conscious choice, or de facto as a result of the particular spin we put on the style and content of what we do. We choose between speaking to the truths of our individual and collective existence or serving mammon by scripting products for the commercial mill. We choose whether to pander to our audiences by concentrating on pleasure and thereby winning applause and popularity or to prod and push our audiences to recognize the reality of our existence and to struggle to improve and beautify the world within which we live. In this regard, a more important metaphor for the Black writer is Elegba, the trickster Orisha of the crossroads.

In the final analysis, writing is a conversation, and even if we cannot tell the pilgrim which way to go, certainly we should tell the pilgrim from whence we have come, what brought us here, and what is the nature of the "here" where we now find ourselves. Moreover, the point is not simply the content. The point is also the conversation. Not just what we are saying but also with whom we are speaking, to whom we are writing.

One of the sad truths of Black writing is that most of us are employed to be guides (some would say pimps) of Blackness. In order to succeed in mainstream terms, serving as a translator of Black life, explaining the exotica (inevitably with an erotic twist) to the non-Black mainstream is almost unavoidable. But who will explain Black life to Black people? Who will break down the whys and wherefores of our daily existence in a language that our mothers and fathers can understand and appreciate, that our children can embrace and learn from?

The question of audience is seldom raised directly in school but is implicitly dictated by the writings suggested as models. When was the last time our people were validated as the authority on our work—not simplistically, as consumers to buy our books and media, nor duplicitously, as voters to determine a popularity contest, but sincerely, as appraisers who determine the ultimate relevance and value of our own literary works?

I believe the question of audience is a dynamic rather than static question. I believe in audience development. I believe that we must both reach out to our people and we must teach our people; we must embrace our people and we must challenge our people; we must elevate our people and we must critique our people—and ditto for ourselves and our peers. I believe in cycles rather than linear development. I believe in constantly doing one's best rather than achieving perfection by creating a masterpiece or two. There will always be contradictions, but our work need not head in a negative direction.

Writing is often defined as a lonely profession. I do not believe it has to be that way. Part and parcel of developing audience is developing community: as writers, we need to create networks and organizations of support for one another. We need to model audience development and not simply leave it to retailers and investors to market us, pitting one of us against another. In order to know what to write about in terms of defining, defending, and developing our communities, we must actively be engaged in defining, defending, and developing community. If we cannot develop community among our colleagues, how then will we be in a position to realistically inspire and/or instruct our audiences?

The question of audience is the ultimate one in our quest to contribute to the development of a Black literary tradition. I do not believe in racial essentialism nor in racial proscriptions. Just because one is a Black who writes, that does not mean that one's work has to be part and parcel of the Black literary tradition. I believe that Blackness is color, culture, and consciousness, and that color is the least important component. Cultural awareness and practice is important, but consciousness—choosing to identify with and work on behalf of Blackness—is the ultimate sine qua non.

Each of us can choose to reject an allegiance to Blackness, howsoever "Blackness" might be defined. We have the right to identify with any, or even with multiple, human social orders. Indeed, one of the hallmarks of Blackness among African Americans is the rejection of Blackness as a determination of self-definition! Moreover, I do not denigrate those who choose social options that I reject: everybody has a right to define themselves. However, for those of us who are writers and choose Blackness, I suggest that we have chosen a difficult but exhilarating path. We have chosen to pass on the torch of that old Black magic, a firelight that started the saga of human history, a mighty burning whose bright Blackness continues to stress the sacredness of love, community, and sharing.

LET'S HAVE SOME FUN

Hey, everybody, let's have some fun.
You only live but once, and when you're dead,
you're done[1].

Pleasure is essential to life. Indeed, the desire to fulfill the pleasure principle is the fundamental hunger of life. Even at the basic survival level of food, we prefer down home cooking that gives us pleasure to dishes that solely give us nutrients. The first law of human nature is survival. The second law is finding a way to enjoy surviving!

While we all know the pursuit of pleasure can lead to excesses such as greed, gluttony, and hedonism, we all also would prefer a smile to a scowl, a caress to a slap, a kiss to a moral lecture. Most of us would prefer to enjoy ourselves rather than grimly go through life rigidly disciplined. Why is this?

Pleasure is essential because life is hard. A grain of sugar (or a proverbial "taste of honey") is never so sweet as when savored by a tongue accustomed to a poverty-enforced regimen of starch and vinegar. Those who have had the harshest experiences possess the deepest appreciation of pleasure. Moreover, for those who live a life of toil rather than leisure, <u>pleasure is not just</u> a salve soothing over hard times; pleasure

1 "Let The Good Times Roll," Decca (1946), Sam Thread and Fleecie Moore.

is also a necessary encouragement to optimistically face the future. Or, as the blues bards sing: *I believe / the sun gonna shine / in my backdoor someday.* We face the future because we believe there will be some pleasure to be gained by holding on, otherwise why stay alive?

In the United States, the pursuit of pleasure is very often linked to popular music, and, in turn, the popular music of the United States is Black music and/or musical forms (such as Broadway show tunes, country & western, or rock & roll) that are strongly influenced by Black popular music.

This little essay will talk a bit about the function of Black popular music, specifically rhythm and blues (R&B)—and by extension rap music, in modern American society. I understand that not everyone will appreciate popular music in America as being one and the same with Black music. Some argue that music has no color. Others argue that Black music is not the only popular music of America—such people, of course, deny any connection between country and western, for example, and rhythm & blues, or between bluegrass and traditional jazz. While I respect everyone's right to their own beliefs, that right in no way negates an accurate appreciation of reality.

In reality there is no popular music in America that did not come from Black music or that is not strongly influenced by Black music. For example, the very notion of a backbeat and of swing is proof of the Black origins of popular music. If the rhythmic emphasis is on two and four, rather than one and three, better believe "Negroes" had something to do with it.

I use the term Negro both ironically and seriously. Ironically, because currently we former Negroes no longer use that term to identify ourselves, preferring African American or Black, and yet both African American and Black are ambiguous with respect to identifying us as specifically and/or exclusively coming from the USA; in reality all Blacks who are born and reared anywhere in the western hemisphere are African Americans. Moreover, just as African does not identify where in Africa our ancestors came from, American does not identify where in the western hemisphere we come from, unless one assumes the great national chauvinism which claims that when we say American, we are ipso facto talking only about the United States, and that anywhere else in the western hemisphere is not also America.

I use the term "Negro" seriously to specify that we are talking about those of us in the African Diaspora who were culturally shaped by and in turn have shaped the culture of the United States of America. The term "Negroes" differentiates us from Afro-Cubans, Brazilians, Haitians, or other "Blacks" born and reared in the Western Hemisphere. Negroes initiated the backbeat and the concept of swing in music. Samba, zouk, calypso, etc., do not have a pronounced backbeat, and those forms that do, such as reggae, do so as a direct result of the influence of "Negro" music.

The upshot of all of this is that when we abandoned "Negro," we actually muddied the water of self-identification, even as we thought we were making things clearer. In one sense we were clearer in identifying with Africa—which "Negro" obviously does not since there were and are no "Negroes" in Africa—but in another sense, we confused the issue of the specificity of our Americaness by simply saying American. The irony is that we dropped one label and picked up another in an effort to be clearer, but our new term is actually more ambiguous than the older term even though the older term had its own limitations.

Although this is an obvious aside, it is an important digression in that it helps us understand how it is that our music can be identified primarily as "Black" music within the USA and primarily as American music outside the USA. Now, let us return to the main thread of our discussion.

Essentially, modern American pop music all started with the ragtime craze and minstrel music. We may not know Scott Joplin, the greatest composer of ragtime, but we do know Irving Berlin's "Alexander's Ragtime Band."

The invention of popular American music is distinct from the various popular ethnic musics—e.g., the polkas of the Polish peoples; the ballads of the English, Irish, and Scottish peoples; the martial music of the Germans—the John Phillip Sousa-inspired marching bands that still parade through downtown Main Street in the American heartland; the light opera of the Italians. All of these ethnically identified musical forms merged into and were subsumed by the wave of popular music unleashed by newly emancipated enslaved Africans (who by the turn of the century had officially become "citizens," i.e., products of the American social matrix).

When people argue the existence of American popular music they are really acknowledging the disappearance of distinct European ethnic musical forms and the emergence of a unique music. By the twenties (which, incidentally, immediately follows World War I, the historical starting line for the rise of America as an international superpower), American music (i.e., "jazz") sweeps Europe and the rest of the world for the "second" time. Before jazz, there was the ragtime craze and there was the near insatiable appetite for Negro spirituals. All of this was represented as "American" music, a music which did not exist anywhere else in the world unless exported by the U.S.A.

Added to this is the technological dominance exerted by American "inventions" and "improvements" on twentieth century technology, specifically the phonograph (1917 was the first jazz recording, 1920 the first blues recording) and the cinema. Although photography was not invented in America, Hollywood is purely American in its exploitation of the technology. Moreover, the first "talkie" and first film musical was *The Jazz Singer* (1927) starring Al Jolson, a Russian-born man of Jewish heritage performing in black face.

To raise the ante a bit, during the period of American ascendancy as a world power, Euro-ethnic immigrants signified their transformation into "Americans" via their (re)presentation of "American" music, i.e., music which had been initially created by "colored people." What do I mean? I mean the Berlins, the Gershwins, the Goodmans, the Whitemans, not to mention Bing Crosby who started off singing jazz or Gene Autrey who sang blues! Check the records. To be an American was to be able to make or emulate some form of Black popular music.

The three major musical branches of "American music" were jazz, blues, and gospel, and the three major musical roots were ragtime, minstrel, and Negro spirituals. Everything we know as popular America music either came directly from these six elements or was indelibly influenced by those roots and branches. I do not claim the Broadway musical is "Black," but I do claim that the origins of Broadway music are directly inspired and influenced by ragtime and the minstrel tradition. The contemporary dominance of "rap" is nothing but a reoccurrence of the dominance of jazz and before that, the dominance of ragtime. That is the history of American music in a cursory but not inaccurate nutshell.

"Black" is not solely a racial designation. For the purposes under discussion here, Black is a cultural designation that refers to a very broad, but nonetheless specific cultural aesthetic. This aesthetic is sometimes misleadingly labeled "always for pleasure." Actually, this music is produced by the same people who literally slaved to build America. Clearly there is more to "Blackness" than the unbridled pursuit of pleasure. At the same time however, in the case of what is popularly known as R&B, undoubted-

ly and unashamedly, pleasure is the primary purpose. And
that's good.

Acknowledging that pleasure is good is a given among
those of us who like our good times hot and loud, but the
philosophical goodness of pursuing pleasure is alien to the
traditional, Anglo-oriented status quo of America. Engaging
the body in dance and celebration specifically for the pleasure of the experience is a concept integral to African-her-
itage aesthetics, and as foreign to the Anglicized, puritan
philosophy as is the distance between tepid clam chowder
spiced with only a pinch of salt and cayenne-flavored filé
gumbo.

Music, song, and dance is the holy trinity of the Black
music aesthetic, and R&B/rap, in particular, is the paragon
of pleasure-seeking within the context of Black music. Plato
never trusted music precisely because music foregrounded
emotion and backgrounded cognition. Christian ministers were always condemning Black popular music as the
"devil's music," pointing out that such music inflamed pagan
passions. When we say that "music" is the first aspect of the
eternal triangle, we mean that music communicates at a
visceral level, connects through sensations, feelings. Popular
music is then a music you don't have to think about; in fact,
any thinking you may do is incidental or secondary. The
first commandment is what is real, is what is felt. This only
makes sense when you consider that feeling precedes thinking—before you can think about the world, you must "feel"
the world, or, as we commonly say in New Orleans, "I feel
to believe."

The second commandment is "sing," express yourself lyri-
cally. Singing represents your conscious thoughts about the
world presented with emotional ardor. When we sing we are
not only making music: we are also expressing our thoughts,
and regardless of how base or ordinary the thoughts may be,
and regardless of how emotionally charged the music may

be, all popular music expresses thoughts as well as feeling. R&B is primarily a vocal music, i.e., the lyrics are sung, whereas jazz is primarily an instrumental music. In the early days of jazz, the music was both sung (vocal) and played (instrumental). In fact, jazz introduced "scat singing," which was a new way to vocalize music. But when jazz ceased being popular music, the emphasis swung heavily toward instrumental music.

The vocal element is then a key element in popular music. It is significant that R&B/rap has lyrics, significant that you can "articulate" (emotionally communicate) your thoughts and feelings without the need of an instrument other than your own body. Popular music is then literally "self"-sufficient: the body is the only vehicle absolutely required for presenting both sensation (feeling) and cognition (thought), whereas jazz is almost impossible without instruments, without the use of material objects (instruments of "noise making") outside of the performer's body. Moreover, it is extremely significant that jazz instrumental techniques mimic the human voice rather than some abstract pure tonality. The jazz "vocalization" emphasis for the playing of instruments points to jazz's origin as popular music based in an African aesthetic. This vocal-orientation is a major demarcation between how one plays jazz and plays Euro-centric musics. "Vocalness" is then the second element of the tri-part focus.

Thirdly, R&B/rap has a strong beat; it is dance music. The emphasis on dance is significant. Indeed, the birth of R&B happened precisely at the same time that jazz ceased being dance music. While I do not argue that dancing is necessary to receive pleasure from music, I do recognize that at the popular level in America, pleasure in music is equated with dance. Initially, R&B was nothing more than a branch of post-World War II jazz that emphasized lyrics (often humorous and/or bawdy) accompanied by a dance beat. A

founding figure of this development was saxophonist/vocal-
ist/bandleader Louis Jordan. Indeed, initially this precursor
of R&B was sometimes known as "jump jazz," a term which
made the dance connection obvious.

America's fascination with Black dance forms began
with the "cakewalk" during the ragtime era and escalated
from there. When we investigate the background of dancers who are considered 100% American such as Vernon and
Irene Castle, who made a career out of teaching popular
(i.e., "ballroom") dance in the twenties, or movie idol Fred
Astaire, we find that they were not only directly influenced
by Black dancers of their time, but they indeed often studied
Black dancers, both directly (as in were mentored by) and
indirectly (as in imitated).

If not directly descendant from or primarily influenced
by Black dance, all forms of popular American dance have
an ethnic origin outside of America—need we point out that
Cajun culture is French-influenced? Although a case can be
made for square dancing, even that has been transformed
by Black contact as any quick perusal of country cable television will demonstrate. When we see contemporary country and western dance, what we are looking at is "cowboys"
doing line dances whose structure and moves are clearly
based on Black forms of dance. They don't call what they do
the "electric slide" or the "bus stop," but the resemblance is
both obvious and unmistakable. In fact, if we look back to
the late fifties/early sixties we find the immediate precedent
for contemporary line dances, like the "Madison" dance
craze touted by *Time* magazine and complete with a chart
demonstrating the steps.

Musicality, lyricism, and a dance beat are the triumvirate
of essential ingredients in all popular American music.

One of the most significant "American" shifts in the
Black music aesthetic is the separation of secular and spiritual forms of music, a separation which is reinforced by the

mutually exclusive association of dance with secular music. Thus, although Black religious music (spirituals and gospel) clearly qualify as embodying the concepts of musicality and lyricism, spirituals are not dance music, and ditto for gospel (a music form which developed in the 1920s, epitomized by the work of composer/pianist Thomas Dorsey and vocalist Mahalia Jackson). The recent attempts of Kirk "Stomp" Franklin and others within contemporary gospel notwithstanding, churches do not allow dancing.

This is a European splitting of the celebration of the body from the celebration of the soul. Moreover, because all Black dance celebrates the erotic, and because Christianity posits the body as sinful (as in "original sin"), there is a further demarcation and separation. But an African aesthetic does not consider the body sinful, nor does our aesthetic consider the erotic to ipso facto be lewd. Thus on the one hand dance and popular music are generally considered beyond the pale for good Christians, and at the same time, within the Black community there is a constant cross-genre traffic.

Many of the major R&B artists originate in and get their basic foundation in the musical liturgy of the Black church and then cross over to the secular side of the street to become popular music entertainers. These musicians carry the gospel way with them, for while gospel may have eschewed dancing, gospel retained a direct identification with emotionalism and with trance, which is a transformation of the body into a vehicle for sacred expression. We call it getting the holy ghost. While the number of R&B artists who started off as gospel artists is too many to shake a stick at, it is important to mention that it was Ray Charles who brought not just the expressiveness but adapted, on a wholesale level, the specifics of gospel and injected it into what then newly emerged as R&B. For all practical purposes, if Louis Jordan was the John the Baptist of R&B, Ray Charles was the "Jesus" who had thousands of disciples, both male and female, following in his wailing footsteps.

At the same time that gospel was used to develop the "soul sound" of R&B, Black religious music was, and is, constantly re-energized by injections of Black secular musical forms. Gospel as we know it initially was spirituals "jazzed up." In the twenties, when Dorsey and Jackson first introduced this music, they were accused of bringing the devil into the church and were actually forbidden to sing "gospel" in some churches because the church elders insisted that what they were really singing was the "devil's music." Mahalia Jackson's retort is classic: Well, that's the way we sing it in the South.

What is even more significant than simply "jazzing up" gospel music, and also even more significant than injecting "rap" into gospel music, is the Afro-centric reintroduction of the drum into sacred musical liturgy. If any one factor represents both dance and Afrocentricity, it is the drum. That the drum is not only accepted, but is increasingly a mainstay of religious music, signifies a move toward the merging of secular and sacred music into an aesthetic (holistic) whole that is a hallmark of the African way of life.

In a very important and Afrocentric sense, music that does not merge both body and soul, feeling and thought, is not complete. Music that is truly a people's music (i.e. truly "popular") ought to contain and celebrate both elements as part of a continuum rather than separate one aspect from the other. What we are witnessing, whether we realize it or not, is the push and pull of African aesthetics toward wholeness.

The sound of Blackness is the aesthetic of psychological freedom. Understanding its psychological impact is the key to appreciating the attraction and importance of R&B specifically and Black popular music in general. This music is both a music of freedom and of honesty.

The freedom: to acknowledge one's self, body and soul, to say that I exist and I matter, and all of me matters, my physical and emotional as well as my mental and spiritual capacities — admittedly, the spiritual aspect of a music of pleasure is usually limited, but that part is there also. And the honesty: to admit that the reality of the self, the spectrum of concerns we inhabit, is a spectrum whose poles are good and bad, beautiful and ugly. We all live on and in that sphere, and the extremes are never fixed—each quality is relative. What is good, bad, beautiful, etc., at any given moment changes as we change.

There are no absolutes except life itself, and even that is speculative, i.e., is there life after death? Many people don't realize that all of this is contained in going up to Slim's on Saturday night and dancing until you fall out and, hopefully, landing in the embrace of a special someone's arms.

What is important to understand is that many of us have been taught that we are ugly, that the physical is sinful, that physical pleasure is wrong, and yet, through the magic of music we resist such teachings with a philosophy that refuses to separate feeling from thought, body from soul. When we dance, we are arguing that life is wholistic.

R&B/rap is philosophically important. To prioritize pleasure, a pleasure that we can produce and reproduce without "buying" something, is extremely important to maintaining mental health. To understand self-production as an activity that each of us can engage, rather than an artifact we own or purchase, such as an article of clothing, or a fat bank account, or even a fine physique: this understanding is key to why we persist in singing and dancing to the music. We do so because ultimately we cannot exist without recreating our sense of self, our awareness of our own beauty and goodness. And that is why we could, indeed "had to," sing a song in a strange land.

In our communities, aesthetic (a sense of beauty and goodness) awareness is generally an unconscious awareness; nevertheless, such awareness is absolutely necessary to the survival of the self, for we cannot go on if we do not believe that there is some good, some beauty within us. That screaming and hollering that the singers do, those songs that move us so, all of that informs us that within each of our lives there has been some good, some beauty; even if only momentary and fleeting, even if we are crying and moaning because that good thing is now gone, even if we believe the exquisite moment shall never return, we are still emboldened by the fact that we can stand and proudly proclaim, "I have had my fun / if I don't get well no more."

Finally, fun is subversive, especially when one is the object of oppression and exploitation. For when the sufferers find a way to have fun, we not only momentarily transcend our suffering; we affirm that there is a part of us, an enjoyment within us which we share with our fellow sufferers that is beyond the reach of the overseer, the master, the banker, our creditors, the boss, the hoss, and any damn other person or thing that is intent on making our lives miserable. This subversive factor is the ultimate meaning of R&B/rap, and is also the source of why the music is always damned by the psychological gatekeepers, i.e., ministers, politicians, educators, and status quo intellectuals. When social pundits argue that R&B, or rap, or any other contemporary popular music is a morally corrupting force, or that those forms "are not music," that our music needs to be censored if not actually prohibited, then what they are saying is that we have no right to decide what to do with our own bodies for good or for ill.

R&B asserts that "I'm three times seven / and that makes 21 / ain't nobody's bizness / what I do." The ultimate determination of self is the right of self-expression, and those who would limit, circumscribe, prohibit, or otherwise legislate our self-expression are the very same people who have no problem with capitalism (and if they were alive during slavery time, ditto, they would have no problem with slavery). In fact, during slavery time there were those who tried to stop enslaved Africans from singing and dancing. The power of popular music is that it asserts our existence centered in a pleasurable, self-determined celebration. When we holler, "let the good times roll / laissez les bon temps roulez," we are actually uttering a war cry against psychological oppression. And when we produce our own popular music and dance outside of the purview of the status quo, then we are (re) creating the/our "living self."

There is more, of course, just as surely as Sunday morning follows Saturday night, but that more is for another time. Right now, I just wanted to share with you the "psychological significance" and "aesthetically-African origins" of popular American music; in other words, I just wanted to tell you why it is so important for us to have some fun!

TAKING CARE

one

There are literally millions of us. We are generally unacknowledged by our communities, our neighbors, fellow workers, social associates. We exist at each level of society. Everyone knows at least one of us; knows us intimately but, paradoxically, does not know us fully. While many of those close to us are aware of some of what we go through, on a day-to-day level, the whole of who we are is seldom grasped, not to mention rarely embraced.

In this nation of over 320 million people, literally millions of us are the primary care givers of family or very close friends.

We function at an intimate level of responsibility for the wellbeing of family members, friends, clients, and the indigent. Dealing with the "wellbeing" of others generally means that we are assisting someone who is sick or disabled; someone who cannot fully care for themselves; someone who needs support.

That much is easy to understand. However, I believe that our caregiving responsibilities extend beyond loved ones and clients, and, yes, beyond individuals who, for a variety of reasons, are unable to fully care for themselves. Caregiving concerns the wellbeing of our society as a whole and also includes the environmental wellbeing of the planet.

But getting to the larger, general issues begins with a deeper understanding of what it means to be a caregiver in a one-on-one case. In that regard, I am using my personal experiences to link the individual to the collective, the specific to the general.

two

Early in my adult life, I had three major encounters with caregiving. The first time, I was totally unaware.

I was newly married to Tayari kwa Salaam, nee Cecily St. Julien; we both were born and reared in New Orleans, albeit from distinct sections of the city, Tayari from the Seventh Ward and me from the Ninth. We were living with my elderly, maternal grandmother below the Industrial Canal in the Lower Ninth Ward.

I don't remember the specifics of how we came to be domiciled with my grandmother, but I do remember that leaving the Parkchester Apartment complex in the Gentilly area where I had moved upon returning home from the army and, subsequently, moving back CTC (cross the canal) to Lizardi Street in the Lower Ninth Ward, was not my idea. Family members must have thought I was in a position to assist in taking care of Grandma Copelin and asked me to go live with her.

I didn't fully understand the importance of my being there. My widowed grandmother, even in her elder years, was an independent woman. I can vividly recall, she had a lovely rose garden beside the house that she was no longer spry enough to dote over by the time Tayari and I moved in; it didn't occur to me to tend to it. I had grown up cutting the grass in the side yard and clipping the hedges out front, but beyond that I was never much good at domestic landscaping.

Moving as an adult into the house where I spent my early pre-teen years while my father was in the army was unavoidably crowded with formative childhood associations, such as playing under the wooden shotgun house that was raised almost three feet off the ground.

The front room of that home was where I first conducted writing workshops. I never asked my grandmother what she thought about those gatherings. I was oblivious to some of the opinions and feelings of an elder with whom I shared living quarters—me and Tayari mostly in the front half of the seven-room home and my grandmother mostly in one bedroom and the kitchen. None of us spent much time in the back room, which had been my grandfather's study when he was alive and active, preparing his Sunday sermons.

Our first child, Asante Salaam (asante = "thank you" and salaam = "peace"), was newly born when we moved. Theresa Copelin loved her great-granddaughter. Although when I reminisce about her formative years I'll remember Grandma holding Asante on her lap; I was unaware at the time of the deep joy that babies and children bring to elders and how, in ways not only physical but more importantly psychological, being around babies and young children gives elders something to hold onto and live for.

After a couple of years living with Grandma, I moved on, although not very far away—literally just around the corner from 1311 Lizardi Street to the 1300 block of Egania Street.

In the sixties and early seventies, a number of us were militantly intent on making fundamental social change. We went far beyond merely *thinking* about making change, far beyond the normal rebellion of breaking away from parents and living on our own. After moving out of Lizardi Street, Tayari and I engaged in a short-lived experiment of sharing a house with another couple. The living arrangement didn't work out, but we soldiered on in our serious pursuit of actualizing our belief in self-respect, self-defense, and self-determination, i.e., Black Power.

I was in Nicaragua when my grandmother died and was totally incommunicado. I didn't know about her death until I returned home a couple of weeks after the funeral. I never had the opportunity to say goodbye nor did I find out the specifics. I just assumed she died of old age. Would she have lived longer if I had been there?

I was in my twenties then. Fired up about participating in revolutionary struggle. My grandfather, Reverend Noah Copelin, had died a handful of years earlier in the spring of 1969. He was addressing a meeting called by the administration of Southern University in New Orleans, who were attempting to quell our student uprising. Grandpa Copelin literally had a stroke while speaking about supporting his hot-headed grandson, who was one of the leaders in the school takeover.

The last time I ever wore a coat and tie was to his funeral. My grandmother asked me to. I felt a responsibility to her. Yet, even then, I did not fully comprehend the extent of my human responsibility to care for others.

My own culpability for my grandfather's death is an issue I never extensively focus on, probably because my grandmother never, in any way, ever made me feel that I was responsible for the death of her husband, Rev. Copelin. She easily could have resented me for causing his death, but she never treated me and my family with anything other than love and devotion. I took her love for granted while never completely realizing that in her own way, she cared for my psychological wellbeing as much as, if not more than, my meager contributions to her homestead. In fact, by cheerfully accepting my limited assistance in our living arrangement rather than resenting me, Theresa Copelin encouraged me to continue the struggle that her husband died supporting.

three

The second time I was deeply involved in caregiving was when my younger brother Kenneth suffered a serious asthma attack. At the time, he was newly married. He had followed me in living at my grandmother's house. One night, desperately seeking my help, his wife Willetta frantically called, saying that Kenneth had fallen out. When I got there, Kenneth was on the floor, wheezing heavily and convulsing. He suffered these attacks as a child so I was not shocked; plus, I had been in the military and was trained to respond to emergencies. Within two or three minutes I had used a spoon to keep Kenneth from swallowing his tongue and then found his medication.

For me, while it was a serious situation, taking care of my brother was almost routine. However, the next time I tangled with death, the experience emotionally jolted me.

four

This third occasion of caretaking occurred well over a decade after living on Egania Street. By then I had literally quit my first marriage; this was one of the three pivotal movements of my early adult life. Relocating from Parkchester back into the Lower Ninth Ward on Lizardi Street with my grandmother was the first move. Then around the corner on Egania Sreet with Kwesi and Femi, and concluding with the move less than a mile away to Tennessee Street, where ultimately five children were reared. And when Tayari and I broke up, I briefly moved in with my father on St. Maurice Avenue, in a far corner of Lower Nine.

Big Val welcomed me home. From birth until after my father died, except for the brief 15 or 16-month period in Parkchester, I lived in the Lower Ninth Ward. Both my brothers also lived cross the canal in the Lower Nine as they were starting their families. The younger of my two brothers is a cardiologist. Some time after I'd moved to St. Maurice, Keith had to go out of town and had left me with specific instructions of what to do if my father had any health problems. Early Friday morning, Daddy complained that he had not slept well the night before. I took him to the doctor as Keith had recommended.

Dr. Wooten did not find anything seriously wrong but admitted Daddy to a hospital as a precaution. I visited later that afternoon accompanied by Debra Campbell, a woman I was dating at the time. Daddy said he was feeling ok but would like to get a good long sleep, so tell anybody who wanted to come see him, to do so on Saturday. I recall that while Daddy and I were talking, Debra spontaneously reached out and rubbed his feet. She was meeting him for the first time. I never would have done that.

Daddy fell into a coma later that night and died two days later on a Sunday morning. He had held on until Keith could get back in town. The doctor took Daddy off life support, and Keith, Kenneth, and I were standing beside my father while he expired. No one could explain what had happened, what was the cause of his demise.

I had never known my father to be sick, in fact never even saw him, as the saying goes, "under the weather." Big Val was robust, active and full of energy. His fatal illness was a mystery. One day he's ok, the next he's in a coma, and less than 48 hours later, he's dead. What the hell happened? We've never received any answers, not even plausible guesses.

As it sometimes does, death came both swiftly and without warning. Caught me totally unprepared. My mother had died several years earlier after a long bout with cancer. We had been prepped to deal with her home-going; indeed, she involved each of her sons in coping with her transition by talking with us when we drove her across town for medical treatments. I had more or less calmly dealt with the loss of my mother but was blind-sided by my father's untimely departure.

We never knew my daddy's mother who had died when he was a child residing down around Donaldsonville, Louisiana. Even though he briefly lived next door to us, I never really knew my daddy's father, who was my namesake. Vallery Ferdinand, Sr. was my daddy's father, and I was born Vallery Ferdinand III. Grandpa Ferdinand died when Hurricane Betsy flooded our neighborhood in September of 1965 while I was in the army.

Well before reaching forty, I found myself as the oldest living member of my immediate family; most of them had died during my physical absence, and none of them had required any major care on my part. I really had no clue concerning what it took to be a day-to-day caregiver.

five

The loss of family and friends reminds us that mortality, paradoxically, is a major part of life. Many years later when I was in my sixties, while helping to care for close friends, death once again caught up with me in a major way. Of course, there were other occasions when I had to confront death in the intervening years, but none of those ordinary instances really shook me as did two particular close friends leaving me behind—Doug Redd and Harold Battiste.

Born in New Orleans but reared in Baton Rouge, Douglas Redd was a visual artist who returned to New Orleans for college and became a fixture on the cultural scene. He and I connected and over time became like brothers. Right after Katrina hit, I had made a major video documentary of the two of us opining about New Orleans culture.

When cancer struck him, I responded. For over a year, I devoted nearly every night, from around seven or eight in the evening until after midnight, to sitting with Doug. We'd talk, watch television. During the last year of his life, illness rendered Doug virtually incapacitated; nevertheless, I mostly remember him jovially laughing and smiling as we bantered about the TV series *24* or whatever else happened to be on that night.

Mostly that was the way each night went, except the time Doug suddenly convulsed and I held him, first shaking him gently and then lowering him to a prone position. Carol Bebelle, Doug's business partner with whom he shared an apartment at Ashé Cultural Center, the organization the two of them founded, called 911. I ran downstairs to the parking lot to make sure the EMTs would be able to arrive without any delay or confusion about how to access Doug, who was on the third floor at the back of the building next to the rear parking lot. The front of the building facing the street offered no way upstairs and no access to the elevator.

Fortunately, help arrived quickly and Doug was stabilized. As significant as that occasion was, another night was more memorable. It was a cliché: a dark and stormy night. Carol was away at a meeting. I asked Doug if he wanted to go outside. He looked at me wide-eyed. I assured him I was not joking.

"But don't tell Carol," I conspiratorially whispered.

Downstairs there was an overhang by the rear entrance facing away from the side parking lot. Lightning and heavy rain. I pushed Doug's wheelchair as far out under the overhang as I could without the rain plummeting down on us. And we silently enjoyed the exhilarating ambience of the New Orleans night shower. There was an electric charge in the air, plus a definite atmospheric odor, as well as a perceptible drop in the temperature. The sights and sounds of the thunderstorm were simultaneously dangerous and energizing. At such times, most people seek shelter; we were two fools reveling in the experience of exposing ourselves to the elements.

Sometime later, I told Carol about being out in the storm with Doug. Although he and I spent numerous nights together, I was not present when Doug passed away early

early one morning in July 2007, one month shy of the second anniversary of Katrina.

six

Both Doug and I were born in 1947, he in December and I in March. Doug was my peer. Harold Battiste, conversely, was more of a father figure.

I was working as the executive director of the New Orleans Jazz and Heritage Foundation, the parent organization of the internationally renowned New Orleans Jazzfest. I knew of Harold Battiste but had never met him. When he came in town for one of the annual Jazzfest activities, I invited him over for dinner. By then I was living in the Midcity area of New Orleans. Harold had produced *New Orleans Jazz Heritage*, a multiple LP set of fifties- and sixties-era jazz music that greatly inspired me. Following up on Harold's example, I would go on to produce *The New New Orleans Music*, a three-volume set of recordings featuring six different groups, one on each side of the collection.

As music producers and cultural activists, Harold and I were two amigos and stayed in touch. Within a year of our dinner, Harold decided to return home to New Orleans after living in Los Angeles for many years that included working with Sam Cooke and serving as the musical director for Sonny and Cher. We started hanging out, usually around dinner at Picadilly's, but also at other eateries.

One place we sometimes chose was a Thai restaurant located in the River Bend area of New Orleans. A scary incident happened there: Harold fell while negotiating the narrow spaces between tables. Although he insisted he was okay afterwards, I was alarmed. The fall had been hard. His health was failing. Within a year or so, Harold was homebound. Although dealing with Harold's physical condition did not bother me, nor fellow musician/guardian angel Jesse McBride, nor Sophia, a distant cousin who became Harold's primary caretaker, Harold was deeply resentful of the deterioration of his strength and mobility.

What he resented most was not being able to drive. Our trio of caregivers was there for him, but eventually we started arguing with Harold about us denying him the chance to drive himself. One time the disagreement was so sharp, I challenged Harold, telling him I would give him the keys to his car if he could come and get them. I went outside his apartment, walked toward the end of the long hallway and, holding up the car keys, patiently waited for him to come to me. It was a cruel gesture; I knew he was unable to walk over sixty feet unassisted.

I knew driving had become too dangerous. In the year prior to that confrontation, Harold had had both a minor and a more serious automobile accident. I was afraid the next collision would be fatal. Emotionally, tough love is sometimes harder on the person giving it than on the person receiving it.

Eventually, our hanging out was curtailed altogether as Harold grew more sick and old age prevented him from doing anything alone. Sometimes, when I would visit, I would find Harold sitting by himself on his bed, looking out over the back parking lot of his building, which ironically abutted a cemetery. Usually we could talk for hours, but now he would silently sit; the only sounds was our deep breathing, as he was mostly unresponsive to me prodding him to engage in conversation.

Sophia had moved in to care for him 24-7. Harold died at 83 in June of 2015. I had known him for over thirty years and when he left us, I was deeply affected. Just as had happened earlier when Doug passed, another part of me was now irretrievably missing.

When you lose decades-long close friendships, especially as you grow into what our people euphemistically call "the sunset" years, you do not live the rest of your life unchanged, whether or not you verbally acknowledge your hurt.

seven

I am not alone in dealing with the existential challenges of caregiving. I decided to reach out to a friend from back in the day, Sylvia Hill. The phone rang and rang, until eventually the answering machine picked up: Once. Twice. Thrice. I called a couple of people I knew who lived in D.C., where Sylvia was, and whom I thought might know her. Still was unable to reach her. A few weeks after giving up, I tried again on a whim, a hope.

She answered and informed me she had been out of town. I told her why I called in the first place: I was in the throes of dealing with caregiving with my wife and Sylvia's example years before had profoundly affected me.

Long story, short: after a marriage and a separation, Sylvia had taken her former husband back in over a decade later when he went blind. When we finally talked, Sylvia told me James had died over a year earlier on January 8, 2017.

We conversed as though we had seen each other last week. Actually, it had been years since we talked but ever since we first spoke on the phone back in 1974 about participating in the Sixth Pan African Conference, popularly known as 6PAC, for which Sylvia was a major coordinator, she and I were close even though we never even lived in the same city.

In the Howard University emergency room, sickle cell wracking his body and sapping his strength, James Hill had remained resolute. Sylvia recalls his last lucid words: "Power to the people. Power to Black people. Keep hope alive." A janitor who happened to be nearby said, "Did I really hear him say that?"

Our friendship grew out of political work. I had first come to know Sylvia when she was working as staff for 6-PAC in Tanzania, following that with ongoing Anti-Apartheid work in the eighties, and eventually assisting with Nelson Mandela's tour of the United States following his 1990 release from prison.

Nearly twenty years before Mandela's world tour, I had been one of the national organizers for FESTAC 1977, the Second World Black and African Festival of Arts and Culture, held in Lagos, Nigeria, and underwritten by Nigeria's oil riches. Coming up out of New Orleans, I was representing the deep south region of the United States. FESTAC held monthly board meetings in D.C. and I would make an effort to call and, if possible, visit with Sylvia whenever I was in town.

Sylvia and I knew a number of people in common including Ed Brown, who was Rap Brown's older brother and who was a former organizer with SNCC (Student Nonviolent Coordinating Committee), working as a field secretary in Mississippi. In 2002 Jamil Abdullah al-Amin (bka H. Rap Brown) was convicted of and incarcerated for the death of a policeman. Rap had converted to Islam, as would Ed during the last years of his life. I had gotten to personally know both Jamil and Ed, when they lived in Atlanta.

Ed Brown and I would journey back and forth visiting with each other. In later years when Ed became terminally ill, my friend Lionel McIntyre and I set off on the six-and-a-half-hour journey 'fore day in the morning to sit with Ed. We spent about four hours reminiscing with Ed and his wife Valinda. Afterwards, we jumped into our vehicle and drove back to New Orleans.

Some weeks later as a pain in my right leg worsened, a doctor asked me had I recently taken a long trip. I said yes. He advised me that long back and forth drive probably contributed to a serious blot clot condition for which I was hospitalized for a couple of days. If I had not received treatment, the blood clot could have been fatal.

Years later, when Sylvia told me about James' death, I thought about my own illness.

Originally from Jacksonville, Florida, Sylvia had been
working with the Institute of African Education, a program
supported by Macalister College. The program was based
in the small but vibrant Black community of St. Paul,
Minnesota. I had spent two trimesters at Carleton College
in Northfield, Minnesota, about 50 miles from St. Paul. I
didn't know many Black folk who were familiar with that
part of the country.

Sylvia was adept at patiently talking with people in a
non-threatening but forceful way. Her goal was to get people
active in education, oppositional politics, and communi-
ty-based health pursuits, all three of which were a necessary
foundation for ongoing political work. Just as legendary
Chinese revolutionary Mao Tse Tung advised: "a dull-wit-
ted army cannot defeat the enemy." Sylvia knew we had to
both study and struggle. Of course, the popular culture of
the sixties and seventies actively encouraged us to be, in the
famous words of James Brown, "Black and Proud," and to
"get up and get involved."

Ninety percent of movement work happens away from
the spotlight and microphones, takes place in the workplac-
es, churches and temples, and home spaces of working class
people. While the churches were important organizing focal
points, during the seventies, activists at community and
cultural centers offered a more radical interpretation of what
was to be done. Additionally, in these spaces one could meet
and interact with regional, national and international figures
who were culturally and politically active. Overall, independent organizing was hard, inching along work, that required
daily commitments sustained over extensive periods of time,
often for only incremental gains.

On the one hand, during this period, as a result of
social ferment throughout our city, this nation, and the
world, there was a rise in the number of Black elected and
appointed officials; but on the other hand, there was an

overwhelming and profound need for economic and health care programs.

From 1973 to 1977, I was the director of the Lower Ninth Ward Neighborhood Health Center. At that time, I did not fully grasp the revolutionary potential of such programs that fulfilled fundamental concerns of our underserved communities. Indeed, although I had been selected to head the newly opened health center precisely because I had a history of community activism stretching back years doing door-to-door civil rights work, my career choices were elsewhere. I was an able administrator but was far more interested in developing myself as an activist and writer.

When I shared with Sylvia my current struggles with caregiving for my wife, Sylvia gave me an insight I can never forget. Yes, caregiving was hard but caregiving also was a means of finding and expressing the deepest part of our humanity.

With neither embarrassment nor restraint she and I are able to talk as only long-time friends can, particularly friends who have shared both political and caregiving struggles.

Politics, especially at the oppositional level, is not only emotionally consuming, the struggle is also both a barrier and a bond. People outside activist circles seldom grasp the depth of experiences held among those who confront dangers, make sharp personal sacrifices, and, most of all, share all the ups and downs, all the twists and turns, and, yes, all the inevitable reverses and contradictions that are inherent to protracted struggle. From arrests by the state and confrontations with both the police as well as with para-military civilian forces, to international adventures and connections with people and places far from home, the politics of struggle more often than not sets one apart from those family, friends and associates who are not active on the front lines.

This voluntary grappling with the powers that be informs and shapes one's individuality in ways that outsiders not only generally don't and can't understand. More importantly, because being in opposition to the powers that be is dangerous and all too often illegal, the details and results of resistance usually remain hidden from others, no matter how close the others may be or, over time, may become. To engage in anti-establishment struggles inevitably means keeping secrets, and keeping secrets alienates you from others.

Paradoxically, caregiving has the opposite effect of pushing the giver and receiver closer together even if they have not otherwise shared activities or viewpoints, which is often the case when one person has been politically active and the other has not.

Moreover, caregiving brings us males closer to another person than does any romance, social/political activity, or even any kinship relationship. Caregiving makes clear that living is no easy task and requires constant vigilance and work. Ultimately caregiving is a nurturing process that is too often preconceived as outside of the realm of manly responsibilities.

Caregiving inevitably humanizes men far, far beyond what is normally expected or actualized by males. In a sense, caregiving enables me as a male to emotionally, as well as intellectually, identify with a whole world of experiences—a world that, in this society, women know intimately, and which we men too often discount or ignore. We men assume some woman—be she family member or paid professional—will do the job.

Most of us not only think of caregiving as "women's work," worse than feminizing a task that more of us men ought to willfully undertake, caregiving in many, if not most, cases is unpaid labor. This is significant. How significant? Try paying for round the clock, 24/7 professional (meaning it is a job) caregiving. Such professional care is far from cheap, indeed, professional care givers are expensive.

The political economy of caregiving is massive. But beyond the labor, the monetary costs, and the time, looms the larger issue: compassion and love for one another. Not only is it true that men don't want to talk about caregiving, and really don't want to be burdened with the constant effort required of care givers, the deeper truth is that because of our socialization we are too often unable to do so even when we want to.

There is a reason that I could call Sylvia after us not seeing each other for over a decade, and we could intimately speak about our separate lives. We didn't have to share day-to-day mundanities; we have shared pivotal and essential struggles: we both were spousal care givers. I had now entered a realm of responsibility that previously I knew of but, for which, I did not have primary and full responsibility.

Just Nia and I live in our home. I had been inducted by unforeseen circumstances into the golden circle of caregiving. I know there are many other men in a similar situation but I have never before at length and in-depth talked about or written about caregiving.

eight

The details may change but the essential challenges remain the same. In 1997 I re-married. In the fall of 2017 when my wife, Nia (Beaula R. McCoy, who was also married for a second time), suffered a stroke, I found myself again in a spousal caregiving role. I had forgotten about the first time. Back in 1985 Tayari had the first of three brain operations over a roughly thirty-some-year period. There was a slow recovery following the first operation.

Although extremely serious, I don't recall Tayari's recuperation being as strenuous as the daily struggles to care for Nia, who is barely mobile with a walker and spends most of her time in a wheelchair.

Nia and I are now in our seventies; in the 1980s both Tayari and I were in our thirties. We were overall, much more-healthy, much stronger, and had much more energy, all of which greatly contributed to the relative ease that Tayari had in responding to the first brain surgery compared to Nia coping with the after effects of her stroke.

While Tayari's recovery was, as the saying goes, no "walk in the park"; afterwards, Tayari could take care of herself. Even though she had to be careful about what otherwise would be an ordinary bump to the head, she was not physically impaired. Nia completely lost her peripheral vision on her left side and also suffered an increasing, although minor, deterioration of her sight in general.

Nia had to give up driving, which required a major psychological adjustment for someone who was used to being independently mobile. Thinking back to Harold's anger at not being able to drive, I could easily empathize with how hobbled Nia feels. It's almost like being permanently grounded. Of course, when faced with ongoing major health issues, not being able to drive doesn't initially register as a great challenge, but it doesn't take long before one feels like a newly caged bird.

Tayari could walk, talk, and, over time, carry on as usual. Although she was not physically restricted there were disconcerting attitudinal changes. At that time, the women in our organization wore either lapas (long, wrap-around skirts) or trousers. Not long after the operation, Tayari announced that she wanted to wear shorts and walk around the block.

Although I didn't particularly like the idea, if I truly believed in self-determination, I knew that I had no right or prerogative to control what Tayari did with her body, even if I thought her decision was a negative result of her operation.

Tayari and I didn't argue about her choice. She went for her walk and returned home shortly.

Tayari's personal decisions were never an issue for me. There is a critical saying from the women's movement of the late sixties, which, incidentally, I think may have grown out of the civil rights movement. That saying is an essential credo of self-determination: "the personal is political". Moreover, I believe that slogan really took off as an outgrowth of the Black Power movement. Indeed, wasn't it obvious, if the lowest strata of society could insist on its rights to self-determination, to power, then why not women, whom patriarchy oppressed and exploited across the board at every level and in as many ways as possible? For example, what is a beauty contest but an appeal to what men consider beautiful? And, yes, President Trump and the beauty contests that he "owned" are a prime example!

The reason that the women's movement was so hated is precisely because empowering women is a direct challenge to patriarchy, a system that implicitly and explicitly is based on the male control of the female: body, mind and soul.

People who knew me in the seventies, on some rare occasions ask: why did you and Tayari break up? Why did I end our marriage? And, it clearly had been my decision. For a long time, I could never really articulate why, however, as I write this essay, a pivotal event from over thirty years ago strikes me in ways I never fully understood at the time. The breakup happened in conjunction with what I thought of at the time as the total destruction of a world I had worked hard to construct.

In reflecting on the situation, I've come to realize that ending our marriage happened in conjunction with me leaving our organization, Ahidiana. To be more precise, I made a decision to leave the organization because I believed that we were no longer primarily about making social change.

Of course, our organizational issues were far more complex than my personal opinion. For over a decade all but one or two of Ahidiana members were either reared in or moved into the Lower Ninth Ward near our school build-ing, which we owned collectively. But over time, neighbor-hood safety deteriorated. My youngest brother Keith and his wife Daphne had a burglary and they decided to move their family away from the area, as it was becoming more and more dangerous. Tayari's brother, Mtumishi, and his wife Shawishi also decided to move out to New Orleans East. Keith was a doctor, Mtumishi was a lawyer. As they were progressing in their professions, they were also moving into a different social strata.

I could sense changing attitudes resulting from chang-ing social circumstances. And just as when Tayari decided to wear shorts, I did not believe I had the right to over-rule the decisions of others. My thinking in regard to our organi-zation was that it would be best to officially disband rather than to slowly wither away as members moved far from the Lower Nine and further from anti-establishment activism.

On the other hand, I had a major blind spot in terms of child-rearing. I did not fully understand how important it was to maintain our school whose students ranged from pre-K to fourth grade.

Part of my blind spot was that I didn't teach in our school. I drove the van doing pickups in the morning or drop offs in the afternoon. I pulled my clean-up shifts at the school and at our small, one-room bookstore. I participated in the lesson planning and the preparation of booklets we used for instruction but I was not a hands-on care taker for the watoto (children).

At Ahidiana the children referred to the adults as mama (mother) and baba (father). Regardless of what I thought, the reality was that I was ready to abandon my parental duties for the children who did not live under the Salaam roof. Of course, any of the organization children who was visiting with us was cared for. They often slept over and didn't even have to ask permission. The Ahidiana children grew up collectively.

The breakup of Ahidiana was a major struggle for me but I was prepared to let it go. I didn't fully understand that care givers shouldn't just walk away. The politics of struggle are far deeper than most of us realize as we make individual life choices; certainly, far deeper than I understood at that time.

I was convinced that rather than gradually disintegrate, Ahidiana should come to a planned halt, but I was not thinking about what that meant for all the children at our school, partially because, except for our youngest, all my biological children were already moving on to public school.

Moreover, there was a deeper truth: Ahidiana had been founded as a result of a painful split. Initially, we were Dokpwe Work/Study Center, founded by my brother Kenneth and Tayari. Roughly half of us broke off from Dokpwe to start Ahidiana because we were pushing for a political organization that also operated a school rather than a staff that functioned solely as a school.

Even though it meant splitting with my brother, I was adamant that the fissure had reached a non-negotiable political position. Dokpwe kept the stove, Ahidiana took the refrigerator. It was a classic separation, emblematic of many, many splits happening in Black America of that period. Although both camps considered themselves Black nationalists, the severity of the separation was akin to the nationalist/Marxist breakdowns that were rife among anti-establishment, political forces in the eighties.

nine

Those of us of the Ahidiana persuasion were particularly militant about participating in community organizing and confronting civil authority. For example, we were actively engaged in addressing the issue of police brutality and were especially motivated after three people were gunned down during police raids in the Algiers area of New Orleans on the west bank side of the Mississippi River in November 1980.

A police officer, Gregory Neupert, was shot and killed in Algiers by an unknown assailant. In attempts to hunt down the killer, the cops enacted repressive, Draconian measures (that included torture, which was later documented in court trials). The word on the street was that Nuepert was a dirty copy involved in drug dealing. In one particularly horrific case, three people were killed by police following the death of Neupert. One of the victims was a 26-year-old woman, Sherry Singleton, whom one neighbor reported hearing beg for her life. Two young men, James Billy and Reginald Miles, who was Singleton's boyfriend, were also killed in gun fights with the police that night. A few days earlier Raymond Ferdinand had been shot by police.

Some of us felt we had to do something, take some action. Mayor Dutch Morial was the city's first Black mayor. We decided to sit-in the mayor's office under the slogan of "Blow The Whistle On Dutch," whom we held ultimately responsible. The take-over was very controversial—and, as the cliché goes, "that's putting it mildly".

Dutch was not only a "first negro", he was a proud man. What we did was a major embarrassment not just for the Morial administration but for him personally. Many years earlier, when I was in high school and an active member of the NAACP Youth Council, Dutch headed the adult NAACP chapter. Back then we had clashed over a boycott of Canal Street, which was the main business district. After over a year of the Youth Council picketing and organizing the boycott, the merchants decided to negotiate but only if the pickets were removed. The adult chapter, which, except for two or three members, had not regularly walked the picket line, were ready to meet the merchant's terms. They gave us an ultimatum: either agree to the terms or be expelled from the NAACP.

Nobody had to tell me twice. I resigned. Years later, following the Algiers murders, Dutch and I were again at loggerheads. Although I did not view the situation in personal terms, there was no denying we had history.

This classic conflict was not actually between two forces contending for the same objective. No. On the one had there was the view that we should push for full participation in the established society. On the other hand, there was the view that we should struggle for an independent alternative, a struggle that included forceful opposition to establishment authority. What to do when the former rebels, i.e. people such as Dutch who had a long history of participating in efforts to improve the conditions of our community, were in conflict with the emerging youth, i.e. those whom we represented and who were staunch opposition elements.

Without any warning, we launched a frontal assault on City Hall. We occupied the mayor's office from Thursday until Saturday afternoon when we decamped, striding out of the building with our fists proudly upraised.

Being an activist is among the higher levels of caring because it moves beyond individual benefit and instead is focused on collective issues. At a philosophical level, I cannot separate caring for individuals from social activism. Living a good and relevant life required principled activity on both a personal and a social plane. Not surprisingly, I often publicly focused on the larger social issues even as I privately paid attention to personal issues.

I believed that there are three levels of power: the political, the economic, and the military. Police brutality made shockingly clear to us not only that we had no military power but also that although the police were nominally controlled by the mayor, de facto, the truth was the police still viewed some of us as runaway slaves. In fact, worse than runaways, a number of us were actually viewed as slaves in revolt. We had to be put down.

Some of us had to be shot as examples in order to keep the bulk of us in compliance with the powers that be. Although his power as the titular head of the city was not negligible, Dutch Morial was not essentially in charge of the city, and certainly was not in charge of the economy of the city.

New Orleans is one of the major port cities of the United States; always in the top ten, sometimes as high as one of the top five. But there was a change in both the national and international shipping of goods that happened a number of years ago: cargo was placed in containers that could be mechanically loaded directly from the ship onto rail or trucks. A large gang of longshoremen was no longer needed for manual labor.

The Black longshoremen had earned significant income (enough to support businesses and pay for college education). They, along with public school teachers, had been the major economic force in the Black community. Longshoremen and public school teachers were both unionized. Technology wiped out the longshoremen and charters attacked the teacher's union, thereby effectively limiting if not totally neutering major economic levers that were under Black control in New Orleans. Although this development took over thirty years to come to full fruition, nevertheless, the destruction of these two forces was a major blow.

Longshoremen and teachers were integral to our collective wellbeing, especially when you consider issues around health care. Caregiving costs money. Adequate health insurance was a major benefit of both professions (and yes being a longshoreman was a profession). Buying medications and paying for direct and indirect medical services can be expensive: from clinic visits to obtaining sturdy wheelchairs and regular purchases of medication. In most cases, while we are young and relatively healthy, we don't consider these issues; but, oh, as we age.

Regardless, as significant as providing compassion-ate caregiving is, far too many of us never get to be elders in wheelchairs and on long term medication. Why? Well, because we instead become early victims of poor health care, and also tragic victims of police brutality. One of my broth-ers is a physician. Another of my two brothers is a business-man. I was the militant.

By taking a public and militant position on police brutality I knew that I was placing a target on myself. We began receiving threatening phone calls at home and after a drive-by with people shouting racial epithets one night, I began sleeping with a loaded thirty-caliber, semi-automatic carbine rifle next to the futon.

Some older friends and associates counseled that it might be prudent if we slowed down a bit; after all, who would take care of my wife and five children if something might happen to me. Although I never surrendered to the social pressure to stop anti-police brutality organizing, I was sincerely concerned about my personal responsibility as the prime care taker for my family versus my commitment to a leading role in caring about our larger community by mili-tantly confronting police brutality and organizing around other issues germane to our collective wellbeing.

ten

During the eighties and early nineties, I was doing a lot of travel internationally, mainly to the Caribbean, but also to England, France, and Germany in Europe; Brazil and Suri-nam in South America, and of course to Africa. I helped organize the first Pan Jazz Festival in Trinidad, and before that took jazz combos and brass bands to a number of the islands. I was also a participant in the 1994 PANAFEST in Ghana, West Africa.

At home I was a fixture on radio station WWOZ, the New Orleans music station. One of my most popular

programs was the Thursday night Kitchen Sink, whose eclec-
tic playlist was just what the name implied. I once garnered
a month-long ban for a show I did featuring Malcolm X
speeches mixed with music from Archie Shepp. On another
occasion, I offended some listeners with my "MJ Special".
We played Mahalia Jackson the first hour and Michael
Jackson the second hour. I was far from programming just
historic New Orleans R&B, popular funk, progressive jazz,
show tune standards, and romantic ballads.

The transfer of the broadcast license from the Nora
Blatch Educational Foundation to the Friends of WWOZ
Inc., supported by the New Orleans Jazz & Heritage Foundation, was my major achievement during my tenure as the
Jazz & Heritage executive director. 'OZ was founded by
brothers Walter and Jerry Brock, who had been active in
community radio in Texas. It literally took them over four
years of organizing and gathering support from the wild and
diverse New Orleans music community to secure the last
broadcasting license available in the greater New Orleans
area. The station began broadcasting on December 4, 1980.

I knew that financial stability was going to be a major
issue. The technical side of broadcasting was covered by engi-
neer Ken Devine with whom I struck up a long-term alli-
ance. Walter and Jerry raised early funding selling member-
ships while at the same time coordinating the programming
talent. Initially, the programs were pre-recorded for broadcast. After shifting to a mix of pre-recorded and live shows,
the station subsequently went predominantly live, 24-hours
a day. The focus on the music with volunteer DJs and mini-
mally paid staff notwithstanding, I knew that the funding
required for daily operation and for equipment purchases
and upkeep was the critical issue.

During my tenure as executive director, I had managed
the considerable funds of the Foundation and became adept
at identifying six-month CDs (certificate of deposit) at vari-

ous financial institutions to make money off of earned interest. Once I even drove twenty-some miles across the lake to Slidell, Louisiana to garner a high interest 100,000 dollar CD. I knew that if I could persuade the Foundation board to actively support WWOZ that would solidify the financial status of the station. Orchestrating the transfer was far from easy and fraught with numerous obstacles, misunderstandings, and conflicts.

The first WWOZ studio was a small room above the famous Tipitina's nightclub. The second location was the Kitchen Building in Armstrong Park. The current home is an upstairs location on St. Peter Street in the historic French Quarter. At one point in the early years following the move to Armstrong Park, the entire staff and many of the programmers went out on strike because of management issues. I joined the strike. Eventually those issues were ironed out and today the station thrives in its French Quarter offices overlooking the Mississippi River.

Coordinating the diverse partners who were needed to get the title transferred and to establish the sound financial footing necessary to keep the station afloat was a tricky proposition, but eventually it was accomplished. Via the internet, WWOZ is now heard worldwide. Very few of the thousands of members and listeners know any of the details about the founding and early struggles of WWOZ. Ultimately, just as I had assumed, despite inevitable ups and downs, as well as internal conflicts, the Jazz and Heritage Foundation proved to be a reliable caretaker for community radio.

Although some may not see or understand the nexus of community work to individually caring for a spouse, a family member, a close friend, or other individual in need; to me, whether for the collective or the individual, my caretaking in either case is philosophically an essential aspect of what I believe is my responsibility to kin and kind. While not denying the differences, I believe community/individual are two sides of the same coin of my essential humanity expressed in terms of how I live with and relate to others.

eleven

To accomplish my tasks as a caretaker with Nia, I take on many of the responsibilities usually assigned to the "house-wife". Beyond culinary duties and cleanup afterwards, there is the daily clothing that has to be washed, plus the significant toileting assistance and waste disposal that requires constant maintenance.

One day Nia told me that she didn't want our home to smell of "urine and feces" as did the houses of some others who were infirmed. She didn't have to tell me twice. Although emotionally taxing, none of the necessary hygiene chores are physically strenuous. The biggest requirement is that you have to deal with the issues quickly and efficiently, especially putting out the trash.

Red Plastic Bag (Stedson Wilshire) is an entertainer from Barbados who combines reggae and soca, and has won national contests in his home country. What a name, I thought, when I first heard the light-brown-skinned performer at Barbados' annual "Crop Over" festivities. Today, taking care of my wife, I use beaucoup plastic bags on a daily basis mainly to line trashcans and to contain waste but, also, to dispose of the plastic-lined padding that is used daily on easy chairs and bedding.

Although the inexpensive plastic bags that the grocery stores and supermarkets now offer, in place of the heavy paper bags formerly used, are inexpensive and convenient, I also know that plastic is non-biodegradable. Plastic bags and plastic packaging are a major pollutant in oceans worldwide, which are too often where hundreds of thousands of these cheap containers end up. Some countries are beginning to actively curtail the routine use of plastic bags, especially for daily use at home. Nevertheless, plastic bags are incredibly convenient even though for the long-term, disposal of medical and human waste, incineration is ultimately required for that. Ultimately, the environmental cost of the proliferation of plastic bags is high. Plastic bags are both a major convenience and at the same time a major environmental hazard.

There is a critical upside and critical downside to much of our modern 21st century lifestyles. The widely-accepted general use of plastic bags embodies both the positive and negative.

Plastic bags offer us immediate short-term solutions but create expensive, long-term problems. Once again, our society is faced with a major question given the conditions that have to be dealt with and the options available to us: "what is to be done?" Dealing with Nia's condition directly presents all kinds of questions for me that I had not previously considered, not to mention, for which I have not yet found suitable answers. I believe stewardship of self, others and the environment is one of our most critical human responsibilities.

twelve

Because my wife is only partially mobile, frequent clinic appointments, doctor checkups, and therapy sessions that happen three or more times a week require hours to prepare for and to complete. As a friend told me in serious jest: growing old is not for wimps!

Imagine: it takes us three or four minutes to negotiate the series of four steps up and down our front porch. There is a whole technique to climbing up, and to climbing down—lead with the good foot, which is Nia's left foot because although her left peripheral vision was gone, the right side of her body was weakened. So, she faces the railing and, standing sideways, painfully steps down or up leading with her left foot. Of course, I am there supporting her but there is also a major issue of encouraging her to do as much on her own as she can.

Indeed, she can grow stronger by pushing herself to do as much as possible on her own. Haltingly moving with a walker is painfully slow but I patiently wait, often next to and slightly behind her just in case she needs support.

Ordinary tasks we do without much thinking about it, such as unscrewing the cap on a bottle of water, is extremely difficult for someone who has suffered a stroke. Picking up the Chapstick that fell on the floor—oh, the floor is so far away.

Your worldview is different when you are mostly confined to a wheelchair. You can't just go out on the porch and check the mailbox. Indeed, you can't reach the mailbox. Of course, you could push the walker out on the porch, maneuver the wheelchair onto the porch, brace the walker against the side of the house, pull yourself up, and hobble over to the mail-box. Nothing there but ad brochures and solicitations from insurance companies.

You get tired of watching network television and cable.

The biggest thrill of the day isn't eating, it's bathing. Sitting on the shower bench that fits into the tub with a set of legs inside the tub and a set of legs outside the tub. The bench is designed with holes in the seat so the water flows through rather than splashes on the floor. To just sit there and take a long hot—but not too hot—shower is totally refreshing. And then being helped into freshly washed, clean clothing is a wonderful feeling.

Yes, you wear the pull-ups that are a combination of drawers and diaper. Thankfully, your caretaker is on the case whenever you say you need to go to the bathroom—oh, why be coy, you need to use the toilet, and you need assistance once you are finished emptying your bowels. You change your disposable underwear, get dressed again, and push yourself to navigate with the walker. The long hallway takes time and you're breathing hard when you finally get to the den, but you know walking is therapeutic.

Decades before, I wrote a poem about two aspects of home care that come back to me now in an altered way. The poem is called "Diapers and Dishes" and is included in my book Revolutionary Love.

Diapers and Dishes

i can thrust
my hand straight
into the toilet bowl, expertly
swirling a soiled diaper around
shaking loose all the stool
as I submerge the cotton cloth
agitating with a firm
back and forth action

i used to recoil
from the touch and texture
of warm masticated corn
kernel hulls and other leavings
smellingly ejaculated
from our babies' behinds
but now it is no bother

i used to be upset
coming home late at night
shake my head and suck
my teeth at the sight
of dirty dishes in the sink
now I willingly wash them

these tasks are so simple
since my thought
has been reformed

Tayari can read now at night
since we share house work
and mutually develop

now, after much self struggle, i
too can change
diapers and wash dishes

i laugh at my old self
sulking about bowel movement
and toilet water on my hands
or dishes that need only
a little time and hardly any
trouble to be made clean

i laugh at my old self
if feels good to improve

Of course, dealing with babies is not the same as caring
for an adult who needs assistance. In terms of psychological
trauma, the swirl of emotions and embarrassment surrounding toileting is more crippling than is the physical-limitation
aftermaths of a stroke. As adults, and certainly as a male
adult, I was not prepared to be an adult caregiver for an
adult.

Bathing, or to be more accurate, showering in the morning is perhaps the most important daily event. Getting on
and off the shower bench means swinging over the edge of
the tub. Plus, I had to learn how to position the shower
curtain to keep the water from splashing all over the floor.
Cleaning the shower bench, the floor, the sink, and, yes, the
toilet, is a daily task, some of which has to be done three or
four times a day.

After getting dressed and breakfast, usually grits or
oatmeal, tea, and toast, there's a moment to slow down a

bit. Finally, Nia relaxes in the wheelchair and, an hour or so later, asks for a bottle of chilled water.

And then, two or three hours later, there is a mischievous moment. Nia requests her favorite cookie: "Do we have any Lorna Doones?"

Being the sole caretaker for what the old folks commonly called "the sick and shut-in" is not a lightweight job. You get no days off and it requires rigorous and sustained follow through on all necessary tasks. Who knew there was so much involved in caregiving? Until we are thrust into caregiving jobs, most of us are totally clueless.

For me, the hardest aspect of caregiving is the emotional impact on both Nia and myself. Yes, I'm sometimes annoyed when I am working at the computer and Nia calls out to me. And I know that Nia would much prefer not to have to ask me to heat up some chicken noodle soup for her. Occasionally the sixth trip of the week to a clinic ten or so miles away taxes my patience. Despite how pleasant and concerned the physician is, I'm sure Nia can't enjoy visits with Dr. Robinson as she goes over the various medications and the regimens required for Nia's prescriptions to be effective. Walking back and forth from the washing machine and dryer in the back room to the hall bathroom on the other side of the house as part of the non-ending daily routine invites me to think about so many other things I would prefer to be doing. I know Nia does not enjoy being confined to a wheelchair day after day, not able to freely move throughout the house because there are rooms she physically can't access. Some days I get up earlier than I want to, or stay up later than I choose to, because Nia is not sleepy at that moment.

Yes, I sometimes wish that this particular phase was ended. But then, I soldier on. I know, not only is no cavalry going to appear to save me, I also know a deeper truth—I don't need mythical or magical saving. Yes, care taking is difficult. The unrelenting day after day struggles take their toll. There is no denying that hard fact. Yes, over time, water can wear down stone.

But there is also a deeper yes. No matter even if I personally momentarily feel sorry for myself, I have been gifted with the example of family and friends who carry on. As my brother, Kenneth, is wont to say: it's in the genes. I come from people who have made a way out of no way. I have it within me to hold on and press on. Indeed, as long as Nia is breathing and resisting, I can and will be a bridge cross these particular turbulent waters. In human affairs, sunshine outlasts rain.

Plus, rain is an eternal fact of life. There is no moral nor ethical failure that links to or causes anyone to suffer a stroke. God is not punishing people. The illness is not karma coming back on someone who has done wrong. Especially, considering that the patient was seventy-years-old when the first in the series of three strokes struck, this illness is actually part of the general arc of life. Our bodies wear down or wear out as we age. While it is true that in the long term, healthy, active lifestyles are far better than the average American sedentary lifestyle, that still does not mean we can live illness-free forever. We are in fact mortal and subject to our heath deteriorating. We all, to one degree or another, encounter a major struggle to stay fit as we age.

Although there is obviously a love for the patient, ultimately, the act of caregiving is unsentimental. Regardless of how we might feel about the task at hand, whatever is required to address the recovery is our responsibility, which we volunteer to undertake regardless of how trying our duties may be. Indeed, too often it is not the impossible that confronts us but rather our reluctance to face up to the difficult, or to the repulsive, the distasteful, the disturbing. Sometimes it's simply the inconvenient. Whatever. When faced with the job of caretaking, it's simply will you or won't you do what is required.

People sometimes ask what they can do to help? Perhaps the easiest and maybe even the most helpful thing family and friends can do is come by and sit for two hours or so to give the primary care taker a break. Not only is that easily doable, also, visitations can actually be emotionally supportive to people who often feel forgotten and depressed about their situation.

Dealing with those who are ill is very different from being ill yourself. I believe it is important that we get over the embarrassment inherent in much of the physical tasks that the caretaker must undertake. Also, and perhaps even more important, is letting the patient know that they are not a burden or a failure, especially when they are struggling to overcome a disability or limitation. One of the most difficult things in the world is to accept our weaknesses, especially in areas where we formerly were strong.

Are we strong enough to acknowledge our weaknesses and are we ready to make whatever necessary adjustments to carry on?

You know what Jerry Butler said: only the strong survive. I believe, for sure, we are strong enough to survive, particularly if we acknowledge and celebrate that just as there are many ways to survive, there are many ways both the care taker and the cared for can be and ought to be strong.

After all, survival is our calling card. Not just the survival of our family and loved ones. Not just survival of our race in this terrible, color-struck society. No. Our individual survival is but a small part of human survival. As a care taker, as well as the person being cared for, we don't have to wish for release. We just need to carry on. We can do this. And we do.

Survival on a global level is what enables the human species to grow and develop. It is human to face whatever music might be sounding. It is human to dance and carry on.

As the primary caregiver, regardless of how I might feel on any particular day, I know: I can do this. I will do this.

thirteen

At the deepest level of existence, we really do need each other. We humans are social creatures. While there is no new news in that truism, most of us generally do not think on what it means to be human. We go through our days without contemplating that to be human necessarily requires us to be connected to other humans. Even for those of us who are hermits, or misanthropes, or monks living in silence atop mountains of our own making. No matter. We don't become whomsoever we are without contact with others: first as babies, dependent on parents or surrogates for survival; second as adolescents growing up and maturing together; third as adult workers and parents, propagating both society and our species; fourth and finally as elders, who generally require physical and emotional support even as we impart wisdom and understanding to our society.

Humanity is not a solitary state; to be human means to be social.

In one sense or another, all of us are like babies: Dependent on others to take care of us but at the same time near totally self-absorbed with our own individuality. But the importance of, and even the psychological dominance of the individual personality notwithstanding, essentially our identity as a human being is initially created, continually shaped, and ultimately fulfilled by our relationships with others. In that regard, taking care of others is the highest expression of our humanity that any of us can achieve precisely because in caring for others we ultimately define who we are as a living organism interacting with our physical and social environment.

The beauty of being human is that, regardless of our condition, we are not alone. Or, as a number of African philosophies correctly assert: I am because we are.

Take care.

WHERE ARE YOU GOING?

I always admired him. The grace of his slow walk, his endless supply of endless stories to simple questions. I once asked him why he couldn't just give me a simple answer; he asked me why couldn't I just ask simple questions. I didn't know I wasn't being simple, I retorted. He just snorted softly before replying in his captivating, gruff voice: it's hard to be truly simple.

I used to like to see him dance, entranced by how light he made his heftiness move, vibrating with the music. And he was always singing to himself. Or trumpeting in the afternoon air.

There was the toughness of his thick skin: bullet-scarred, knife-scarred, old and wrinkled but nonetheless attractive. His eyesight was dim, but there was always a twinkle gleaming forth. I guess you could say I really liked him.

When we set off, I wanted to walk near him, but at the crossroads I became confused when all of us kept going and he turned off. I stood transfixed for a moment and then rushed to catch him, to call him, to tell him he was going off. But my mother called me back.

Where is he going, I asked her. She simply said, he is going where he needs to go. Come, we must stay together.

But why didn't she tell that to him. He was the one going off somewhere. And where is that, I asked her. Oh, she sighed, you'll know when it's your time to go. But how would my time answer a question for where he was going in his time.

And then she said, after a while, we all have to go. And with that, she fell quiet, and we moved on.

ACKNOWLEDGEMENTS

I would like to thank the staff at University of New Orleans Press - Abram Shalom Himelstein and GK Darby for publishing, Ann Hackett for interior design, and Chelsey Shannon, Thomas Price and Matt Knutson for editing and copy editing.